W9-BPJ-234

THE
GOLD
RUSH

THE
GOLD
RUSH

by
George F. Willison

Indian Head Books
New York

To my Mother and Father

Originally published as *Here They Dug the Gold*

This edition published by Indian Head Books,
a division of Barnes & Noble, Inc.

1992 Indian Head Books

ISBN 0-88029-896-0

Printed and bound in the United States of America

M 9 8 7 6 5 4 3 2 1

FOREWORD

FROM one source or the other, historical or fictional, perhaps rather more from the latter than the former, each of us has his own conception of the almost incredible hardships, the wild excitements and even the more prosaic concerns of pioneer life in the early West. Some no doubt have been moved by curiosity to speculate upon the correspondence, if any, between the actualities of that life and their conceptions of it. Out of such curiosity has grown this volume which, for want of a better term, may be called a chronicle of early days in the Pike's Peak country — more particularly, of the great Pike's Peak Gold Rush of '59 and of the manner of life prevailing in the larger mining camps which boomed there before the passing of the Frontier some thirty years later.

This chronicle could not, nor does it, pretend to be an exhaustive social history of early Colorado. But it may fairly claim, I hope, to represent the life and spirit of the time and place in not only significant but authentic detail. Although I have not burdened these pages with the usual scholarly apparatus, nothing has been presented as fact except upon good authority. Nowhere have I wittingly colored what was, by my own literary or dramatic notions of what should have been. Undoubtedly I have slipped into error here and there — but not, I trust, into the kind of literary "romance" which has bedeviled most literature about the West from the beginning. I have faithfully followed the record, for, to me at least, the truth here is stranger than fiction. Whenever I have had occasion to relate anything as a "story," it has been so indicated.

My goal has been to portray a whole society by presenting a group of persons whose lives were all more or less related but of very different kinds. So far as possible these have been allowed to tell their own stories, although it must be admitted that all have been edited. A background for these main characters I have attempted to recreate with materials drawn from many sources — published memoirs, public and private collections of manuscripts and letters, newspaper files and conversations with a number of old pioneers who lived through those eventful years.

With pleasure and gratitude I desire here to acknowledge the kindness of all whose advice, criticism, encouragement and actual manual labor assisted me in the making of this book. More especially am I indebted to Mr. George Frisbie of Leadville for invaluable aid in imaginatively recreating the old camp as it once was; to the Honorable H. M. Butler, Editor of the Leadville *Herald-Democrat,* for placing the files of the old Leadville newspapers at my disposal; to Miss Helen Teats, Mrs. G. H. Ferrall and Mr. Walden Sweet of Denver for granting me access to books, papers, letters and original manuscripts in their possession; to Mr. E. W. Milligan of Denver for many old photographs and cuts; to the Colorado Historical Society for both photographs and manuscript material; and to Mr. Thomas Hornsby Ferril of Denver and *Books* of the New York *Herald-Tribune* for permission to quote at length from Mr. Ferril's poem *Ghost Town,* from which came both the title and sub-title of this book.

G. F. W.

Croton on Hudson,
New York.

Contents

ILLUSTRATIONS

THE
GOLD
RUSH

I. The Shining Mountains

". . . would be found to contain more riches than those of Indostan and Malabar, or the golden coast of Guinea, or the mines of Peru."

For centuries England envied Spain her loot from Aztec and Inca temples, her vast stores of bullion from deep mines in Mexico and Peru. Always the English hoped that their own less favored colonies on the cold North Atlantic might somewhere — some day — pour forth native gold in fabulous amounts. No search of theirs came to more than Captain John Smith's.

But in 1799, less than twenty years after the English departed, a twelve-year-old boy wading a creek on his father's farm in the North Carolina mountains stumbled upon a strange heavy stone, picked it up and carried it home. There it excited sufficient curiosity to be kept as a doorstop for several years until sold to a goldsmith for $3.50. Similar stones were found from time to time on neighboring creeks, but without inspiring any general excitement.

Thirty years passed before a North Carolina negro known only as Charley, journeying south on foot along the mountains, picked up gold on Duke Creek, Georgia. Veins of gold quartz were soon traced back into the Carolinas and across northern Georgia into Alabama. A gold rush developed. The richest diggings were found to lie in Georgia on lands belonging to the Cherokee Indians, many of whom had already been transported across the

Mississippi into Indian Territory (Oklahoma). With the discovery of gold upon their lands the remaining Indians were customarily dispossessed.

From the Georgia field came the first considerable amounts of gold to be mined in the United States. Here at Dahlonega a branch mint was established in 1838, for the Georgia diggings remained the richest in the country until Tom Marshall in far-off California chanced to see a yellow glint in a mill pond and fished out the nugget which, far from enriching his friend and employer Colonel Sutter, brought him suddenly and completely to ruin. For the nugget conjured up a mighty human flood to sweep him away and shatter forever an immense, almost independent empire built up by long years of patient toil.

The first experienced miner to reach the famous mill race on Sutter's Creek was Isaac Humphrey, an old Georgia digger. It was he who proved the whole region rich with gold and more than any other precipitated the great California Rush of '49. It was likewise an old Georgia digger, William Green Russell, whose discoveries at the base of the Rocky Mountains incited the great Pike's Peak Gold Rush ten years later — as brave, as exciting and as glamorous an adventure as any in our history. This frenzied rush to the Pike's Peak country and the rise and fall of the earlier mining camps which boomed there form the body of this chronicle.

Green Russell, too, had joined the rush to California, journeying there with two brothers, Levi and Oliver, the former a doctor. With them had gone a band of Cherokees to whom they were closely related. Green Russell, for one, had married a Cherokee squaw. In California the Russells appear to have done rather well. Dr. Levi, in fact, is said to have made $60,000, which may well be doubted. In any case, the Russells soon exhausted their claims and were certainly not rich upon their return home to Georgia in '52.

The Russells, according to the more probable account of their hazardous five months' journey from coast to coast, did not entirely follow the main roads. They first joined the stream of gold-hunters pouring West along the Santa Fe Trail. But at Cimarron Crossing where the trail bore off toward the Southwest, they left the traveled road and pushed on alone up the Arkansas River. Striking the mountains near Pike's Peak, they turned north to follow along their base to Fort Laramie and the Overland Trail. Panning for gold in every stream they crossed, they first " raised color " on the South Platte at the mouth of a small sandy creek lined with choke cherries — the renowned Cherry Creek of later years. Again their pans showed color at the mouth of Cache la Poudre Creek forty miles to the north. But in neither instance were the colors sufficient to divert them from their goal.

Few other adventurers California-bound turned aside from the main roads as the Russells did to explore the intervening plains and mountains. When the rush passed, consequently, there remained between the Santa Fe and Overland Trails a great island of virgin territory. Almost virgin rather — for the Spanish had known it, the French had known it, American trappers and traders had long since pried into every nook and corner of it. But what all these learned they kept rather well to themselves for reasons of their own.

Into this island between the Platte and the Arkansas, Coronado had early penetrated in search of fabulous Quivira — where all plate was of solid gold — where the king napped every afternoon under a great tree hung with little golden bells which lulled him to sleep with their tinkling. More than a half-century later — but still many years before Captain John Smith set sail for America — Leiva Bouilla and Juan de Humana came north in another ill-starred search for Quivira. Then, a decade before the Pilgrims landed, Santa Fe was founded to become the capital of all the plain and mountain country. From it was dispatched expedition after expedition to hunt for gold and silver treasure in what is now Colorado, for the legend of Quivira was stubbornly rooted in men's minds and was long in dying.

The French early heard of it. Joliet and Marquette in their explorations westward from Quebec were instructed not only to seek the passage "to the sea of China by the river which discharges into the Vermilion, or California Sea." They were also to verify "what has for some time been said of the two Kingdoms of Thequaio. And Quivira, which borders on Canada, and in which numerous gold mines are reported to exist." Soon the French were pushing west from Vincennes, Kaskaskia and New Orleans. By 1750 French *coureurs de bois* have penetrated to the mountains up every large tributary of the Mississippi. But soon the French are seen no more in the West. New France falls a prey to England and Spain who advance their outposts to the Mississippi. It is not long before Spain sees the British Redcoats disappear from the river. Now Spain herself retreats. With Napoleon at her throat she disgorges all of Louisiana Territory and with some misgivings sees it sold to the aggressive young Americans who each year come surging westward in greater and greater numbers. Americans have little enough idea of Jefferson's bargain, but already their eyes are upon the distant prairies and mountains. And they have their own notion of the site and nature of Quivira.

"These mountains are supposed to contain minerals, precious stones, and gold and silver ore," reads a book of the day. "It is but of late that they have taken the name *Rocky Mountains;* by all old travelers they are called the Shining Mountains, from an infinite number of crystal stones of an amazing size with which they are covered and which, when the sun shines full upon them, sparkle so as to be seen at a great distance. These same early travelers gave it as their opinion that in the future these mountains would be found to contain more riches than those of Indostan and Malabar, or the golden coast of Guinea, or the mines of Peru."

Lieutenant Zebulon Pike is the first to be sent officially to inspect the Shining Mountains. He reaches them late in 1806 to make an unsuccessful attempt to climb what he mistakenly calls the " Highest Peak " — famous Pike's Peak. Pike then wanders mysteriously about the mountains with no apparent aim unless, as seems likely, he is involved in Aaron Burr's treasonable conspiracy to found an independent empire in the Southwest. Pike is seized by the Spaniards and carried off a prisoner to Santa Fe. After him come other official investigators, notably Major Long in '20 and four expeditions led by General Fremont, the last in '45-'48.

The vogue of the white beaver hat has meanwhile sent forth hundreds of bold trappers and traders to seek peltries in the West. Many a famous name is associated with this curious trade — Kit Carson, Jim Bridger, Jim Beckwourth, Uncle Dick Wootton, Bill Sublette, Louie Vasquez, Ceran St. Vrain and, perhaps greatest of all, Colonel William Bent, son of Silas Bent of the Boston Tea Party. With two brothers Bent has been on the Plains since '24, building one fort after another up and down the Arkansas. These trappers and traders have long known of gold in the mountains from the Indians. But the latter, according to Bent, have always remonstrated " against this knowledge being made known to the whites, for they are afraid, and we believe with good grounds, that this, their last and best home and hunting-grounds, will be appropriated by the white man, and they themselves be finally exterminated." Traders and trappers have no desire for their part to see the country settled and guard the Indians' secret well.

Reports of gold in the mountains begin to multiply nevertheless. One circulates in '35, another in '43, a third in '49. Stories begin to be less circumstantial. In '50 Indian traders definitely place gold in Clear Creek and two years later in Ralston Creek nearby. Finally in '54 or '55 a band of Western Cherokees, accompanied by two Ralston brothers from Georgia, come north from Indian Territory in search primarily of good buffalo country in which to settle. But as all know something of mining, they have an eye out for gold as well. The Cherokees succeed in penetrating as far as the mountains and there raise color on the Cache la Poudre before the Arapahoes and their fierce cousins the Cheyennes drive them home.

Through the Ralstons or his Cherokee wife Green Russell hears of this Indian expedition to be reminded of his own operations on the Cache la Poudre. He is soon in communication with the Western Cherokees. A joint party is agreed upon, and early in '58 Green Russell, his two brothers and six other miners set out from Georgia for the rendezvous in Kansas. Two months later the combined party, now more than one hundred strong, is plodding slowly up the Santa Fe Trail, leaving it as formerly at Cimarron Crossing. Green Russell follows the Arkansas River for a time and then boldly turns north up Black Squirrel Creek to strike across a dry treacherous trackless waste. At last, late in

May, the Georgians and the Cherokees come rolling down the sandy banks of Cherry Creek to the Platte — "camping that first night in a large grove of cottonwoods that three years afterwards began to bear fruit with boots on."

Early next morning the men go to work excitedly panning the creek — but to little profit. Nor do the sands of the Platte yield more. Within a few days many begin to grumble and complain. Within two weeks half the company deserts. All the Cherokees flee in fear of an Arapahoe attack. The bolder of those who remain now approach the mountains to prospect Ralston and other creeks. Others venture north to Boulder Creek. All return empty-handed and discouraged. Matters reach a second crisis with muttered threats of violence against Green Russell. Gentle of speech and manner, tall and rather handsome, perhaps even a little vain of his comparative elegance and neatly braided whiskers, Russell calmly faces the mutineers and attempts to quiet them, pointing out the folly of having come so far at such a sacrifice to do so little.

"I have faith in this country," he tells them, "and I will remain until I satisfy myself that there is no gold here, if only one man will stay with me, no matter if it takes all summer. Who will stay with me?"

A mere dozen from more than fifty choose to remain, and at Russell's suggestion they break camp immediately to pan their way slowly up the Platte. Loitering behind one day a youngster begins to "strip" a sand bar to bedrock. Green Russell chances to come up, judges the sand bar likely, fills a pan with dirt, kneels by the stream to wash it. The water and coarser gravels disposed of, he examines the "crease" for pay-dirt. He quickly washes another panful before raising a great shout to bring all the Georgians running. Russell has them finger the pay-dirt carefully to satisfy themselves. They glance at one another with shining eyes and smile — and laugh — and shout, dancing wildly.

"Our fortune!" echoes the cry, "Our fortune is made!"

Their fortune, unhappily, is not made, as they themselves are the first to realize. Here they wash out less than $100 of gold. But they are encouraged to go on. They find one gold pocket and then another on Dry Creek. But these, too, are soon washed out. Green Russell calls a general council. This free gold on the Plains, he argues, must have been washed down from outcropping veins on the mountains above. If they would be rich, they must find the source of the gold.

The party divides in two. One half undertakes to trace the Platte to its headwaters in South Park — dangerous territory, for the savage Utes jealously guard it as their one good hunting ground. The second group prospects north along the mountains almost as far as Fort Laramie. Snow soon begins to fly, and both parties hasten back to safety at Cherry Creek. Neither can report the slightest luck. As days grow shorter and colder, a few scattered cabins go up among the cottonwoods — the beginnings of a primitive settlement called Auraria by the Russells after a little town of that name near their home in Georgia. Here, some seven hundred miles from the nearest settlements on the Missouri, the Georgians anticipate months — even years — of isolation. After all, as the result of their long journey and a summer of hardship and toil, they have less than $800 of "dust" to be shared among thirteen. Certainly they are not rich save in hope — every gold-hunter's one certain treasure.

II. ARGONAUTS, INC.

". . . . masters of the popular Anglo-American art of town-making, understanding to perfection how to turn little or nothing into real or supposed fortunes."

MEANWHILE, unknown to the Georgians still absent in the mountains, a half dozen prairie schooners have drawn up and stopped at the abandoned Dry Creek diggings. This is John Easter's party from Lawrence, Kansas, launched upon adventure by Delaware Indians. Until reaching the mountains, it had never heard of the Georgians and Cherokees.

Late in '57 Chiefs Little Beaver and Fall Leaf led a band of Delawares into Lawrence to excite the town by displaying a quill or two of gold dust. When asked its source, the Indians pointed vaguely toward the sunset. This apparently satisfied John Easter, local butcher, who began to organize a small party. Thirty or more adventurers from neighboring towns joined it before its departure the following spring. Chief Fall Leaf, one of Fremont's guides, had agreed to lead the party but so injured himself in a drunken frolic on the eve of departure that he refused to go. Without him, on almost the very day the Georgians first pitched camp on Cherry Creek, eleven prairie schooners rolled out of Lawrence and were soon lost in clouds of dust as they headed toward the Santa Fe Trail. The party was joined by two men and a woman at one remote prairie settlement, and at another gained three more men and a second woman, the latter with a six-months-old child.

As Pike's Peak was the one landmark they knew in the wilderness, the Lawrence party hastened there to prospect the Fontaine qui Bouille and other creeks. Ignorant of mining, the Kansans found nothing. Soon weary and disgusted, they harnessed up and started for New Mexico. But along the road they somehow learned of Green Russell's operations on the Platte. A majority wheeled about and a week later reached Dry Creek only to find it abandoned.

On a knoll nearby John Easter and his friends stake out a townsite. A few cabins soon mark the beginning of Kansas Row. After a town company has been organized, the tiny raw settlement is dignified as the City of Montana — which is Spanish, say its promoters, for "Little Mountain." Here most of the party spend the winter. But a few move down the Platte five miles to Cherry Creek where in the absence of the Georgians they find but three men — Atwell, John Smith and Jack Jones. All are squaw men, each with numerous half-breed children. Smith and Jones soon rise to prominence in the gold fields. Smith, the Kansans learn, has been on the Plains since '26, first as a trapper, later as a war chief of the Cheyennes. At the moment he is working the Old Spanish Diggings up the Platte. Smith's partner and inseparable companion is "Jack Jones," the usual alias of William McGaa, son of a Lord Mayor of London. Educated for the Church, McGaa early disqualified himself as a shepherd of the flock by his passionate devotion to whiskey. Drifting to America and into the West, he fell in with Smith to settle down beside him with an Arapahoe squaw. When the Georgians return, they and the Kansans and squaw men settle down together for the winter.

For four months Lawrence has heard nothing at all of John Easter's party. Men speculate variously upon its fate. The bright cool days of Indian summer come before a solitary horseman rides in from the West one afternoon on a lean footsore pony. Word flies about that John King has returned from the diggings. All Lawrence presses forward for news. In public King talks with vague optimism of the diggings. But to a favored few he privately exhibits a quill — a quill filled with dust.

King's secret is not long kept. All Lawrence quickly knows it and neighboring towns as well. It early reaches the ears of the Larimers, private bankers and dealers in land warrants at Leavenworth. Here at Leavenworth the greatest excitement prevails. Street corners are crowded far into the night with men eagerly discussing routes and equipment necessary for a dash to the "Kansas Gold Fields." Leavenworth, it seems, is about to be depopulated. But when preparations actually begin, less than eighty men prove ready for adventure. In the end nine tenths of these withdraw. Some fear the uncertainty of wood and water along the way. Others argue the lateness of the season, citing the real danger of freezing or starving to death in the blizzards likely any day to sweep the prairies. All recall bloody tales of the Indians near the mountains. Six resolute men persevere and shortly take the road under the command of General William Larimer.

This Larimer group, although typical of every gold rush, differs materially from other parties of Argonauts, as the pioneers of '58 soon begin to style themselves. Neither General Larimer, nor his son Will, nor his chief lieutenant Dick Whitsitt are interested primarily in the mines. They are business men — land speculators and town promoters by training and preference. The General himself has been many things and was once a man of influence in western Pennsylvania, amassing a considerable fortune there from Conestoga wagon lines, wholesale groceries, real estate developments, railroads and coal mines — a varied career crowned at last by appointment as Major General of Militia. Wiped out in the panic of '54 and pathetically eager to regain a responsible and respectable station in life, Larimer came West to found La Platte City on the Nebraska prairie, an ambitious but soon abandoned settlement. He then retreated to Omaha, served a term in the territorial legislature, immediately transferring his allegiance to Leavenworth when that town began to boom. The General as speculator and promoter objects on principle to squatters' free and easy ways. As he races' toward the mountains, he only hopes they have not preempted all choice lands.

Up the Santa Fe Trail the Larimer party slowly plods from fifteen to twenty miles a day. Before them and to either side stretches the boundless rolling prairie, brown and dry at this late season, with nothing to be seen but occasional clumps of bare cottonwoods in creek and river bottoms. One long weary day of travel is much like any other — except that each grows colder. Nor do they dare light campfires at night, for the Indians worry them by following their wagon constantly. Every day Indian bands can be seen on distant ridges riding a parallel course. Several times a day the warriors come charging toward the wagon to beg trinkets, coffee, tobacco, sugar and firewater. They sorely try Larimer's patience, but he never quite dares deny his friendly but unwelcome outriders. Late every afternoon the Indians ride off not to be seen again until the party is breaking camp next morning. They ride off because they have good reason to distrust the whites. But the General is not one to appreciate this and lives in constant dread of a night attack. Cold as nights are, all fires are regularly stamped out before sunset.

The Larimers meet and are joined by a small party of gold-hunters from Oskaloosa, Kansas. Some days later the combined party is surprised to see three horsemen riding down the trail on their way to the States. They stop to talk. One rider identifies himself as Green Russell. Larimer is shocked. What does this mean? Russell explains that he is returning to Georgia to bring out a large party in the spring. More reassuring, he shows them several small bottles of dust. But he tells them frankly how matters stand at the diggings.

" If I'd met you in Leavenworth," he concludes, " I would have advised you to stay where you were. But as you've started, I would say, go on and see for yourselves."

Even so little encouragement renews enthusiasm, and the party presses forward to the Picketwire (Purgatoire) River near which stands Colonel William Bent's great stone fort at Big Timbers. It mounts four cannon on its walls, covers more than an acre of ground and houses a number of hunters, trappers, traders, teamsters and general hands — the nucleus of Bent's private army, small but formidable. The Colonel is induced to sell the travelers a dozen apples for $1, their first fresh food in a month, and his fort somewhat quiets their fears as they pass into wilder country beyond.

Nearing the mountains they note signs of travelers ahead and come up to find campfires burning in the river bottom near Pueblo, a cluster of adobe huts occupied chiefly by Mexicans, all that remains of Jim Beckwourth's old trading post. A few years previously Utes boldly raided it to kill and scalp more than a dozen men, only one escaping alive. Larimer sends his party off across country to the north before advancing to the campfires by the river. There he finds eleven men from Lecompton, Kansas, under the command of " Colonel " Ed Wynkoop. They announce

their intention of wintering where they are. Larimer is not dis-
pleased until informed that they have been authorized to organize
the gold fields as Arapahoe County, Kansas, and have had themselves appointed its chief officers. These men are obviously needed
as allies. Larimer now pointedly argues the necessity of proceeding immediately to Cherry Creek before everything of value is
preempted. But the Lecomptonites still hesitate. It is too late,
they fear, to cross the high divide between the Arkansas and
South Platte valleys where a large military command had been
almost overwhelmed by disaster not five months previously
—in fact, late in May, when a terrible blizzard suddenly de-
scended from the mountains. The soldiers had suffered cruelly.
Two had perished and all had been badly frost-bitten. Many
ponies and mules, not to be replaced within a radius of many
hundred miles, had also been lost to the great peril of the
survivors.

But the General finally prevails and the combined Leavenworth-
Oskaloosa-Lecompton party, praying for good weather, hurries
north past Jimmie's Camp and Fagan's Grave, ominous names.
On the crest of the Divide the wind rises suddenly, clouds come
scudding over the mountains, flurries of snow sweep round the
wagons and before camp can be made, the storm breaks furiously
upon them. Huddled together in the wagons, the Argonauts
scarcely dare think of what may happen as the oxen, maddened
by the driving sleet, plunge and kick and break from harness.
All night the blizzard rages as the wind and cold increase. But
the morning fortunately breaks clear. The cattle are found
to have taken shelter under a rock ledge nearby. By noon the
wagons are again moving forward and on November 16th, almost
fifty days out from Leavenworth, the Larimer party and its
allies descend the Platte and pull up in the cottonwood grove

Green Russell
Discoverer of Gold in Colorado

Larimer Street, Denver, '59

where Auraria is rising to busy sounds of axe and saw and hammer.

Camp is no sooner made than Larimer goes on a round of inspection. Decisive measures taken that very night reflect his disappointment. Already an Auraria Town Company has been formed. Already thirty or more log houses are built or building to either side of the Jack Jones-John Smith double cabin. As it is obvious that no time is to be lost, the General calls a council. Whitsitt and a partner are sent up the river to the town of Montana. Two others are dispatched downstream to survey the situation there. Larimer and his son sit quietly in camp until nightfall when the General, shaking off the fatigue of his long journey, slips quietly from camp, crosses the dry bed of Cherry Creek and spends a chill fireless night on the far bank where he proposes to stake out a rival townsite.

His son Will joins him at dawn and together they hastily begin building a cabin, for no claim is recognized without one. They are only well started, however, when a horseman comes galloping up the Platte to order them off. Several of the Lawrence party, it seems, have made precisely the General's estimate of the situation and have already laid claim to the sand flats as the townsite of St. Charles. They have already organized a town company with Jack Jones and John Smith as members. Shares were given the squaw men for the curious but adequate reason, so a St. Charles promoter later explained, " that we thought they might help protect our interests to a certain extent, for the land belonged to the Arapahoes."

The Larimers, having " jumped " the sand flats like any squatters, defy the horseman and stubbornly refuse to move. They form a town company of their own, debating long and earnestly about the best name for the still nebulous city. Golden City rules as favorite until some shrewder person suggests the desirability of honoring Governor James W. Denver of Kansas. Denver City they name it, only to have all hopes of favors from that quarter dashed when word comes at length of the Governor's resignation a month previously. The St. Charles promoters now press the Kansas legislature to pass a bill incorporating their company and granting it title to the land. This the legislature is expressly forbidden to do, for Congress in creating Kansas Territory specifically denied it the right to alienate any lands owned by the Indians by treaty with the Federal Government. The legislature nevertheless passes the St. Charles bill. Larimer dispatches an agent in a frantic attempt to persuade the governor to veto the bill. He fails for reasons perhaps not then known to him.

"On the last night of the session, at 11:30 P.M., I went to the Governor's office and stated briefly that if anyone had any rights, we had priority," wrote a leader of the St. Charles group. " Knowing the Governor had a son, I said to him, ' If you will sign this bill, I will give your son one hundred lots.' — He signed the bill."

The General, still refusing to admit defeat, now desperately proposes that the two companies compromise and unite to promote a larger and finer Denver City. It is so arranged. The St. Charles Company accepts $250 in cash for its rights and each member receives a share in the reorganized town company. The Indians are given a barbecue of three whole oxen.

By spring the two rival camps on Cherry Creek can boast of perhaps one hundred small cabins, all similar in style and construction like the cabins of every early mining camp. Logs, round or hewed, are laid up to a height of seven or eight feet. These support a flat roof frame of split timbers, covered first with dry grass and then with six inches of dirt. Doors are covered with canvas stripped from the hood of prairie schooners. Oiled cloth stretched over window openings admits some light. Such cabins are very dark, very warm and also very wet, " the rain usually continuing three days indoors after the weather has cleared up outside." But they are not too uncomfortable and life in them offers a number of simple pleasures.

" You have no idea how nice Will and I are fixed up," Larimer writes his family. " We have plenty of everything to eat. Today we had nice cakes, venison, beans and molasses for dinner. We have a nice door with an old-fashioned wooden latch, with the string on the outside of course. The fireplace, as is the custom in this country, is made of sods. In the southeast corner is the bunk; in the northwest corner the window, four panes of glass with sash. On the north side, between the end of the bed and the fireplace, we have two shelves and a bench, all made with a nice slab. We cut the meat on the bench and set water buckets on the other two shelves. . . . I have the remaining hams hung up; also, the saw, auger and hatchet, also the two bed cords and two pairs of boots and sundry little matters. On the northeast side and corner we hang our coats, guns and things. I have a nail box, shovels and old boots and buffalo overshoes under the bunk. . . . I am writing on a nice pine table under the window, covered with the gray horse blanket as nice as the day we started. On this table I have my books and papers, ink stand and all the other nice things, together with a candlestick and candle, with some matches ready to light. Will scoured up the candlestick today; it looks clean and nice.

" We have also another pine table to eat upon. Will has on it a nice table cloth of muslin. We have four nice stools with my trunk and waterbag to sit upon. I have the comb and hair brush on the window sill. Will made a nice willow broom. I have David Copperfield, my Bible and your Prayer Book together with some old newspapers and a lot of Mr. Collier's books on this table.

"We have three sacks of flour and some crackers with plenty of candles, soap, dried apples, rice, onions, about three gallons of molasses, 100 pounds of bacon, 50 to 60 pounds of sugar, 30 or 40 of coffee, 1/3 of a bag of salt and nearly a bushel of beans. . . . You have no idea how comfortable we all live. We sleep warm and nice."

The General indeed is prepared to speak well of almost everything but the lack of news from home, a want soon filled by Saunders' Express, the first and most important institution of the day. Late in November Jim Saunders and his squaw depart in an open wagon for Fort Laramie. Upon their return two months later the entire camp crowds about their wagon. As names are called, men fight their way forward to pay twenty-five cents for each newspaper and fifty cents for each letter. Larimer stands confidently to the last and can scarcely credit his ears.

"Our mail is in," he writes his oldest son in great anguish, "and only think, John, we did not get either letters or newspapers from you or any other. . . . Oh! the sad disappointment when the next thirty days will have to pass without another mail. I never felt such a sore disappointment. I have no heart to write more today."

"Congregate one hundred Americans anywhere beyond the settlements," remarked one with an eye to the local scene, "and they immediately lay out a city, form a State constitution and apply for admission to the Union, while twenty-five of them become candidates for the United States Senate."

Little more than a month after Larimer's arrival, at a time

when the entire region does not contain more than two hundred persons, an ambitious attempt is made to cut the gold fields from Kansas and organize them as the Territory of Colona. A delegate to Washington is chosen at an election marked by considerable irregularity. In general, Denver City is aligned against Auraria, but drink is also an issue. Party lines are rather confused, however, with abstemious General Larimer campaigning for " wet " William Clancy. But as Clancy also represents the General's town company, Larimer can forgive him his morals.

On election day a great blizzard is howling so that few in Denver City come to the polls, a deficiency which Clancy decides to remedy himself. With a few supporters he slips away to a secluded cabin. There the younger Larimer, according to his own story, reads a long list of names from a Kansas directory as the candidate and his friends cast votes. But if congratulations are exchanged, they are rather premature.

With the approach of evening Aurarians come valiantly to the support of their candidate. " After supper," so one relates the story, " I told the boys I was going to fix up a ballot box, and, taking a cigar box, I soon had a good one. Then arose the question as to who would administer the oath of office to the election board. Some contended it would make no difference in this far-off country whether they were sworn in or not. Others made it plain that everything should be regular. They finally put it to a vote that I should administer the oath. After supper, in the midst of the blizzard, we wrapped up our books and ballot box and started out to the different cabins for more votes from those who had failed to brave the storm, and by nine o'clock we had enough votes to beat Mr. Clancy — I think it was about a seven majority — and thus we prevented the sending of a drinking man to Congress."

Delegate Graham inspires only smiles at Washington, but the Cherry Creek camps do not lose hope. Within a few months a number of self-appointed delegates assemble, with General Larimer in the chair, to proclaim "many strong reasons why a State government should be adopted." They resolve that the " name of the proposed new State shall be Jefferson." This movement fails when the working portion of the population — the miners — refuses " to take the slightest interest in these political maneuvers." But aspiring politicians are never easily gainsaid. They call another convention of self-appointed delegates who proceed to establish a provisional government for the Territory of Jefferson. As the proceedings have no constitutional warrant whatever, this extra-legal provisional government is recognized neither at Washington nor by Kansas which continues to administer the region as the County of Arapahoe. The gold fields remain subject to two rival sets of authorities till '61 when Congress organizes them as the Territory of Colorado, spurning the name Jefferson as smacking too much of Democracy, then fatally identified with the slave-holding South.

No mining at all is done along Cherry Creek during the winter, and gold-hunters dare not venture into the mountains before spring. Although they do not quite believe, miners are not yet prepared to deny trappers' tales of winter there — of fabulous blizzards sweeping down without warning from the high white ranges to bury the pines under forty or fifty feet of snow. All have lost faith in the local diggings. During the long winter the only mining in the entire region is done at the mouth of Dry Creek by one Andrew Jackson of the Oskaloosa party, who works every pleasant day with an occasional profit of a few dollars. In fact, as the younger Larimer once declared without great exaggeration, "there were only a few prospect holes on Cherry Creek, and in all the region around there was never found (as long as I was in the country) enough gold to fill a goose quill."

Restlessly awaiting spring to be off into the mountains, miners turn to the few simple pleasures at hand. Drinking and gambling prove the most congenial. For months there has been little whiskey in camp. No doubt many a demijohn started from the Missouri River, but few survived the arid prairie and thirsty Indian. On Christmas Eve, however, a wagon loaded with all kinds of merchandise is driven in by Richens Lacy ("Uncle Dick") Wootton, old trader and trapper, friend of Colonel Bent, Kit Carson and Jim Bridger and once as renowned as any of these. Wootton has come north from Taos to trade with the Arapahoes and Cheyennes who know him both affectionately and fearfully as "Cut Hand." The miners crowd round his wagon and beg him to sell flour, sugar and all that he carries. Greater profit is to be had from the Indians, but the miners prove so clamorously insistent that Uncle Dick at last agrees and in the end remains several years to become a leader in camp.

Auraria, he finds, has "no such thing as a store or anything like one." He moves into a log cabin and starts business "without waiting for any such things as shelves or counters to be put in." But there is no need of counters, for the miners' eyes are fixed upon three large barrels in his cargo. All contain "Taos Lightning," a staple of the early days — a raw rank Mexican distillation of which it was said that none indulging ever lived long enough to become an addict. Wootton rolls the barrels inside his cabin, ranges them on end as a bar, taps one, fills a number of tin pans from the gurgling bung and with a friendly open-handed gesture endearing him to all but a few, invites the miners to drink their fill. The " Lightning " strikes fast, hard and often that first Christmas Eve but with no fatalities.

" You have no idea of the gambling carried on here in Auraria," Larimer tells his wife. " They go it day and night, Sundays and all, and Oh, how they drink. You cannot conceive of anything as bad as they carry on here. . . . Neither Will nor I go out at night."

Nor do the Larimers appear to have dissipated their quiet evenings at home with *David Copperfield* or Mr. Collier. Practical matters fully occupy their minds. With four shares and twenty choicest lots in Denver City they now seize two large tracts abandoned by the town company. They also envisage the necessity of still another townsite. One cold morning at dawn they hasten to the Platte, ford its icy waters, clamber up the bluffs on the far side and there stake out the City of Highlands. A few cabins are erected, but development is slow and Larimer turns to other things. The diggings need a hotel. At first sight it seems certain to pay handsomely. On second consideration the General decides not: a floating population of miners is not apt to pay its bills.

Late in January, to the amazement of all, six men from Michigan come stumbling into camp " with their hand-carts, . . . a most destitute lot." They have almost miraculously fought their way to safety up treacherous Smoky Hill, pushing their heavy handcarts more than seven hundred miles through deep sand and snow. The first of thousands of even more reckless gold-hunters, they come bringing news of a virulent gold fever sweeping the States. Men are everywhere talking of the new Eldorado and preparing to rush to the Cherry Creek diggings.

Larimer hastily writes his son John at Leavenworth and exhorts him to expand his land and banking business to include a whole-sale and retail grocery, " with iron and nails on the side." For, as the General declares with less exaggeration that he can ever have dreamed possible, " All the world and the rest of mankind will be fitting out there by early Spring."

III. PIKE'S PEAK OR BUST!

". . . a glaring illustration of human recklessness, avidity and folly, a powerful effect of an insignificant cause, the strongest possible proof of the almightiness of gold."

ALMOST incredibly General Larimer's prophecy comes true. Long before it is safe to travel the snowbound prairies, excited reckless gold-hunters by the tens of thousands begin to fill up the Missouri River towns. The South Platte diggings have yet to produce $1,000 of dust, but this deters none. Green Russell himself made an attempt to stem the rising tide. On his way home to Georgia he publicly warned Leavenworth that as the gold fields had yet to be proved, all could afford to await receipt of better news. He prophesied maddening hardships and death itself for many if a great human flood suddenly descended upon the tiny camps on Cherry Creek. But Leavenworth turned a deaf ear, charging him with a sinister desire to monopolize the diggings by frightening others off.

Not yet recovered from the panic of '57, the country offers little resistance to the gold fever. Unemployment is widespread. Thousands of farmers and merchants are bankrupt. Like Larimer many turn their eyes hopefully toward the West. There in the foreground looms Pike's Peak — bright and alluring enough in itself, but now most extravagantly gilded by hundreds of editors and town promoters. Cherry Creek speculators have not done all, or even the most part, of the gilding. The brightest patches have been contributed by the Border towns along the Missouri, all of which have been especially hard hit by the panic. As an increased population, even a transient one, is a matter of life or death to all of them, they seize upon the gold excitement with a determination to make the most of it, each loudly crying itself up as the best point of departure for the mines.

For months every Border town has had agents busily canvassing city and countryside, trains and river steamboats. Throughout the country, the Middle West especially, they gratuitously distribute publications " containing either false or fabricated evidence of the richness of the mines." These publications consist largely of Pike's Peak guidebooks revealing little but the ignorance and dishonesty of their authors and sponsors. " Gold exists throughout all this region," one announces. " It can be found anywhere — on the plains, in the mountains, and by the streams. In fact, there is no end of the precious metal. Nature herself would seem to have turned into a most successful alchemist in converting the very sands of the stream to gold." A second insists " that at least as far as to the summitt of the Rocky Mountains the journey is one of the most delightful and invigorating." The St. Louis Chamber of Commerce becomes so excited that it addresses a memorial to Congress demanding a local branch mint. As it has its information " from gentlemen so well known in the West for their truth and veracity," the Chamber declares it a fact that the " country on the headwaters of the Platte and Arkansas, to the extent of three hundred miles north and south, and from forty to fifty miles east and west, is richly covered with gold deposits of great purity and fineness."

Even more extravagant reports fill the Border press and are copied uncritically by newspapers throughout the country. In fact, according to the younger Larimer, the gold rush is stimulated largely by falsified reports of Andrew Jackson's occasional operations on Dry Creek during the winter. Letters reporting his gains are seized upon by Kansas editors who swell his profits from $2.50 to $25.00 a day. It is these same editors who name the gold rush, for their confident knowledge of the richness of the diggings is not matched by knowledge of their location. They place them vaguely at the base of Pike's Peak, almost one hundred miles south of Green Russell's abandoned diggings on the Platte.

At St. Louis enterprising promoters publicly exhibit three-ounce nuggets ostensibly from Cherry Creek. " Now there is *Shenanigan* going on," protests a Denver City miner indignantly but in vain. " This thing is being done by speculators in town property out here and on the Border, and should be denied by all the papers; it was never found in such lumps, within a thousand miles of Pike's Peak, and the originators of such stories, to advance their own interests, *should be lynched,* and the emigrants who come out here next spring, will, if they find out the originators of these stories do this thing. Now, tell any of my friends who may think of coming out here next season, that they will curse the day they started; tell them to *stay at home* and not listen to all the stories they hear. There is a bare possibility that enough gold may be discovered here next season to pay for the emigration. If so, it will be a wonder."

From end to end the country is swept by the gold fever. During '59 more than one hundred thousand people, all conservative estimates agree, abandon their homes in the Middle West, East and South to join the rush to the new Eldorado. In a mounting flood they converge upon the Missouri River towns — by train, by river steamboat, by stage coach, by covered wagon, on horseback and on foot. Early in the spring before the snows are melted, long lines of prairie schooners come wallowing axle-deep in mud across Iowa and Missouri. On every canvas top appears, painted in large black letters, *Pike's Peak or Bust!*

Every prairie schooner is crowded with gold-hunters from every walk of life. Hal Sayre and a friend, two young engineers from the East, arrive at the Mississippi by train and lie stranded there for days, unable to obtain passage in any of the crowded wagons passing by. They are picked up finally by two farmers in an old battered wagon drawn by a single yoke of feeble oxen. As the price of their passage they buy a year's provisions for the party. Captain Peleg Bassett finds times dull on the lower Mississippi and persuades three fellow-steamboat pilots to resign their commands and ship with him on a prairie schooner. Far away in Georgia the Reverend Hezekiah Porter recruits sixteen hardy souls among his Methodist congregation and leads them forth toward Canaan. By Horace Greeley's *Tribune* the excitement is imparted to a quiet Connecticut village where an unemployed youth of nineteen decides to join the rush. Young Ryan works his way to St. Louis hoping to find a job there and earn enough to carry him on to the diggings. But times are bad and jobs are not to be had. One day as he is idling away an afternoon upon the levee, he spies the *S. S. New Monongahela* loading for a trip up the Missouri. From stem to stern runs a large white streamer with immense black letters crudely painted upon it: *Ho! for the Gold Fields of Kansas!* From another youth, a chance acquaintance, Ryan borrows money and both take passage. The steamer, large as it is, is densely crowded. There are " seven hundred people aboard," the majority bound for the gold fields. As there are not berths for so many, almost all have to sleep on deck.

Five days later Ryan and his new friend Rice disembark at Leavenworth to drop from sight for a time in the seething confusion reigning in every Border town.

In how many thousands of farmhouses in the East and Middle West occurred scenes similar to this on the homestead of Robert Teats in Michigan when the Detroit *Free Press* and New York *Ledger* first brought news of Pike's Peak gold — scenes which profoundly affected the lives not of adventurers alone but of their families for generations.

" How vividly I recall the interest of the family in the news," wrote Eugene Teats of these exciting days of his boyhood. " Father, after a hard day's work in the fields, going out to the gate to get the mail from the hired man whose duty it was to go for it every Saturday afternoon — and how we children would be allowed to sit up later than usual to hear him read of the great unknown country beyond the Missouri. Each week through the winter the news became more interesting and finally by Spring, after most of the hard work on the new and only partly-developed farm had been performed, Dad decided to go to Detroit (some 20 miles away) and make a more careful study of the conditions reported in the papers. In a few days he returned, fuller than ever of enthusiasm. That evening he and Mother sat up later than usual talking the subject over. We children, of course, were sent to bed early, but my own enthusiasm would not allow me to sleep. So, waiting until my elder brother who slept with me had dropped off into a sound slumber, I carefully slid out of bed and tiptoed across the floor to the stove-pipe thimble and putting my ear to the holes, found I could hear perfectly all that was being said in the room below. The upshot of their talk was that Mother thought she could handle the farm that year with the help of two trusted hired men and us boys, if Father wanted to go, which was surely his desire."

The question of finance bothered as did the problem of the family in case the crops failed, which was all too possible. But these matters were finally arranged. Then Uncle Phillip, the father's only unmarried brother, was summoned to a general family conference. " As I knew what was going on, my interest in the conference can easily be imagined," said Eugene, " for absurd as it may seem, I had hopes that I might soon be drawn into the adventure although at the time I was just past eight years old. No such luck, however, for Uncle Phillip took up the scheme with the greatest enthusiasm. Then all fell to studying such maps of the West as were available in those days, discussing routes and deciding upon necessary equipment, for the journey would have to start at our own front door and with our own animals, and it was one of considerably more than a thousand miles."

A bright new " dead-axle " wagon was bought and when wheeled under the carriage shed to be remodeled, became the focus of the eyes and energies of all. The farm itself furnished tough young hickories to be dressed down and bent into the great bows which, when spread with canvas, transformed a plain farm wagon into as romantic a schooner as ever sailed the seas. Eugene had his part in the glamorous adventure. He helped bend the bows. " This was accomplished by selecting a level area in the yard where stakes were firmly driven in in the shape of a great letter ' U,' around and between which the tough pliant slats were slowly bent by means of hot water, which it was my duty to heat and pour over them.

" Next, on each side of the top of the wagon box, shelves were extended out over the wheels to serve as beds for the travelers.

At the ends, cupboards were built for clothing and other uses. So, gradually, after the long hickory bows were set in place and covered with stout canvas, the little home on wheels began to look so inviting that I could not resist frequent pleading to go. But I was always reminded that Mother depended more upon me than some other members of the family. And at last, early in the summer, with Nell the pet mare of the family in harness with her mate, Father started off one bright morning for the long drive to the Rocky Mountains. Little conception had any of us of the magnitude and perils of the undertaking. It was fully six months before we heard of his safe arrival in Auraria, the little settlement on the left bank of Cherry Creek."

What gold-hunters require as equipment and what it costs may be learned from one of the more reliable guidebooks of the day, which thus lists a minimum outfit for a party of four persons for a period of six months (see opposite page).

More, a fast saddle pony on which to scout for wood and water is almost a necessity — an additional item of $100. Expense is further increased if horses are used in harness. In general oxen are preferred to horses on the Plains for several good reasons. They are cheaper. They can subsist wholly on pasturage along the way while both horses and mules require grain in quantities rather too heavy and bulky to carry. And as compelling a reason as any, oxen are less frequently stolen or stampeded by the Indians.

Such a minimum outfit, even with its cost shared among four, is beyond the means of thousands. Many poorer men fell into traps set by such concerns as the Gold Mine Emigration Office of Chicago. Here one W. H. Horner, author of a Pike's Peak guidebook, advertises that " parties who can raise FIFTY to

Spirit of American Progress

Stagecoach on the Plains

PROVISIONS, ETC.

1,000 lbs., flour	($30.00)	4 gallons, vinegar
400 lbs., bacon	($40.00)	2 gallons, pickles
200 lbs., sugar	($18.00)	2 dozen boxes of matches
150 lbs., beans	($ 4.00)	1 coffee-mill
100 lbs., dried beef	($12.00)	1 frying pan
50 lbs., salt		1 Dutch oven
50 lbs., coffee		3 camp kettles
40 lbs., dried fruit		6 tin plates and cups
30 lbs., rice		1 set of knives and forks
25 lbs., soap		1 butcher knife
10 lbs., pepper		8 sets of spoons
8 lbs., tea		50 lbs., lead for bullets
6 lbs., cream of tartar		1,000 gun caps
3 lbs., soda		

Total

$158.30

TOOLS, TEAMS, ETC.

8 yoke of oxen	($240.00)	4 axes
1 wagon, cover, etc.	($ 85.00)	6 lbs., wrought nails
1 tent, etc.	($ 15.00)	3 augers
10 pairs of blankets	($ 40.00)	1 chisel
4 gold pans	($ 2.00)	1 hand-saw
yoke, chains, etc.	($ 9.00)	1 drawing knife
4 steel picks		1 half-inch file
4 steel shovels		

$410.35

Provisions 158.30

$568.65

SEVENTY-FIVE DOLLARS can reach the mines with sufficient provisions to sustain them for three or four months." Others make use of the more legitimate services of such concerns as the Pike's Peak Transportation Company which widely advertises that on April first it will start " its first train of Ten Wagons from St. Louis, Mo., via Leavenworth City, for Pike's Peak, for the purpose of transporting Passengers and their Baggage. The price of Passage, including fifty pounds of Baggage and Mining Tools, Provisions en route and thirty days after arrival, will be One Hundred and Twenty-five Dollars ($125)." What such companies studiously refrain from advertising is that they contract only to carry gold-hunters' baggage. As thousands bitterly complain, all " passengers " have to walk.

Great hazard attends any attempt to cross the Plains before the first of May, especially if oxen are used. Only then do the prairies offer fresh green pasture. Only then are blizzards unlikely. But fevered gold-hunters, ignorant of even the rudiments of pioneer travel, begin to rush blindly forward as early as February. A large number trace the steps of the Lawrence and Leavenworth parties up the Santa Fe Trail. A larger number follow the Overland Trail as far as the South Platte up which they turn to toil through long stretches of deep sand to the diggings.

Up the Overland Trail races William N. Byers " with his shirt tail full of type " in a frantic desire to establish the first newspaper in the gold fields. One day he spies a strange white object astern. A wagon with two great sails bellied out by the wind bears down upon his slow-moving schooner, flashes by and is soon lost in the sunset. Next morning it is seen again — a total wreck in a deep ravine. Many parties along this route are snowed in for weeks at a time. Soon the entire trail from the Missouri to Cherry Creek is lined " with cooking stoves, clothing and mining tools, thrown away to lighten loads " — with the rotting carcasses of oxen, horses and mules which have perished along the way. It is not long before gold-hunters find the road marked with " many fresh graves." Upon a secluded island in the Platte the " bloody remains of a little girl with a broken skull " is discovered by a Boston journalist who finds it " difficult to surmise the motive of the murder of the poor child."

Two other routes are soon opened to the gold fields. Both are shorter than the roads up the Santa Fe and Overland trails but many times more dangerous. One ascends the Republican Fork and the other the treacherous Smoky Hill Fork of the Kansas River. Up the former toils Horace Austin Warner Tabor with his wife and year-old baby, both weak and ailing.

Although wholly undistinguished now and destined to remain so till late in life, Tabor is a man to mark — with his large head and great black moustache, his heavy thick body and his slow fumbling speech and thought. After long bitter years of failure and defeat he will awaken one morning to discover himself, thanks to a jug of whiskey, Colorado's first great Bonanza King. He will become banker and patron of the arts, of the drama in particular. He will grace the United States Senate. In his life, in fact, he will epitomize a colorful era now gone forever.

A poor stonecutter from Topsham, Vermont, where he was born in 1830 of Sarah (Ferrin) and Cornelius Tabor, small farmer and country schoolmaster, Horace was early driven from home by a stepmother. In Massachusetts he joined an older brother who taught him his trade. Tabor later drifted to Portland,

Maine, where in the panic year of '57 he married his employer's daughter, Augusta Pierce. A frail and delicate girl, she was rather angular perhaps both in figure and manner as New England girls are apt to be. But whatever Augusta may have wanted in physical strength, comeliness and charm, none ever denied her remarkable moral stamina, steadfast loyalty and great unpretentious courage. As times were bad, Augusta immediately acquiesced in Tabor's desire to seek fortune in the West. They journeyed by train to its terminus at St. Louis and thence by five-day boat to Westport (Kansas City). There, said Augusta, "we purchased a yoke of oxen, a wagon, a few farming tools, some seed, took my trunks and started westward. The trip was not very pleasant, for the wind blew disagreeably, as it always does in Kansas."

At Zeandale, near Manhattan, the Tabors claimed an abandoned homestead and started housekeeping in a deserted cabin standing solitary and alone upon the open rolling prairie. "To add to the desolation of the place the wind took a new start. Our only furniture was a No. 7 cook stove, a dilapidated trunk and a rough bedstead made of poles, on which was an old tick filled with prairie grass. I sat down upon the trunk and cried," declared Augusta. "I had not been deceived in coming to this place. I knew perfectly well that the country was new, that there were no saw mills near and no money in the territory. But I was homesick and could not conceal it from the others."

Here Tabor broke the ground and put in seed, exchanging day labor with neighbors to save hiring help. Augusta worked in the fields as well until brought to bed with her first and only child, Nathaniel Maxcy. During that first summer no rain at all fell. When harvest came, there was nothing to gather. That winter Tabor went to Fort Riley nearby to work at his trade.

Augusta remained at home to mind her baby and raise chickens. Indians and snakes infested the neighborhood and Augusta lived in dread of both, especially of the rattlesnakes which she occasionally found coiled in her cabin. The next summer brought much rain and an abundant crop. But the Tabors were but little better off than before as they could find no market for their produce. What little money the family had was earned by Augusta who " kept boarders and made some butter to sell." Certainly Kansas seemed to offer little hope of fortune.

" In February, 1859, Mr. Tabor heard of Pike's Peak through someone of Green Russell's party who was returning, and at once decided to try his luck in the new Eldorado. He told me I might go home to Maine, but I refused to leave him, and upon reflection he thought it would be more profitable to take me, as in that case the two men would go along and board with us, and the money they paid would keep us all. . . . Mr. Tabor worked at the Fort through March and April, earning money for the outfit. The fifth day of May we gathered together our scanty means, bought supplies for a few months, yoked our oxen and cows, mounted to our seats in the wagon and left the town of Zeandale with the determination of returning in the Fall, or as soon as we made enough money to pay for the one hundred and sixty acres of Government land and buy a little stock."

Unsuspecting their destiny — their separate tragic destinies — the Tabors drive off never to return. Soon they are plodding up the Republican River through lush green prairies starred with crimson anemones and blue larkspur, shadowed with dark belts of purple bunch grass. Timber along creek and river bottoms gradually thins out and finally disappears. Now they are among the buffalo, antelope and Indians on the high brown Plains. The Tabors pass Hurricane Creek just a few weeks after it has been named from a tornado which "overturned heavy freight wagons, blew a light buggy into fragments, tore open boxes and scattered dry goods for several miles and rolled cooking stoves forty to fifty yards." The Tabors encounter no hurricanes or cloudbursts such as imperil the lives of thousands traveling this road before and after them. But every afternoon they anxiously watch towering white thunderheads gather in the west to cast an indigo shadow over the suddenly hushed and sultry afternoon. Great shafts of rose-colored lightning flash across the sky. Thunder crashes with a deafening report to roll heavily off into the distance. Suddenly with a cyclonic rush of wind the storm bursts upon them. Not even white squalls on tropic seas, according to a world traveler following this road a few years later, equal the sudden violence of these thunderstorms which often shoot down hailstones big as pigeon eggs to whiten the ground for miles around.

Day after day the Tabors follow the strenuous, almost invariable routine imposed upon all gold-hunters. By seven o'clock they have breakfasted, struck their tent, repacked the wagon, captured the grazing cattle and yoked them. They drive a full five hours before lunch. During the heat of the day they usually rest an hour or two, sometimes amusing themselves with a game of cards, more often creeping under the wagon to nap in the shade. In the afternoon they drive three or four more hours before one of the men is sent ahead to scout for a campsite. Again the cattle are turned out to pasture while supper is preparing and the tent is being raised. More often than not, there is no wood. Buffalo dung must serve as fuel. Occasionally even this is hard to find. It sometimes requires an hour or two to gather sufficient to cook coffee, beans and bacon. The weary work of gathering buffalo chips falls to Augusta's lot, for the men have all they can do in caring for the teams and in making and breaking camp. Supper is finished before dusk. The oxen are herded back once more to be tied securely to the wagon wheels. The wagon itself is frequently staked down against the wind. Smudges are built to drive off the clouds of insects which harass both themselves and the cattle. White stars are out before Augusta and the men make ready for bed. The watchman for the night takes his post. Rifles and revolvers are looked to and placed within easy reach. At last all lie down to rest as best they can — to be up again next morning at daybreak.

"Indians followed us all the time," declared Augusta, " and though friendly, were continually begging and stealing. Every Sunday we rested, if rest it could be called. The men went hunting, while I stayed to guard the camp, wash the soiled linen and cook for the following week." But Augusta often accomplished nothing at all on Sundays, for the departure of the men emboldened the Indians in their worst practices. When not begging and stealing, they wallowed in the water courses from which the party drew its supplies and were generally pretty filthy, said Augusta. " My babe was teething and suffering from fever and ague, and required constant attention day and night. I was weak and feeble, having suffered all the time I lived in Kansas with the ague. My weight was only ninety pounds. . . . What I endured on that journey only the women who crossed the plains in '59 can realize."

Altogether it was a searing experience, but years later Augusta looked back upon it without regret. " I can almost see the approach of each night's camping ground. I can tell how, when, where and how many buffalo my husband killed. I can see just how the Indians looked as they came on begging expeditions to our wagon. The antelope, the great herds of buffalo, the wild flowers I gathered, the prairie chickens, the bright mornings, the fragrant atmosphere. . . . I was a girl then, filled with enthusiasm. I feared nothing."

Augusta almost alone among her contemporaries, it should be said now rather than later, looked upon the antelope and buffalo and prairie chicken as something more than meat for the pot. She was one of the few who saw more in the lush green prairies than potential real estate. No other later recalled gathering wild flowers on fresh spring mornings warmed by a bright yellow sun. And never in later years did she come to look upon the mountains merely as heaps of earth and rock piled up perversely by the gods to conceal gold and silver treasure.

There soon comes another with eyes to see and ears to hear. On the far side of the Missouri suddenly appears Eugene Teats, now all of nine years old, in " red-topped boots (long hoped for), a suit of blue overalls, one just a little better and a little carpetbag well loaded not only with a change of underwear but good home-cooked food." Eugene has left home alone for St. Joseph, Missouri, where he is to meet his father's partner, Colonel John Wanless, who will take him on to the diggings. Eugene has just arrived by train.

" What a crazy old road it was in those days, that Burlington and St. Joe. First ride aways, then walk aways, and those able to do so were expected to be prepared to help put the cars back on the track everytime they slipped off, which was often. We were all day, all night and until four P.M. of the second day in reaching St. Joe. The slow run was very tiresome, and I will admit that I was ready to turn my back on Pike's Peak after listening to the talk of the passengers, many of them bound for the P.P. country. When I heard of the discomforts and dangers they were looking forward to, more than ever did I long for home and Mother and consider going back while I still had money enough in my little belt so securely fastened around my waist. So when we landed and I strutted about the rickety old platform, expecting someone to grab me, and no one even inquired who I was or where I was going, my feelings do not have to be explained. So I went to the agent and told him my troubles, asking for a ticket and the time the train went back."

The kindly station agent smiles and takes the boy home with him for the night. Next day Eugene gets trace of the Colonel by making inquiries among the horse dealers. He learns the hotel at which the Colonel's family is stopping, knocks on their door and is " at once invited by Mrs. Wanless to come right in." The Colonel is off in the country buying stock, but several days later returns with horses and two farm hands who in their desire to reach the gold fields have signed on as teamsters without pay. Within the week the party departs in two heavy wagons, each drawn by two teams of horses, and the Colonel's ambulance, a light strong vehicle favored by army officers crossing the Plains. Eugene is given a place on the box beside the driver of the leading wagon. With the Colonel's ambulance bringing up the rear, the party is ferried across the Missouri and drives off into Kansas. They pass first through a thick forest, with cultivated clearings here and there, and are soon in open grass land. That first night they camp near a deserted cabin offering wood and water and shelter for the stock. After supper the Colonel orders nine-year-old Eugene to stand watch till midnight, under strict orders to call the next watch at that time. Although he does not pretend to know what is to be done or why, Eugene obeys without asking questions.

"Being very proud of the confidence placed in me, I had no difficulty in keeping awake. The night was fine, the camp fire was alive, and the fragrance of fried ham and pancakes still lingered around. It was not at all unpleasant; besides, I had a double-barrelled shotgun and was already feeling myself a man among men as a boy will under such circumstances. But about ten o'clock I was startled to attention by a long-drawn-out howl that seemed far away, followed almost immediately by another coming apparently from exactly the opposite direction, then by a succession of howls, each seemingly nearer than the one before. To say that I was alarmed would be to put the matter mildly. None of the sleepers seemed to hear the sounds that were so terrifying me, or if they did, did not take any notice of them. Nor were the stock in the least disturbed. So I managed, though badly scared, to stand my ground and refrain from calling for help. After a while, as usual, the chorus died out or came from such a distance that my courage revived. But the experience drove all thought of time out of my mind. Midnight came and went and left me still tensely listening for repetitions of what I still fancied to be a threatened attack by a troup of pernicious wild brutes. At last, close to four A.M., the horses, being more or less strange to one another, began to quarrel and move about uneasily. This finally resulted in a kicking bee which culminated when one big animal broke the rail to which he was tied in his stall, which of course made such a racket that the whole camp came awake. Three of us at once saddled and started in pursuit."

Several hours later Eugene finds the horse. But he is lying prostrate, with his back broken. In attempting to vault a small stream he had been thrown and killed when trees along the bank caught and held the dragging rail. The Colonel delivers the boy a " well-deserved lecture " before turning back to St. Joseph to procure another animal, leaving the party in camp at the deserted farm. Eugene improves the interim with sly questions to establish the cause of his alarm and is somewhat chagrined to see his " troup of pernicious wild brutes " turn into a band of sneaking coyotes. " But those who know what kind of a noise one coyote can make when on his mettle will understand the impression made on a youth (under ten) on hearing hundreds of them at night for the first time."

After more than a week of monotonous travel the driver of the leading wagon, a powerful young Scotch blacksmith, Eugene's favorite in the party, asks permission to quit his job. He wants " to strike out with some others on foot and get to the mountains and mines sooner." The Colonel is greatly upset and points out the difficulty.

" No trouble about that," says Scotty, " for that boy can beat me to death driving and caring for the teams. Let him try for a day or so, and I'll stay along until you satisfy yourself that with help in greasing the wagon and in handling the feed, he can take my job to your advantage."

Scotty departs, and Eugene now reigns alone upon the wagon box. But the Colonel orders him to drop back to second place in line. As they are plodding forward four days later, they come upon a fresh grave by the roadside. Eugene is overcome when he discovers it to be Scotty's. " But whether he was killed by whites or Indians we never learned but we inferred the former because the grave was evidently not the kind of one a savage would have given him. We knew that he had a good-sized wad of money when he left us, and as he was gifted with a love of whiskey like many of his countrymen and a rather loose tongue, we reached the conclusion that his new companions were in some way responsible for his death. But in those days when laws had not yet crossed the Missouri and a man was supposed to take care of himself or suffer the consequences, no one had the time or inclination to follow up a matter of that kind."

Colonel Wanless has chosen to proceed by the dangerous route up Smoky Hill. Now the party is struggling through the Ridge Country, barren and stony. Grass is thin and water scarce, most of it alkaline. Their grain supply, even at half rations, is rapidly disappearing. All that cheers them is sight at last of the snow-capped mountains far on the horizon. Eugene is in raptures. But more than one hundred difficult miles yet separate the party from Cherry Creek and safety.

The horses have now become too weak and footsore to go on. The Colonel decides to lighten up the ambulance and push on for help. Eugene and the driver of the other wagon are left to make what progress they can after allowing the horses a full day's rest. But when the teams are harnessed up again, one of Eugene's leaders collapses. They have to remain in camp on the hot dry Plains another day. Eugene is "pretty blue."

Next morning they learn of a station some miles in advance. But they have no money and Eugene says nothing of the gold in his belt, having long ago resolved not to be parted from it. He is persuaded, however, to ride forward to use his wiles upon the station agent. He returns soon with corn and hay received on credit. Good feed so quickly restores the horses that they are hitched up for a drive during the cool of the evening. Progress is so rapid that it is decided to keep moving all night. Guiding themselves by the white stars, they roll slowly forward through the dark with nothing to be seen and nothing to be heard but the heavy breathing of the horses and the creaking of the wagons.

But about midnight they hear a distant tramp of horses, apparently in the rear. Eugene is frightened, thinking the station agent is pursuing them to demand his pay. Now the sounds shift and appear to come from the front, and now someone rides up close by in the dark. A voice rings out.

" Is there a Eugene Teats in your party? "

The boy is too overcome both by fear and joy to reply. The driver of the other wagon answers for him. Eugene is soon in his father's arms, sobbing loudly. " You can imagine the reunion there in the middle of the night on the barren plains. Father was riding a beautiful little Indian pony that he had bought for me, and on another horse had a sack of grain for the animals and some lunch for us. We proceeded at once to feed ourselves and the animals, while McKnight rode back to pay for what we had procured from the agent. Well, to make a long story short, we started off in good shape the following morning, I on my new mount, Father driving my team, and with old Long's Peak rising up majestically higher with every mile we made, until, late in the afternoon several days later, we drove down Cherry Creek and into the little town of Auraria. What a relief it was to have someone of my own blood to talk to about home and family, and for a few days every leisure moment was put in in that way. We all lived at the Elephant Corral. My bed was on the ground, made of a few soft pine boughs known as ' Irish feathers,' then some hay with a blanket over it, with my clothes for a pillow or sometimes my saddle. What more could a boy desire? "

Whatever their trials, hardships and dangers, the Teats and the Tabors experienced the gold rush at its best. At its worst it was one long feverish delirium and nightmare. Poorer gold-hunters by the thousands, unable to buy wagons or even adequate supplies, resorted to the most desperate measures to reach the diggings where they had been led to expect that nuggets might be gathered as readily as pebbles on a beach. If it was madness to attempt to cross the Plains before May in wagons carrying food and clothing and affording some little shelter, it was nothing short of suicidal folly to attempt it as thousands did early in the spring — hitched to handcarts, pushing wheelbarrows or trudging along on foot with a few day's provisions on their backs.

" One came almost hourly upon hand-carters and footmen slowly journeying over the sandy undulations of the plains," wrote Henry Villard, later a railroad king of the Northwest, who first crossed the Plains at the height of the rush. " Not a few started with such clothing only as they wore on their backs and small bags containing a few pounds of corn-meal and meat. We met two individuals, one fifty, the other sixty-two years old, who had left Leavenworth with just twenty pounds of corn and $1.68 in money. Nor was this reckless infatuation confined to representatives of the less well-informed classes." Young lawyers and doctors, young clerks in remnants of broadcloth and patent leather, could be seen toiling with farm hands and laborers across the apparently endless prairies.

These poor handcarters and footmen, wantonly deceived by guidebooks and editors, were soon " hungry, in rags, shoeless, with sore and swollen feet and without shelter from the rains, snows and chilling winds. Not a few had to meet death in its most awful form, starvation, and, what was worse still, were driven by the maddening pangs of hunger to acts of cannibalism, such as living on human flesh, and alas! as in the case of the wretch Blue, even on brothers' bodies. . . . It is doubtful whether such scenes of human misery, as were enacted on the Plains last Spring, were witnessed even at the height of the California excitement."

Young Ryan and Rice were among those who attempted the journey with handcarts. After disembarking from the *S. S. New Monongahela* they sought work in vain at Leavenworth. Finally in despair they bought a handcart, having heard that the Mormons in '47 "had used such go-carts, one to two men, with one pushing and one pulling." Ryan and Rice set out in high spirits but soon found "that it was hard work pushing the cart and progress was slow." Rice lost heart shortly and turned back. Ryan pushed on alone up the Smoky Hill road to be overtaken some weeks later by the Reverend Hezekiah Porter and his party of Methodists from Georgia. They, too, have been having their difficulties. To their increasing alarm several oxen have recently died, and all are feeble and ailing.

Although he knows as little about the proper care of oxen as the Georgians, Ryan offers his services and is accepted. The Georgians swear at him occasionally as a " damned Yankee," but all goes well until they reach the Ridge Country where the greatest suffering occurs during the rush. Many have lost their way here and perished in the sandy waste. The country frightens the Georgians. After violent quarrels all turn tail and flee except Ryan and three others, who at length reach Auraria late in May in the midst of a driving snowstorm. The tired hungry cattle cannot be turned out to graze and it proves quite impossible to buy, beg or borrow any feed for them. Ryan thereupon decides to bake them bread. " We took some of our flour, baked a number of large pones, let them cool and fed them to the cattle — this notwithstanding the fact that flour was twenty-five cents a pound and hard to get at any price."

"Letters from Denver City state there is a great scarcity of provisions in the mines at Pike's Peak and much suffering among the emigrants," runs a dispatch to the New York *Tribune* early in May. "Several deaths are reported from starvation and emigrants continue to arrive in a destitute condition. No remittances of dust or rich discoveries are announced."

None have starved to death, in point of fact, but gaunt hunger stalks the gold fields. As Green Russell prophesied, the tiny Cherry Creek camps lie overwhelmed and paralyzed by the frenzied rush. Prices of all things soar. Flour soon rises to $40 a hundred pounds. But even at lowest prices thousands could not have bought, for they are penniless. It is no uncommon sight, according to Villard, to see men picking up the very offal at the doors of the more fortunate. Starving handcarters and footmen soon exhaust Larimer's patience with their begging. They "come here without money, provisions, guns or anything else," he complains bitterly, "and their number is so great that they annoy us very much." But he quickly circumvents them by an ingenious ruse. A friend and wife have exhausted their supplies and have difficulty finding more. The General offers to sell them his if they will board him and his son. The scheme works admirably: "While we kept house we had to feed everybody, now we avoid it."

Hunger considerably aggravates the gold-hunters' other grievances, many legitimate. All have sacrificed much, many their very lives, to reach Cherry Creek under the impression that gold is to be gathered by the handfuls. It takes no time for even the most naïve to discover how shamelessly they have been deceived and exploited. Feeling begins to run dangerously high between aggrieved "Pilgrims" and incorporated Argonauts. The latter, sinking mutual jealousies for a time, draw closer together to maintain "their precedence in importance as well as time," as the younger Larimer phrases it. So angry and bitter are outraged Pilgrims that Captain Peleg Bassett and a friend constitute themselves Larimer's personal bodyguard upon overhearing in the street threats of violence against him. The Captain is murdered in a dispute bearing upon the conflict, but no violence is done Larimer. Reports of his murder circulate so persistently, however, that the General is at great pains to deny them. Do not be "annoyed by the ridiculous stories about hanging and shooting me and other town speculators as we are called," he cautions his family, adding, "I am blamed for writing letters to induce people to come here."

Disgruntled gold-hunters are soon denouncing "all the Kansas gold excitement as the most stupendous humbug ever perpetrated upon the American people." One experienced miner exclaims indignantly that he "visited all the claims and diggings and saw no man who made more than twenty cents a day, or found dirt yielding more than one percent per pan."

Suddenly panic seizes the destitute Pilgrims along Cherry Creek. A stampede back to the States develops, as wild and reckless as the rush itself and in its day as famous. Every morning Villard is awakened by the clamor of auctioneers in "all the principal streets of Denver and Auraria, offering rifles, pistols, clothing, boots, picks, shovels, etc., etc., at prices that did not in most instances cover one tenth of the original cost. And then the last spare shirt, the reserved new boots being sold and the proceeds pocketed, off they went afoot, their packs on their shoulders, on horseback and in wagons." A large boat yard springs up on the Platte, and departures from the port of Denver are so numerous for some time that the *Rocky Mountain News* devotes a special column to local shipping news. Accidents on the swift shallow river happen frequently. The correspondent of the *Daily Missouri Democrat* barely escapes drowning while young Ryan reports five men lost when their crude leaky boat strikes a snag, overturns and sinks, pinning all beneath it. For weeks the Stampede sweeps all before it, hurling back even the more determined and adventurous. Every trail is crowded with long wagon trains carrying home thousands of hungry ragged men, all " swearing mad." On every canvas top can still be read *Pike's Peak or Bust!* But to this has been added *Busted, by God! —* or some such sentiment as *Bound for America!*

Along the way angry Pilgrims talk earnestly of lynching all editors in the Border towns. Every westbound traveler is stopped and told the most harrowing tales. The Cherry Creek camps have been sacked and burned — thousands are dying of starvation there — all town promoters have been shot or lynched. One sullen band of Pilgrims chances to meet a traveler westbound with sawmill machinery. They stop him, as they do all, to relate their grievances and persuade him to turn back. The stranger's face seems somehow vaguely familiar and at last one Pilgrim recognizes it. This is unfortunate, for D. C. Oakes of Denver City is well known — at least by name — as author of a popular Pike's Peak guidebook. At the moment he is returning from a hurried trip to the Missouri to obtain means of exploiting the excitement.

The Pilgrims with a common impulse seize Oakes and prepare to lynch him. In the end he comes off with nothing more serious than a rough handling and is allowed to proceed. Several days later he comes upon what seems to be a fresh grave by the roadside. Above it stands a " headboard made of a polished shoulder of a buffalo — in those days a favorite bulletin board of the Overlanders." Oakes stops and is somewhat surprised to read his own epitaph:

> Here lies the body of D. C. Oakes,
> Killed for aiding the Pike's Peak Hoax.

IV. GULCH GOLD AND BLOSSOM ROCK

"Hell! I expected to see them backing up carts and shoveling it in."

In the black days of the Stampede a single hope shines bright. Gold may be found in the Shining Mountains. As a matter of fact, it has — months ago. But only two men as yet know the secret.

Ten miles west of Denver stand two high table mountains between which tumble down the waters of Clear Creek, once sweet and sparkling but long since discolored and polluted by tailings from mine and mill. Here where plain meets mountain, there once stood the City of Arapahoe. It never numbered more than a score of cabins strung irregularly along the creek bottom. But in its day it appears to have sheltered a hardier lot of Argonauts than any of its rivals. While Denver City and Auraria were idling away the winter of '58 with whiskey, cards and dreams of fortunes in real estate, Arapahoe sent forth into the cold forbidding mountains two bold prospectors to find treasure at last.

One white morning in the dead of winter George Jackson, cousin of Kit Carson, Indian trader and miner, sets out up the creek with his friend Tom Golden and a character known only as Black Hawk. Jackson takes with him his two dogs, Kit and Drum. It is bitterly cold. But the men are warm in heavy windbreakers, fur caps, high leather boots and buckskin gloves. Under packs heavy with provisions, blankets, gold pans, skillets and rifles, they stumble up the creek between the table mountains and on into the foothills. After hunting deer a few days Golden and Black Hawk turn back. Jackson goes on alone, striking north to Ralston Creek, trudging up it through deep snow to its source, stopping occasionally to dig down through the drifts to try his luck. Raising no color, he crosses south and comes back down the North Fork of Clear Creek. He raises no color here. His provisions are running low. " Mountain lion stole all my meat today in camp; no supper tonight — damn him! " Jackson writes in his diary early in January, adding next day, " Killed a fat mountain sheep and wounded a mountain lion before sun-rise; ate ribs for breakfast; drank last of my coffee."

Realizing that he must hasten home, Jackson decides nevertheless to try his luck on the other fork of Clear Creek. He scales the high intervening divide and is now hurriedly working his way down a small tributary. Just above its junction with the South Fork his practised eye falls upon a long low sand bar which seems worth the risk of stopping to prospect thoroughly. He builds a great fire upon the sand bar and keeps it blazing all night to thaw the frozen sand and gravel.

" Clear day," reads Jackson's diary for January 7, '59. " Removed fire embers, and dug into rim on bed rock; panned out eight ' treaty cups ' of dirt, and found nothing but fine colors; with cup I got one nugget of gold. Dug and panned today until my belt-knife was worn out, so I will have to quit or use my skinning-knife. I have about a half ounce of gold, so will quit and try to get back in the Spring. Feel good tonight, dogs don't." The dogs are ill and hungry.

Jackson fills up the hole with charcoal and then builds another large fire over it. With belt-axe and knife he marks a large fir tree nearby and cuts the " top off a small lodge-pole pine on a

line from the fir tree to the hole, 76 steps in a westerly direction
. . . all fixed now; will be off down the creek tomorrow." Next
morning he starts hurriedly for the Plains only to be caught in
a blizzard. " Storming like Hell! " he records three days later
with increasing concern, " high wind and cold; in camp all
day."

Once again in Arapahoe Jackson slips quickly into the routine
of camp with not a word or gesture to betray him. " Spent the
night playing poker for buckskins; won 20 green hides and 7
dressed ones." Next day he grains the best of these to fashion
them into coat and trousers. He cuts up old flour sacks and sews
them in as lining. The pants, he remarks, " fit like a dish rag on
pot hooks." Then Jackson calmly drives off to Fort Laramie to
bring back the mail, taking with him a curious sinister figure,
Big Phil the Cannibal, whose shadow occasionally falls across the
records of the day. Jackson remains away several months but
is not worried. " Tom Golden is the only man who knows I
found gold on the head of the creek, and as his mouth is as tight
as a No. 4 Beaver trap, I am not uneasy."

A richer strike, unknown to Jackson, has been made on the
North Fork of Clear Creek. It was made, in fact, just a few days
after Jackson himself passed down the stream prospecting it in
vain. Here rich beds of spangle gold have been discovered in a
narrow side gulch by John H. Gregory, another miner from the
Georgia fields. By all accounts Gregory was a lazy good-for-
nothing fellow — an " ignorant corncracker," according to several,
who objected that he was " very profane, talked loud and a very
great deal." But he showed no want of energy and courage in the
winter of '58 when he found himself stranded at Fort Laramie
on his way to a gold excitement in British Columbia.

Coming south along the mountains, Gregory panned every stream between Cache la Poudre Creek and Pike's Peak, tracing many to their source. Apparently he found something to interest him in Clear Creek, for he returned from the Peak to stop for a time at Arapahoe before plunging into the mountains. Three days after Jackson's strike Gregory made his and hurried back to the Plains to await spring and obtain supplies.

At the height of the Stampede early in May, Gregory falls in with an Indiana party led by Wilkes Defrees. He tells them his story and they offer him a grubstake — provisions and a little working capital in return for equal shares in his discovery. Gregory accepts and with his new partners flounders up Clear Creek through deep snow. At the mouth of the gulch soon to take his name, Gregory stops to dig for " float " gold washed down from veins on the mountains above. Although he here finds gold as he did in January, he decides now to prospect further.

" Bring your shovel and come with me," Gregory commands Defrees, leading the way up the narrow timbered gulch.

" Stick your shovel in there," he suggests. With considerable difficulty Defrees turns over a few shovelfuls of gravel.

" Here, give me some in this pan." Gregory washes the dirt in the cold small stream which comes leaping down the gulch from the snow and ice fields above. He becomes more and more excited as he washes other panfuls. Defrees is commanded to dig here — and here — and here. Every panful proves richer than the last.

" The ice and snow prevented us from prospecting far below the surface," Gregory informs Horace Greeley several weeks later, " but the first pan of surface dirt on the original Gregory claim yielded $4. Encouraged by this success, we all staked out claims, found the 'lead' consisting of burnt quartz, resembling the Georgia mines in which I had previously worked. Snow and ice prevented regular working of the 'lead' till May 16th — From then on until the 23rd, I worked it five days with 2 hands, result, $972."

Within a week Gregory pans more gold than Green Russell's party in an entire summer. But now Green Russell, just returned from Georgia, makes a third rich strike. Gregory's discovery has confirmed his own theories about gold in the mountains. He hastens up Clear Creek to strike it rich in a side gulch three miles below the Gregory diggings. Within a month nine hundred miners are working in Russell Gulch, panning more than $35,000 of dust a week — a better initial average than the best of the Californian and Australian fields.

George Jackson has meantime returned, distributed the mail and paid off his friend the Cannibal, who loses " his $50 the first night, Big Wallace getting it all at Twenty-one." Jackson walks to Arapahoe to find Tom Golden has kept faith. He meets several Chicago men with money and seeks to interest them in his prospect. An incorrigible optimist, Jackson later enjoys a reputation as the " damndest liar in the mountains," leading his friends into one fiasco after another. But in this instance he can scarcely have exaggerated. The Chicago Mining Company is formed and on May 6, '59, begins the first profitable gold mining in the Pike's Peak country.

Denver City and Auraria learn of Jackson's operations within a few days. Shortly comes word of Gregory's strike and then Green Russell's. So thoroughly discredited a few weeks before, the Pike's Peak country suddenly becomes " richer than California in its palmiest days," according to Larimer's report in a triumphant and somewhat exuberant letter home. " From $4 to $16 a day is now taken out from a single pan of dirt about thirty-five miles from here. One party took out $1,950 in three days last week. Plenty of men are making from $50 to $100 a day."

With one accord destitute Pilgrims loitering along Cherry Creek hurl themselves into a second mad rush. Even stampeders homeward bound across the prairies face about and race again toward the mountains. By the thousands gold-hunters swarm into narrow Clear Creek canyon. Dangerously overcrowded but the day before, Denver City and Auraria become deserted almost overnight. Merchants lock up their stores, saloonkeepers pack up their bottles, gamblers pocket their cards, the few carpenters busy building cabins throw down saws and hammers as all, including the " county judge and sheriff, lawyers and doctors, even the editor of the *Rocky Mountain News*," join the general rush. Even the Larimers are swept along into the mountains. Happy enough to be relieved of the menace of so many desperately hungry men, they are nevertheless in a quandary. What if Denver City becomes merely a way-station on the road to the mines? — another La Platte City early falling to ruin as the Frontier sweeps on? In his perplexity the General makes his first and last trial of mining. His small party struggles up Clear Creek and does a little prospecting. But as no one among them is " much inclined to undergo the hardships and labor of digging and washing gold," according to the younger Larimer, all return within the week to more gentlemanly pursuits.

At the height of the Clear Creek excitement the parties of Hal Sayre and Horace Tabor arrive, pass directly through Denver and on toward the mountains. Both pitch camp above Arapahoe. Sayre and his friends, thinking gold is likely to be found anywhere, divide off into pairs to prospect all the surrounding country. This way and that they run " over the ground like fox hounds seeking a trail and almost as rapidly, stopping to stick a pick in here and there, but without any knowledge of indications as to where to go to work." Everywhere they meet raw prospectors making search much as they are doing. Always they stop to talk but learn nothing. At last Sayre's party reaches Chicago Creek to interview George Jackson. In battered old hat, red flannel shirt and high boots, Jackson impresses the tenderfeet and shows himself kindly and affable. They are most impressed by his easy lush profanity. The diggings themselves prove a sore disappointment.

" Hell! " remarks one, echoing the feelings of all, " I expected to see them backing up carts and shoveling it in." It is not long before Sayre and his friends return, one by one, to their respective trades and professions, early learning that prospecting as such is the least profitable of callings.

It takes Tabor many years to learn this truth. Certainly at the moment his hopes are at their highest. Inquiring the way from a miner down from the diggings, Tabor sets out with Augusta's two boarders to dig his fortune. " Leaving me and my sick child in a seven-by-nine tent that my own hands had made," said Augusta, " the men took a supply of provisions on their backs, a few blankets, and bidding me be good to myself, left on the morning of the glorious Fourth [of July, presumably]. How sadly I felt, none but God in whom I then firmly trusted, knew. Twelve miles from a human soul save my babe! The only sound I heard was the lowing of the cattle, and they, poor things, seemed to feel the loneliness of our situation and kept unusually quiet. . . . Three long weary weeks I held the fort. At the expiration of that time they returned.

" On the twenty-sixth of July we again loaded the wagon and

started into the mountains. The road was a mere trail; every few rods we were obliged to stop and widen it. Many times we unloaded the wagon and by pushing it, helped the cattle up the hills. Often night overtook us where it was impossible to find a level place to spread a blanket. Under such circumstances we drove stakes into the ground, rolled a log against them and lay with our feet against the log. Sometimes the hill was so steep that we slept almost upright. We were nearly three weeks cutting our way through Russell's Gulch into Payne's Bar, now called Idaho Springs. Ours was the first wagon through, and I was the first white woman there, if white I could be called after camping out three months.

" The men cut logs and laid them up four feet high, then put the seven-by-nine tent on for a roof. Mr. Tabor went prospecting. I opened a ' bakery,' made bread and pies to sell, and sold milk from the cows we had brought. Here one of our party, Mr. Maxcy, had an attack of mountain fever, and for four weeks he lay, very ill, at the door of our tent, in a wagon bed, I acting as physician and nurse. A miner with a gunshot wound through his hand was also brought to my door for attention."

Here Augusta first tastes the isolated life of toil and care she is to lead in the mountains almost without respite for twenty years. Here she masters the arts which enable her to support her family and keep it together through the long period of discouragement and defeat which follows. Tabor stakes a claim on the creek near the Jackson diggings and works hard. But his prospect here, like many another later, comes to nothing. The Jackson diggings themselves, in fact, begin to decline rapidly as the summer advances. Soon Chicago Creek has an air of delapidation and premature decay as miners desert for the richer diggings in Russell and Gregory gulches.

One morning early in June when thousands of miners are busily at work along Gregory Gulch, all hands drop pans, picks and shovels at the approach of a curious figure mounted precariously upon a mule. His face is almost concealed under a " variety of extemporized plasters." A battered old white hat is pulled down tightly about his ears. He bounces forward from group to group announcing that he is Horace Greeley come in person to inspect the diggings. His plasters and bandages cover painful bruises received in an accident on the Plains a few days before. Eager to visit the gold fields on a tour across the continent, Greeley secured passage (at $125) on one of the first of the Leavenworth City and Pike's Peak stages which within a short time are plying tri-weekly up and down the Republican River. Attracted by the new coach, bright red with canvas top, friendly Indians came charging up with a whoop, frightening the horses which sheared off the road down the side of a gulley. The coach toppled over to give Greeley a " pretty smart concussion generally."

On either side of Greeley ride Henry Villard of the Cincinnati *Commercial Enquirer* and A. D. Richardson of the Boston *Journal.* They ride slowly forward through a hopeless confusion of tents, cabins, wagons, oxen, horses, mules and excited bustling men, all literally breathless in the high thin mountain air as they work feverishly at stripping sand bars, shoveling pay-dirt, building dams, digging ditches, felling trees, sawing riffle boards and sluices. Some have mounted their pans on barrel staves or rockers to form a " cradle." Others are using the " Long Tom " — a large log hollowed into a trough and rolled from side to side with a long stick as a handle, a variation of the cradle. More are using sluices — long wooden troughs, usually three or four in series, each with a riffle board along the bottom. Behind the wooden cross bars of the riffle frame lie pools of quicksilver. These catch and hold the heavy gold sinking to the bottom as pay-dirt is shoveled into the sluices to be washed down by a steady stream of water from ditch and dam.

Through their sluices Greeley finds the miners running not only bedrock gravels but broken " blossom rock." This blossom rock — white quartz streaked and seamed a rich orange-brown — is found up the mountain sides in surface veins so soft and decomposed that to a depth of several feet they can be mined with nothing more than pick and shovel. Gulch gold loses its allure as all turn to search frantically for this rich " burnt " quartz. Soon it is coming down the slopes by the ton, usually in rawhide sacks on the backs of miners themselves. Only the richest can afford to keep a horse, mule or even a small mountain burro with hay, when obtainable, selling at $100 a ton.

Greeley is frankly impressed with what he sees. But the miners have no great faith in tenderfoot journalists and have decided to take no chances. " The boys," so the story goes, " took an old shotgun and fired dust into a partly worked mine until it had all the richness of a Golconda." Greeley, carefully directed, fills a pan and goes to the creek to wash it. He is amazed, as it was intended he should be. He washes a second panful and a third, and is even more astonished.

" Gentlemen," exclaims Greeley, " I have washed with my own hands and seen with my own eyes, and the news of your rich discovery shall go forth over all the world as far as my newspaper can carry it."

As good as his word, Greeley sits down with Villard and Richardson that very afternoon to start writing his famous report on the Gregory diggings. First published in a special edition of the *Rocky Mountain News* early in June, the report is featured in Greeley's New York *Tribune* and reprinted throughout the country. Although it ultimately becomes a " source of slander and abuse to its authors," as Villard complains, it immediately brings the Pike's Peak rush to its greatest excitement. The journalists first of all deny specifically any personal interest in local mines or real estate and then go on to list what actual profits they have been able more or less to verify — among others, these:

Defrees & Co., (from South Bend, Ind.) have run a small sluice eight days, with the following results: first day, $66; second day, $80; third day, $95; fourth day, $305. . . . Have just sold their claim for $2,500.

Zeigler, Spain & Co., (from South Bend, Ind.) have run a sluice, with some interruption, for the last three weeks; they are four in the company, with one hired man. They have taken out a little over three thousand pennyweights of gold, estimated by them as worth at least $3,000; Their first day's work produced $21; their highest was $495.

S. J. Jones & Co., from Kansas, have run own sluice two days, with three men, yield, $225 per day. Think the quartz generally in this vicinity is gold-bearing. Have not seen a piece crushed that did not yield gold. . . .

John H. Gregory, from Gordon Co., Georgia. . . . Arrived in this vicinity, May 6, . . . found the ' lead' consisting of burnt quartz, . . . worked it five days with 2 hands, result, $972. Soon after, I sold my two claims for $21,000, the parties buying, to pay me after deducting their expenses, all they take from claims to the amount of $500 per week until the whole is paid. Since that time, I have been prospecting for other parties, at about $200 per day. Have struck another ' lead' on the opposite side of the valley, from which I washed $14 out of a single pan.

Conscious of having dealt rather handsomely with the diggings, Greeley and his colleagues feel free therefore to assert their humanity and good sense by protesting most earnestly against a renewal of the gold rush. " There are said to be five thousand people already in this ravine, and hundreds more are pouring into it daily. Tens of thousands more have been passed by us on our rapid journey to this place. For all these, nearly every pound of provisions and supplies of every kind must be hauled by teams from the Missouri River, some seven hundred miles distant, over roads which are mere trails, crossing countless unbridged water courses, always steep-banked and often miry, and at times so swollen by rains as to be utterly impassable by waggons. Part of this distance is desert. . . . To attempt to cross it on foot is madness — suicide — murder. To cross it with teams in midsummer, when the water-courses are dry and the grass is eaten up, is possible only for those who know where to look for wood and water. . . . A few months hence — probably by the middle of October — this whole Alpine region will be snowed under and frozen up. . . . There then, for a period of six months, will be neither employment, food nor shelter within five hundred miles for the thousands pressing hither under the delusion that gold may be picked up like pebbles on the seashore. We charge those who manage the telegraph not to diffuse a part of our statement without giving substantially the whole; and we beg the press generally to unite with us in warning the whole people against another rush to these gold mines as ill-advised as that of last Spring."

Tired as he is from several weeks of hard travel, Greeley cannot resist an opportunity to address the miners the evening of his arrival. Several thousand collect — many out of curosity, some to participate in the disturbance expected. The many Southerners in the gulch know and hate Greeley for his anti-slavery views. But the slavery question is not mentioned — apparently one of the few subjects neglected. Greeley first advances a theory of his own about the original formation of the quartz beds. He then mounts his "usual cold-water hobby," gives the gambling fraternity a scorching, recommends industry and thrift, expounds the blessings of an agricultural community and concludes with a "description of the present condition of the political world of America and Europe." Rather more interesting than all this, according to Villard, was the scene itself.

"The illumination of the place of meeting by dint of pine torches, the unique and picturesque costumes of the audience, the vigorous vibrations of the voices of the speakers and the cheers of the crowds from the surrounding mountains, the frequent discharge of firearms and the distant songs of those encamped in the upper part of the valley — all united to heighten the grandeur of the spectacle."

After several other long speeches the miners proceed to the real business of the evening. This is to institute some few fundamental processes of orderly government, for "only those who have lived in a mining country can form any idea of the petty warfare that is instigated and constantly kept up by the jealousy and egotism which prevail among gold-hunters." On the model of the California camps the diggings are organized as a mining district with a president, sheriff and recorder of claims to execute its few simple ordinances. To prevent monopolization, it is decreed that no miner (except the original discoverer of a field, who is allowed two of each) can hold by right of discovery more than one creek, one gulch and one mountain claim. Once staked, a claim must be worked within ten days to establish title — a

Gregory Gulch, '59

Central City, '60

decree aimed at mere speculation. Any number of claims can be owned by purchase.

" A claim," read the minutes of this meeting, " shall be construde to mean whenever applide to a Load, One Hundred feet running the length of the same and fifty feet in *width*. When applide to a Gulch. One Hundred feet following its meanderings and extending from Bank to Bank. When applide to Patch or placer diggings. One Hundred feet squair. . . . When applide to a water claim, the exclusive right to use water for mining purposes upon any ditch or Stream not exceeding in distance two Hundred and fifty feet. When to a Farming Or ranch claim, One Hundred & Sixty acres. When applide to a building claim fourty feet front and One hundred feet deep."

All disputes in regard to claims must be submitted to the recorder who by a complicated process selects a jury of three disinterested miners to try the case both as judge and jury. If protested, the jury's verdict is submitted to a general meeting of miners. They can order the case retried or confirm the verdict. If confirmed, the verdict is final and must be obeyed by disputants upon pain of forfeiting all claims in the district.

The criminal code adopted by the miners is simplicity itself, consisting of five short laws. The penalty for murder is hanging. For manslaughter and homicide — as a jury of six may direct. For " shooting or threatening to shoot or use any deadly weapons " — by " as many stripes on the bare back as a jury of six may direct," by a fine not to exceed $500 and by banishment from the district. For grand larceny — not less than fifteen nor more than three hundred lashes on the bare back, by a fine double the amount stolen and by banishment from the district. For petit larceny — by a fine double the amount stolen and such other punishment as a jury of six may direct. Men guilty of misdemeanors must work in chain gangs for varying lengths of time upon roads and bridges.

Although Greeley's famous document on the Gregory diggings is reported fairly by newspapers throughout the country, its concluding warning, needless to say, is ignored. From day to day the rush increases until the gulch is black with prospectors and fortune-hunters of every kind. For five miles along the narrow rough road winding up the ravine are strung cabins, tents, wagons and the crudest kind of shelters — some made of hand-sawn boards, many covered merely with pine boughs. Stores and saloons are opened and prosper exceedingly. Bad whiskey sells at fifty cents a glass, gritty Taos flour at $44 a hundred pounds. Grocery tents charge extravagant prices for scanty supplies of sugar, coffee, bacon and " beef " — butchered from " ill-fed and well-whipped oxen just in from a fifty day's journey across the Plains." Blacksmiths grow rich sharpening picks at fifty cents each. A cobbler's shop is opened at Gregory Point by William L. Douglas, later rich and famous as a manufacturer of cheap shoes. Soon a few doctors and lawyers hang out shingles. Richardson finds but twelve women in the gulch, including seven squaws, most of them busily washing clothes in the icy creek at $3 a dozen. Two black slaves toiling at the sluices are pointed out to Ryan by his Georgia friends who inform him of others in the gulch. Here, too, are Mexicans in wide sombreros beating and cursing stubborn burros. Somewhere in the throng wander W. A. Clark, later an Anaconda copper king, and W. H. Stanley, adventurer and explorer, one day to go searching Africa for Dr. Livingstone.

Thousands of disappointed prospectors are soon forced by necessity to abandon all hopes of sudden wealth and hire themselves out to the more fortunate. From twelve to fourteen hours a day they labor in the gulches for an average wage of $1.50 — or $1 a day with board, which the wiser choose as the better real wage. Every night brings the serious problem of where to sleep. Every small cabin shelters an astonishing number of miners packed tightly away in short hard bunks ranged in tiers along the walls. In these cabins, according to local tradition, the idea of the Pullman sleeping car is born. Gregory Gulch can be held doubly responsible, for George Pullman lays the foundation of his fortune here, coming early in the rush to buy and sell gold dust, speculate in mines and loan money at the prevailing interest rates which range from twenty to twenty-five per cent per month. Soon he acquires the stake of $150,000 which enables him to perfect his million-making marvel.

But cabins, crowded as they are, are too few to house so many. Thousands must seek any floor available. Eugene Teats comes on a visit to the diggings and is forced to sleep in the general store at Central City kept by Charles Post, his father's new partner. Post's general store, like all of its kind, is also a gambling saloon open day and night. Eugene finds it crowded with boisterous men and nauseating with stale fumes of tobacco and whiskey, but he must stretch himself out on the rough dirty floor.

" I recall how Judge Post pleaded with the men to give me a place near the big wood stove and how I begged food for my pony. Crackers were about all that could be had, so the Judge bought a lot, which I shared liberally with the pony. Some men in the place more kind-hearted than the rest saw me doing this, and rustled some grain from somewhere and some bacon and flapjacks for me until we were both contented and a little more comfortable. Several nuggets were given me by miners that I talked to, who were pleased to see a boy so young in camp, for the place was practically bare of women and children."

But most gold-hunters must continue to live and sleep in tents and wagons or in the open by blazing campfires. Even in midsummer nights are chilly, especially to tired sweaty men after a long hot day in the gulches. Rolled up in a blanket or two on hard stony ground, they find it " utterly impossible to keep warm," as many complain, and " get up at daybreak, almost benumbed with the cold, build a fire and try to thaw out before breakfast."

Breakfast — in fact, every meal — consists of bacon (" Billy Russell ") or sowbelly (salt pork), flapjacks and coffee, with the occasional luxury of dried fruit. Few can afford fresh vegetables, worth almost their weight in gold. Scurvy and dysentery appear, and other disorders, mountain fever particularly, a baffling disorder of typhoid character induced by bad whiskey and worse water. Loud but vain complaints arise that all streams are contaminated by piles of filth and ordure accumulating about tents and cabins and crawling with ants, bugs and flies. Gold-hunters themselves, for the most part, are dirty and louse-ridden — " to be expected," writes one, " when men pay so little attention to personal cleanliness, going from week to week without ablutions or changing their clothes, which they wear continually, both day and night, sometimes until they drop off."

Hazards to health, life and limb are many — pneumonia from exposure to all kinds of weather and extreme fluctuations of temperature, falling rock in mine shafts, falling timber and forest fires. " We have tidings," writes Greeley, " of one young gold-seeker committing suicide, in a fit of insanity, at the foot of the mountains; two more were found in a ravine, long dead and partially devoured by wolves; while five others with their horse and dog were overtaken, some days since, while on a prospecting tour not far from Gregory's, by one of those terrible forest fires and were all burned to death, and so found and buried, two or three days since — their homes, their names, and all but their fearful fate unknown."

But the Clear Creek camps are fortunately spared any Vigilante storms. They have their share of vice, crime and merely playful shooting, but among early Colorado camps they stand out as relatively quiet and well-behaved. As they grow larger and more respectable, each cluster of cabins up the gulch takes itself a name — Black Hawk, Gregory Point, Mountain City, Central City, Nevadaville, Missouri City, Springfield City, and Bortonburgh. The first five constitute one long attenuated community twisting uphill along the single narrow road. The green mountains to either side are now bleak brown hogbacks, covered with fallen timber and raw stumps, scarred with dumps from shaft and tunnel. The pines are gone. The gulch rings with the clang of stamp mills pounding quartz ore to dust. Crystal streams run discolored and befouled with milk-white tailings from the mills. But all is well so long as claims on Gregory Lode continue to sell at $1,000 a linear foot, and blossom rock continues to come from the Kansas, Bates, Gunnell, Bobtail and other rich lodes.

Mountain City in its day is better known than Denver. In the flush of youth Missouri City demands to be made the terminus of the Leavenworth stage line. Central City grows gradually at the expense of its rivals and soon has a theater and a few more pretentious houses. Some lie half buried in excavations in the hillsides. Others, perched high on stilts, jut forth from the steep slopes at a dizzy height to overhang road and creek. Most are cottages " in the calico style, with all sorts of brackets and carved drop-cornices." Grocery tents everywhere give way to more permanent wooden stores, each with a great rectangular facade concealing the small crude main structure behind, the characteristic false front of the Frontier. All in all, the prosperity of the Clear Creek camps seems assured for many years.

It is not long, however, before the future begins to darken. Many claims along the creek, hastily and recklessly exploited, are soon exhausted. Lack of water impedes work generally. As claims multiply, the tiny streams high in the mountains have proved wholly inadequate for washing operations. Miners in desperation subscribe $100,000 to Green Russell's project of a ditch to bring water from Fall River, more than ten miles distant over the mountains. The project is delayed first by tedious expensive litigation and then by want of money. Fewer and fewer miners are to be seen working creek bottoms for gulch gold.

Blossom rock comes down the slope no more as surface quartz veins are rapidly stripped. As miners dig deeper, the quartz becomes too hard for pick and shovel. Almost all veins begin to taper off and many " pinch out " entirely. Without machinery it is a herculean task to dig inch by inch through solid granite to " contact " the quartz again. But many miners prove equal to it and pierce through only to see the vein pinch out a second time.

And as mines go deeper, ores grow more and more refractory. Miners try the arastra — a crude Mexican grinder for pulverizing ore between two heavy millstones, the upper turned slowly round by mule or water power. Heavy stamp mills are tried with little more success. Finally Black Hawk experiments with a primitive smelter. But it recovers so little gold from baffling iron and sulphur compounds that it soon devotes itself altogether to manufacturing lead bullets to exterminate the Indians. Stimulated by the general speculative mania accompanying the Civil War, Gregory Gulch enjoys one last flurry of excitement before the first great boom collapses. Individual properties, some valuable and more not, are bought up by speculators who organize large corporations interested chiefly in selling stock. This bubble bursts in '64. Mines and mills close down one after another until but one or two are working. For years the Clear Creek camps lie paralyzed and "in cap."

A brief period or two of renascence will come to enliven them. The smelting problem will ultimately be solved by Professor N. P. Hill, who will quickly make a fortune and pass to the United States Senate, the goal of every bonanza king. Shafts will be opened and mills begin to clang again. But the return of prosperity will find the Clear Creek camps staid and respectable. They will have much the color and character of a coal camp, "with shapeless houses dumped here and there among the excavations." Organized strikes and lockouts will take the place of the wild exuberant individualism of earlier days. Absentee ownership will flourish. With every foot of ground staked and claimed, almost all old prospectors will be driven into the wage system "to toil day and night, weekdays and Sundays, in darkness, begrimed with dirt, amidst the clatter of machinery, under the drippings of shaft and tunnel." As local watchdogs for the corporations will come a number of able engineers and lawyers — among the latter, Edward Wolcott and Henry Teller, both to be United States Senators, the latter also to be Secretary of the Interior in President Arthur's cabinet — a fact not without influence upon Tabor's political and social career in later years. But the brief periods of renascence in the Clear Creek camps fade one after another. Today all lie ghost towns smelling of the long slow processes of ruin and decay.

The early difficulties which beset Gregory Gulch first appeared not three months after Greeley's report had spread its fame throughout the country. By the end of the summer gold from gulch sands and blossom rock did not total one tenth of the production of May and June. As owners even of rich claims became increasingly discouraged, utter despair seized luckless thousands whose long desperate search for treasure had not paid them for having their picks sharpened. Not one in twenty had made expenses. Not one in many hundreds had acquired even the most modest fortune. Gold-hunters in great crowds were soon deserting the gulches. " The gambling, which for a while prevailed in this place, has almost ceased," wrote a miner from Nevadaville. " The gamblers could not live as we have to — on hope — and so have cleared out to a man."

A second Stampede back to the States develops. The Plains are again white with prairie schooners carrying home thousands of ragged dispirited men. The more sanguine join the rush to South Park where the camps of Tarryall and Hamilton boom for a few brief summers. Even George Jackson and John Gregory abandon their claims and depart. Jackson pushes on over the Continental Divide to prowl the mountains there unsuccessfully for almost thirty years until in '97 he accidentally shoots and kills himself. Gregory decides to return South. His mind, it is said, has been almost unhinged by good fortune. Never had he known anything but the bitterest poverty. Never had he tasted even the simplest luxury. Now, with $21,000 in his pocket, he can neither eat nor sleep. " All night long he muttered in a wandering way of the ' old woman ' and of the change in her life money would make, and of what a strange thing it would be to see her a ' lady,' and of how the ' brats ' would scream with delight at the pleasures their dad could now buy them." Again in Georgia, Gregory soon spends his money, comes back to the mountains to prospect vainly, attempts unsuccessfully to operate a sawmill and within a year passes from sight to an unknown, or at least unrecorded, fate.

Late in September, '59, the few miners remaining in the Clear Creek camps awakened one morning to find the gulches buried deep in snow. As none had experienced winter in the mountains, all feared the worst and hastily packed up for flight to the Plains. Among the first to flee were the Tabors. "With the first snow came an old miner to our camp who told dreadful tales of snow-slides," said Augusta, "and advised Mr. Tabor to take me out of the mountains immediately. Those who know anything of the surroundings of Idaho Springs will smile at the idea of a snow-slide there. But we, in our ignorance of the mountains, believed all the old miner said, and left for Denver. I had been very successful with my bakery in that camp, making enough to pay for the farm in Kansas and to keep us through the winter. Arriving in Denver, we rented a room over a store. It was the first roof I had slept under for six months. . . . I took in a few boarders."

Tabor had struck no gold on his claim but was so far from being discouraged that he left Augusta in Denver and returned to the mountains in the hope of working his mine through the winter. But within the week Tabor came trudging back to Denver dejectedly. His claim, he found, had been jumped in his absence by the solicitous old miner, "and so he lost all his summer's work," said Augusta, "and had to sell the cow to buy supplies for the new camp. . . ."

V. The Elephant Corral

" Cool in summer, cozy in winter . . . the center of civilization in Denver."

By every conservative estimate, the Pike's Peak Gold Rush of '59 swept more than one hundred thousand fortune-hunters from the security of home toward the distant Shining Mountains. Not more than forty thousand of these ever reached Cherry Creek, for many turned back or stopped to settle along the way. Perhaps twenty-five thousand penetrated into the mountains that first summer, but never were there more than fifteen thousand in the gold fields at any one time, according to Villard, who was in an excellent position to judge. The second Stampede carried off many of these. The approach of winter frightened away many more. By the time the prairies are again snowbound, there remain behind in all the Pike's Peak country not five thousand adventurers who have either actively resisted or been left stranded by the gold rush as it ebbs to pass into history.

What little life remains on plain and mountain during the winter of '59 is centered in Denver City and Auraria. Here some seven or eight hundred men settle down in scattered cabins along the creek or in tents and wagons among the cottonwoods where many large campfires blaze on frosty nights. Times have been very bad along Cherry Creek since the first days of the rush to Gregory Gulch. So dull is business that it " cannot get any worse unless sales stop entirely," reports one offering such indispensables as smoking and chewing tobacco, pipes and snuff. But even at the worst of the depression " signs of Progress — Improvement — Manifest Destiny " are not wanting.

" There was a man about town yesterday who had lettuce to sell," writes Greeley, " and I am credibly assured that there will be green peas next month — actually peas! — providing it should rain soakingly meantime. . . . To the bread, bacon and beans, which formed the staple of every meal a short time ago, there have been several recent additions: milk, which was last week twenty-five cents a quart is now down to ten cents, and I hear a rumor that eggs, owing to a recent increase in the number of hens within five hundred miles, . . . are about to fall from $1 to fifty cents." Game begins to come in, too — deer and especially antelope at four cents a pound. And the fact is long remembered that a load of watermelons arrives late in the season to sell at $3 each.

As miners flee the mountains in fear of winter there, Denver City and Auraria begin to fill up again. Larimer and his colleagues take heart once more. Upon the straggling settlements they impress the usual gridiron pattern. Indian Row in Auraria is extended and dignified as Ferry Street. Here stands the town's original building, the double cabin of Jack Jones and John Smith, both grown rich during the Gregory rush by their rope ferry across the Platte. Down the street Uncle Dick Wootton erects a large two-story log building with a general store and barroom on the ground floor. Here Uncle Dick dispenses Taos Lightning day and night to crowds of noisy men whose uproar frequently disturbs the local court in solemn session on the floor above. Around the corner is the blacksmith shop of " Noisy Tom " Pollock, first City Marshall and official executioner, soon to be busy indeed.

Auraria boasts of three other main streets — Front, Cherry and

St. Louis. Front is graced with the Temperance Hotel, within a short time better and more favorably known as the Tremont House. Cherry has a temple devoted to Masonic mysteries. From a tall pine flagpole in St. Louis Street floats a white silk flag visible for miles to guide the hungry and thirsty to the Eldorado Hotel kept by Smoke and "Count" Murat, who claims to be a nephew of Joachim Murat, Napoleon's King of Naples. Nearby, Uncle Dick Wootton builds a second large cabin and opens it as a hotel. It is well patronised, for the camp is full of hungry men. But the hotel fails financially, for neither he nor his manager, according to Wootton, "could ever understand that only men with money have a right to eat."

Although Cherry Creek is generally regarded as the boundary between the rival camps, both town companies lay claim to its treacherous sandy bed. Indeed, many buildings are erected there by business men who hesitate to identify themselves too closely with either community. On a sand flat in the very middle of the creek, reached by a wooden foot-bridge from either bank, stands the office of the *Rocky Mountain News* founded by William Byers, who at last arrived with "his shirt tail full of type" only to find a rival project under way. The *Cherry Creek Pioneer* already had its presses in place. Byers quickly and quietly rented space in Wootton's building and frantically set to work. "Before midnight the Washington hand press was up, the cases were in place and type was being set. The men worked all the first night, all the next day and at ten o'clock on the night of April 22 — twenty-eight hours after the outfit had reached its destination — the first copies were run off in the presence of a large number of citizens." Next morning the *Pioneer*, taken completely by surprise, published its first and last issue. Byers bought it and merged it with the *News,* which continues as a weekly for several years and is "welcomed almost as a god-send by the community," even at twenty-five cents a copy.

The bitterest jealousy marks the relations of the camps, but Larimer now stages a coup to end the rivalry. Ten shares in the Denver Town Company and twenty lots are judiciously distributed among influential members of the Auraria Company who soon reciprocate. The citizens of Auraria are then assembled at a mass meeting and are finally persuaded to take the desired action:

> WHEREAS, the towns at or near the mouth of Cherry Creek, are, and ought to be one; therefor, be it
> > *Resolved,* That from this time forward, Auraria proper, shall be known as Denver City, West Division, and we hereby authorize the board of directors to change the name on the plat accordingly.

The directors of the two companies thereupon summon prominent citizens of both communities to a meeting of ratification "held on the Larimer Street bridge by moonlight." The union is effected and on the motion of General Larimer the meeting adjourns "with three hearty cheers for Denver."

Improvements are likewise going forward on the far bank of Cherry Creek. Larimer has laid out Blake, McGaa, Larimer, Lawrence and Arapahoe streets. The few cross streets have been lettered from E to H. Even more bleak and wind-swept than Auraria, wanting even the cottonwoods which somewhat soften the latter's ugly profile, Denver City is a "forlorn and desolate-looking metropolis." But it quickly outstrips its rival, centering within itself every frontier activity, throwing together and mixing indiscriminately men of all kinds from all parts of the world.

Blake is the principal street, important alike for its business and sporting houses. None is better known than the Denver House, later notorious as the Elephant Corral. Across the street, Gasnier, a Parisian, has his blacksmith shop. Next door a Jewish merchant has hung out a sign advertising " White, Red and Orange Flannels." Down the street stand warehouses, groceries and Vienna bakeries, a drugstore, the office of the Pike's Peak stage line, primitive cabins with dirt roofs, and a chair factory. McGaa Street has " many tenements occupied as dwellings," the Exchange Coffee House, the " place of Episcopal worship in the Library Reading Room," many livery stables and corrals, and at the far end of the street a large block of stores with the corner one " occupied as a drinking and billiard saloon by American citizens of African descent."

On Larimer is the General's cabin, a theater, Simm's Eating House and Billiard Saloon where the territorial legislature first meets, and the Broadwell House — " the first thoroughly finished frame building in the city, it being plastered, painted and grained throughout." Lawrence has but a few scattered buildings — a powder magazine, several stores of Indian traders, a large white house first turned into a brothel and then into a Methodist church, and the " neat Gothic cottage " where law is practised and the affairs of the town company managed by Secretary Dick Whitsitt. Even fewer buildings grace Arapahoe. " A half dozen cabins and two or three frame dwellings comprise their number," according to the town's first historian, " and with them is finished a full account of Denver as it stood in the month of March, 1860."

The historian fails to summarize. Every fifth building is a saloon and every tenth a gambling hell. There are as yet few brothels. The twin camps together, in fact, contain not a half dozen white women. In want of more the men take freely to the charms of negresses and squaws. Altogether, it is a male society amusing itself as best it can in drinking, gambling, fighting, racing and shooting.

Up and down the dusty streets wander groups of weather-beaten men. All are young and vigorous. There are no old people and but few in middle life. None shave. " Some of us bathe and some of us do not." Even those well clothed on arrival are now long since out at elbow and knee. Store clothes can be had but are expensive. Most are dressed in moccasins and buckskin trousers, woolen shirts, tattered coats and faded black slouch hats. The very poor have fashioned themselves pantaloons from sugar bags. All openly carry at least one revolver and perhaps a knife suspended from their belts. For the most part they saunter along idly, for jobs are scarce.

In the drifting crowd appear a number of familiar faces — Uncle Dick Wootton with his powerful figure and stiff black hair, John Smith, Jack Jones with watery blue eyes and red nose, prim Larimer and his son Will. With his braided whiskers one cannot mistake Green Russell, down from the mountains for the winter. Somewhere lost in the throng wanders H. A. W. Tabor with curious loping gait. But if any notice him here, all signally fail to record the fact.

Suddenly the crowd parts to stand clear of George Jackson's curious friend, Old Phil the Cannibal, a filthy monster, as he comes staggering from saloon to saloon, trailed by a large mangy dog almost as dangerous as his master. A fugitive from justice, wanted in Philadelphia for several brutal murders, Big Phil openly boasts of having in emergency turned cannibal, according to Byers of the *News*. " Said he had killed and eaten two Indians and one white man (a Frenchman.) Upon being asked about the taste of human flesh, he answered that the head, hands and feet, when thoroughly cooked, tasted good — not unlike pork, but the other portions of the body he did not like; they were too grisly and tough."

Down the street, with black cassock flying, harbinger of a different order, now hurries good Father Machebeuf, later a bishop, who has just come north from the episcopal seat at Santa Fe to build a chapel and in time establish St. Mary's Academy. Of a somewhat different stripe is "Professor" O. J. Goldrick, who never appears but in silk hat, frock coat with large shining buttons, white cravat and lemon-colored gloves. His coat buttons are "not of brass but of gold — solid gold — Colorado gold fresh from the mines." On his starched shirt front blazes a "solitaire diamond as big as the end of your thumb." Although he creates the impression of a lackey, Goldrick is, as his epitaph declares, the "Founder of the First Sunday School and the First Public School in Colorado." He has established himself in a primitive log cabin in Auraria and at an entirely reasonable fee of $3 a month, for the Professor claims to have taken honors at Trinity College, Dublin, undertakes to instruct more than a dozen restless pupils, including several Mexican and half-breed children. From time to time he contributes to the *News*. His flowery effusions, masterpieces of their kind, one of which will be noticed later, finally gain him appointment as city editor and the Professor promptly gives up schoolmastering.

And here approaches one of the first to rebel against Goldrick's instruction as both dull and irrelevant. Happy at last in buckskins, "just about the proudest boy in the settlement in a new suit made by the Indians, complete with all the fringes and brass buttons, etc., etc.," Eugene Teats gallops by on a wall-eyed pony given him by his friend Left Hand, Chief of the Arapahoes.

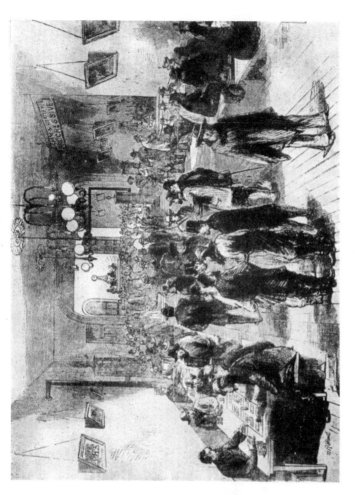

Chase and Heatley's "Progressive" Gambling Saloon

Arrest in a Denver Saloon

Eugene never considers himself dressed now, he declares, without belt, revolver and knife. The boy soon knows everyone in camp from Father Machebeuf to the Cannibal. He is especially fond of Chief Left Hand. He helps the Chief and his braves scour the gutters of the town for the dead dogs to be found there every day, shot because there are so many and food for them is scarce. The Chief invites him to the camp of the Arapahoes just down the Platte where Eugene marvels to see them " cut off the legs of the dogs at the second joint, stand them on their stubs, roast them intact and have a regular feast, eating hide, hair, tail and all." Chief Left Hand proudly shows him still bleeding scalps taken in the mountains from their traditional enemies the Utes. Eugene watches them prepare the scalps and mount them on poles used only for the ritual. As soon as it is dark, the boy rides back to town with the Indians who there collect boxes and barrels, pile them high at some crowded street corner and light a huge bonfire. With weird song and dance the painted warriors, carrying the scalps high, circle round the fire faster and faster as the wives of lost braves moan loudly and slit their breasts with knives until the blood runs. To Eugene it is " not a very inviting spectacle to see them dance and yell with their knives flashing in the firelight," but he reflects philosophically that it is " only their way of mourning the dead."

The Elephant Corral where Eugene lives for several years is the old Denver House, the " Astor House of the Gold Fields." Horace Greeley was entertained and lodged here while on his way to the diggings. Originally it was a crude log building with neither floors nor ceiling. Flimsy canvas covered windows and the roof as well. Still flimsier cotton sheathing served as partitions within. In front was a large gambling saloon. Behind it were ranged six bedrooms, mere canvas cubicles, each containing a rough bed frame with grass mattress, a sawed-off barrel or stump as a chair and a tin wash basin. Guests were invited to fill the basin for themselves from a barrel in the corridor and empty it of dirty water by sprinkling the earth floor to help settle the dust.

Here, so Greeley found, " every guest is allowed as good a bed as his own blankets will make him. The charges are no higher than at the Astor or other first-class hotels, except for liquor, twenty-five cents a drink for dubious whiskey, colored and nicknamed to suit the taste of customers. . . . I had the honor to be shaved by the nephew (so he assured me) of Murat, Napoleon's King of Naples — the honor and the shave together costing me but a paltry dollar. Still, a few days of such luxury surfeited me, mainly because the drinking room was also occupied by several blacklegs as a gambling hall and their incessant clamor, persisted in at all hours up to midnight, became at length a nuisance. Then the visitors of that drinking and gambling room had a careless way, when drunk, of firing revolvers, sometimes at each other, at other times quite miscellaneously, which struck me as inconvenient for a quiet guest."

The Denver House soon passes into the hands of Robert Teats who improves, enlarges and renames it the Elephant Corral. By him it is transformed into a complete caravanserai. One unhitches in the corral proper and leaves one's wagon there to be guarded from thieves. Horses are stabled in a large barn to one side, while the House opposite offers not only food, drink and shelter but the usual amusements of the Frontier. Hal Sayre steps in to find its public room crowded with several hundred men, all " engaged in drinking and bucking the tiger vigorously and in a variety of ways."

A curious arrangement exists at the Corral between the house and the professional gamblers who run the games there. Teats, contrary to custom, has no personal interest in the games, merely renting tables and other accessories by the day, week, month or year. This leads to much scandal, for " transient " gamblers bring in a tenderfoot, fleece him at three-card monte or some such confidence game and then quickly vanish. When the dupe complains, the house refuses to accept any responsibility. In one of the first petitions submitted to the Denver People's Government, "One Hundred American Citizens" unite to demand immediate action " to abate the nuisances existing in this city under the guise of games of chance, to wit: *Three Card Monte,* the *Strap Game,* the *Thimble Game* and other confidence games of a similar character." At the same time merchants on Blake Street ask the City Council to prohibit "from the streets and sidewalks all gambling and selling of liquor." The City Fathers pass such ordinances but without appreciable effect.

"Here you are, gentlemen," cries a three-card monte expert at the Elephant Corral. " This ace of hearts is the winning card. Watch it closely! Follow it with your eyes as I shuffle. Here it is, and now here, now here and now — where? If you point it out the first time, you win; but if you miss, you lose. Here it is, you see. Now watch it again. This ace of hearts, gentlemen, is the winning card. . . . I take no money from paupers, cripples or orphan children. The ace of hearts! It is my regular trade, gentlemen, to move my hands quicker than your eyes. The ace of hearts! Who will go me twenty? " He seldom asks in vain.

Play goes on at the Corral day and night to a repetitive series of tunes offered by a screechy orchestra sitting within a small enclosure at the far end of the hall. Every better gambling hell has its orchestra, which usually consists of four pieces — fiddle, cornet, piccolo and asthmatic piano, with occasionally a banjo substituted for any of these. Mingled with the clink of glasses at the bar and the call-song of the gamblers come the strains of *Lily Dale, Twenty Years Ago, Yellow Rose of Texas* and *Sweet Betsy from Pike.*

One evening when hilarity is at its height and the music at its loudest, a miner enters, approaches a faro table, takes a large pouch of gold dust from his pocket and places it on the five-spot. The dealer asks, " Does it all go? " The miner grunts assent. The dealer begins slowly turning over the cards. Not a half dozen are played before the pouch is lost. The miner grabs desperately for his gold. The gambler whips out his gun and shoots. The musicians with a single practised motion drop both their instruments and themselves behind the low enclosure which they have thoughtfully lined with sheet-iron. For a few moments the air is blue with smoke and bullets as three hundred men dive frantically for cover or dash madly toward the street. The instant shooting ceases, the orchestra is on its feet with Jones, the leader, singing,

> *Ha, boys, ho!*
> *Ain't you glad you're out of the wilderness,*
> *Ain't you glad you're out of the wilderness?*
> *Ha, boys, ho!*

When a guest is killed, as many are, his body is dragged to the rear to be buried at the expense of the house by one McGovern — undertaker, cabinetmaker, gravedigger and sexton. McGovern is a lean lank man given to melancholy when business is dull. " But a full-priced customer would always set him whistling and jigging." McGovern owns his own cemetery up the Platte where he buries, so it is said, many a corpse but never a coffin. His apprentice, a " camel-backed youth with a taste for the grave business," later hung as a horse thief, once declared that the same box was used "thirty times for customers and that the Old Man himself was finally buried in it."

The Elephant Corral has a single serious rival as a gambling hell, the famous Progressive built by Ed Chase not many doors away. With a stake of $1,500 won at poker while working as a railroad brakeman in and out of Saratoga Springs, New York, Chase came West in the rush to spend a fruitless summer prospecting Clear Creek. Realizing the disabilities of ignorance as few did, he quickly abandoned mining for more familiar pursuits. With two Ford brothers he first established a small gambling saloon on Blake Street. An impressive ceremony marked its opening. William Chivington, presiding elder of the Methodist Church in the Territory and Colonel of the Third Colorado Cavalry, attended with his staff in full regimentals. "His benediction was reverently received by the Fords' guests. All bowed their heads and silence reigned as prayer went forth from our soldier-preacher."

Showered with blessings, Chase soon set up shop for himself across the street. "Furniture was scarce and the boys considered themselves lucky to have benches to sit on, while the card tables were covered only with woolen blankets." But profits were large, and with them Chase built the Progressive. "There were seats for all comers. The tables were the best that had been known in Denver up to that time. The entire lower floor, twenty-five feet by one hundred, was devoted to gambling, with the exception of bar space. The second floor was also used by the sporting fraternity, but in a more quiet way. There were private rooms there which were rented to those who could afford to pay for them. The tables were run practically without limit. When one of these big games was on, I generally sat at the head of the table, so arranging it, that a customer could place as high as $200 on double cards and $100 on singles. But they never broke any bank of mine. My profits were big at times."

But the police soon began to annoy Chase, demanding then as now an increasingly larger share of the spoils. "I generally found it cheaper in the end to meet the demands of the officials than to try to evade them. I was often 'held up,' but I never found it profitable to kick about it. I would simply give them the money and forget about it." When their demands became preposterous, Chase closed up the Progressive and departed to try his fortune in Montana. The Vigilantes there proved even more troublesome. Chase finally returned to Denver to amass a fortune first at the Cricket and then at the Palace, famous gambling saloon and variety theater, where in later years he will be found entertaining many notables — Eugene Field, Oscar Wilde, Horace Tabor and almost all the mining, smelter and cattle kings of the day.

The Elephant Corral with its many sources of revenue is paying Father Teats and Uncle Phillip rather well. But they decide their livery business might be improved with a light wagon service. Two small drays are brightly painted and placed on the streets behind fine large horses in shining harness. In an unexpected manner they prove an immediate success — "especially with lucky men who came down from the mines for a good time with their buckskin pouches filled with dust. When they wanted to show off a bit, they would make up a little party, hire both drays, decorate the harness with bottles and cans, and then drive from saloon to saloon until they were all sufficiently soaked to be ready to turn in and sleep it off. As we charged them a dollar an hour for each dray and as hardly a day passed without a gang of them coming to town, the drays proved fair money-makers."

Eugene's education at the Corral continues apace, for he finds himself "like all boys with ordinary ambition in wanting to become as proficient as the other fellow in most things." He first sets himself to master the Western style of riding, finding it "easy after a while to pick up things from the ground while loping along at a rapid rate, which is done by catching a spur in the hair cinch and locking it in with the rowel." He then learns to throw the lariat and manage the "half-wild stock" brought to the Corral to be cared for. Every morning at seven he drives a large herd of horses to one of the three outside ranges where they are pastured during the day. Late in the afternoon he herds them back again so that those wishing to ride or drive in the evening may have their ponies.

Eugene next applies himself to the bullwhip — "built very much like a rattlesnake, about twelve feet long, although many used them longer, with a short handle, a swivel and a long loop on the lash end." Finally possessed of one "with up-to-date qualifications, having a buck-popper fully two inches wide," the boy begins to scourge the barn men. When he can find no fly on which to practise, he pins a "piece of paper to the pants' seat of some of the good-natured ones." At other times he refines his technique upon lazy mules and ponies until at last he can do "almost as good a job as some of the professional bullwhackers, many having eight, ten or sometimes sixteen bullocks to chastize, each with the name of a famous man, their song beginning this way — Up ahha there, Brigham, and you too, Old Abe, and what's the matter with you there, Franklin, that you're not doing your share to help Old Daniel Boone! And you, Washington, and you, Adams, get into the yoke there! "

" During the days when Porter, Raymond and Company had their mule and bull teams moving in and out of Auraria, they used to have about fifty bull teams to a wagon train, with five or six yoke to each wagon and trailer. I used to go out to meet them at the place where they camped until they were ordered in. The drivers would prepare for the occasion by trimming up their bullwhips or ' persuaders ' with new poppers — the wider, the louder the noise. Well, when orders came and they harnessed up, it was like the firing of guns all the way in. How I did enjoy snapping flies off the left hip of good Old Brigham. Great days and good ones, I tell you, with gambling and booze shops running wide open day and night. Everybody had mostly gold dust as money. A pinch between the first finger and thumb was twenty-five cents, and you weren't supposed to have long nails either or dig down too deep in the buckskin pouch. Occasionally some fellow would try the big-pinch act only to find himself looking down the muzzle of a cannon and hear someone say, ' Now, partner, just drop that pinch back and play the game square, and don't try that again in this joint, see! ' "

Into the Corral one day ride two strangers astride a large bay gelding, gaunt and footsore, caked with sweat and dust. They have manifestly ridden fast and far on this one horse. Eugene eyes them with some misgivings as he leads their hungry mount off to the stables. As the strangers continue to live for a time at the Corral, Eugene soon knows them well and learns their story long before they, and their horse as well, become the talk of the town.

One is Tom Hunt and his partner is the gambler-desperado, Charley Harrison, in his day the most accomplished gunman in the West. They have just come from Salt Lake City, they explain, because of a little trouble with the Mormons. Tom Hunt, as a matter of fact, was almost on the gallows when daringly rescued by Harrison. Stealing Border Ruffian, a champion racer, and leading Hunt's big sorrel, Harrison rode down upon the lynching party, freed his partner and away they rode toward Denver with the Mormons in pursuit. They outdistanced these only to meet a band of outlaws who attempted to halt and rob them. " Once more their horses and guns saved them from capture. But in the running fight Hunt's horse was disabled, and he was obliged to abandon him and get up behind Harrison on Border Ruffian — two men aggregating four hundred pounds on poor Ruffian! But he was equal to the emergency, and in good time the trio landed in town and were housed in the old Elephant Corral."

A powerful and enigmatic figure, Charley Harrison looms large in the annals of early Denver. Although broke upon arrival, he and his partner are not long in acquiring a " big wad of money " at the Corral's gambling tables. " About forty years old and compactly built, with dark hair and a well-kept silky beard," Harrison always dresses well but modestly in black. In fact, the attention of the rough camp is first drawn to him by his grooming and quiet elegance which give him the " appearance of something better than a professional gambler." A Southerner — from Arkansas, some say — Harrison has great personal charm. His slow quiet voice and gentle manners are often remarked. Usually he is most suave, amiable and kindly. " He would give his last dollar to a friend," according to Eugene who is soon devoted to him. " Often I would find myself short of funds and only a hint was sufficient. He would generally ask how little I could get along with. If I said a couple of dollars, it was likely to be twenty."

But Harrison is also subject to strange homicidal frenzies. He is said to have carried a pistol with eleven notches filed on one side for the number of men he had killed and three notches on the other for his women victims, remarking that "counting the three women as equal to one man, there would be a competent jury waiting to try him in Hell." Certainly no one shoots faster or more accurately than Harrison, as Eugene declared in relating stories of his prowess.

"One morning some fellow from the gold fields with an overload of booze pulled his gun and began popping it off in the street. Leaning against the porch posts of the Elephant Corral was the colored cook of the Ford brothers' gambling saloon. He was just returning from marketing with a basket on his arm. One of the stray bullets found a vital spot in his frame and he was a cook in our town no longer. The rowdy mounted his pony and started up the street with a number of men shouting, *Stop him! Stop him!* Just then Harrison came walking along quite early for him and noticed the fellow. Realizing that he was the man wanted, Charley pulled his old reliable and although he was quite a distance away, dropped the rowdy from the pony with his shot. Harrison did not even wait to learn what had happened. But that was his disposition. He would walk a long way to avoid trouble, but if he thought he was in the right, no one ever lived who could intimidate him. He feared neither God, man or devil, was the way his friends put it. He was never known to take advantage of any man, gambling or shooting. Never could anyone get a drop on Harrison if he had an equal or an almost equal show, and never would he shoot without giving his opponent the call, *Pull your iron!*"

The gambler and Eugene spend many hours down by the Platte where the boy is taught to shoot "with Harrison's two pets, pearl-handled Colts." Harrison himself practises upon tin cans thrown into the air by Eugene. Often he puts two or three holes in a can while in the air, " and that with either hand or with both guns at once." Eugene pronounces Harrison the best shot he ever saw, an opinion echoed by " Bat " Masterson, Denver gambler and peer of two-gun fighters. After knowing or meeting all the gunmen of the early West, Masterson declared that Harrison " with all his dazzling speed was the most brilliant pistol-handler I ever saw and a far more deadly shot than most of the great gunfighters."

Harrison's guns are the old Colt cap-and-ball revolvers, the original type of the formidable six-shooter renowned in song and story, for the metal-cartridge revolver does not come West until the 'Seventies. The cap-and-ball is not such a clumsy weapon as would at first appear. It is necessary, of course, to load separately each chamber of the revolving cylinder with percussion cap, powder and ball. By means of the small lever-ramrod hinged under the barrel the lead ball is " seated " against the powder. This operation obviously takes time and is never attempted when shots are flying. Hence the necessity of a second gun. Many gunmen also carry in their pockets extra cylinders previously loaded and dipped in beeswax to keep the powder dry. As it takes but a few seconds to insert a loaded cylinder, a man with two guns can fire twenty-four shots in one almost continuous fusillade.

The speed of the old-time gunman is the more remarkable because these first Colts do not have double action. They have to be cocked with the thumb for each shot. But this is considered a positive advantage, according to Masterson, who declares that all better gun-fighters of the West ever scorned the double-acting revolver, complaining of the trigger pull as too hard for accurate shooting. And the cap-and-ball can be fired almost as rapidly, particularly when the trigger notch is filed away so that the hammer drops the instant the thumb releases it. This also allows the more accomplished to " fan " their guns by moving the hammer with their free hand which, palm down, flashes rapidly back and forth above it. Good shots invariably file away the sights. Not only are they apt to catch in holster or pocket when life depends upon a quick draw, but they are considered useless, for a Western gunman's weapon is as much a part of his hand as his index finger and he points it as readily. He cocks his revolver in the single flashing motion with which he draws and, as Masterson declares, " delivers his first shot in a half second, six shots in less than two seconds " — and another six shots in even less time from his second gun which he has meanwhile drawn.

Colts of this day range in size and caliber from the heavy " Dragoon " to the " Suicide Gun." The Dragoon is none other than the well-known Forty-four, the favorite of cowboys and plainsmen because it shoots the same cartridge as their .44-.40 Winchester rifles. With its long barrel and weight of four pounds it requires a holster and is rather too cumbersome for any but horseback use. In mining camps the .41 is generally preferred to the .44, for it is quite as powerful and with less weight has less recoil — " hence faster action at close quarters." Harrison's pets are of this caliber. Although properly a holster revolver, gamblers usually carry the .41 concealed under vests or in pockets sewn inside the waistbands of their trousers.

But early boom towns and mining camps generally prefer the Colt " Navy " (.36), so named from a naval scene engraved round its barrel. This and the .38 Smith and Wesson are pocket revolvers, and are variously and ingeniously concealed. Liable at any time to challenge, confidence men and the worst class of gamblers adopt a weapon peculiarly their own, the derringer, a light gun of large caliber, so small that it can easily be concealed in a vest pocket or even in the palm of a large hand. As it has the shortest of barrels, its accurate range does not exceed five or six feet. But it is deadly within that range, which is ample to embrace all at even the largest gambling table. As derringers fire but a single shot, they are always carried in pairs. Although it bestows an obvious initial advantage, the derringer is nevertheless a dangerous gun to use. For if its one shot goes wild, its user is left at the mercy of the slower but more accurate and powerful six-shooter. Lastly, there is the " Suicide Gun," the Colt .32, which is thought to lack power. " When two men got into a smoking argument, the one with the .44 always killed his man, while the one with the .32 gave his foe merely a skin complaint, as the grimly humorous saying went."

Eugene learns all this and more from Harrison and under his instruction is soon a remarkably fine shot.

Now Eugene becomes a jockey.

One day not long after Harrison's arrival three Greer brothers from Iowa drove into the Corral with four large horses tied to the tail of their wagon. " I paid little more than the usual attention to the bunch," said Eugene, "but when Bill Greer called Father into the room called our office and I overheard him say that he wanted three of the best stalls we had, and for a long time, and would we fix it so that they could be together, and if possible boxed-in, so that one of the brothers could sleep in the stall, well, so unusual a thing created new interest in the horses to be so carefully guarded."

Eugene soon learned that one of them was a champion half-miler, Bay Chief. When asked by the Greers to exercise the racer, the boy accepted delightedly and every day went speeding through the streets and along the nearby roads. It was not long before a race against Border Ruffian began to be talked of. Hunt still had his half share in Ruffian but Harrison, not interested in horses, had sold his to a certain Colonel Miller, " a Southerner of rank ideas called a Secessionist, who was near being invited at times to stop talking or get out of the country." Finally a race was arranged. " For a couple of months nothing else was talked about, and it seemed that about every week a goodly sum would be added to the first amount of $40,000, all in gold, which was taken down to the old Clark and Gruber mint and lumped together in one retort."

To his great surprise and delight the Greers chose Eugene to ride Bay Chief, now renamed Rocky Mountain Chief. Colonel Miller had already announced his intention of bringing a professional jockey from Kentucky. Every day Eugene rode down the Platte to the racetrack on the old McNassar Ranch where Chief Left Hand's Arapahoes were encamped at the moment. As Eugene put Chief through his paces, the Indians "would come running out with blankets, shaking them and yelling to scare my horse and see him run away." Hunt and Miller went to work earnestly as well, training Ruffian secretly at a private track on the far side of town. But they spent quite as much time in "thinking up every little underhand trick which might advance their chances of making a big winning," according to Eugene.

" Two weeks before the race, Hunt appeared at the Corral and very secretly gave out that he had quarreled with Miller and had given him until the next day to retract his words or he would leave him or challenge him to fight or possibly stop the race altogether. Our trainer, McKnight, never thought of Hunt's possible treachery and told him to come back and tell us how his troubles panned out. Poor fellow, he had it in his mind to gain some valuable pointers and have a good two-hundred pound man to help him hold Chief down, for he was becoming very hard to handle when excited. True to his dishonest principles, Hunt showed up on the third day full of abuse of Miller, who had threatened to have Hunt arrested or possibly shoot him on sight. So it is easy to imagine how Chief's true and honest supporters in their eagerness to gain every possible advantage saw the good to come from having Hunt's assistance. He was hired as an assistant starter and immediately began his work. He secretly reported to Miller our speed, endurance and every move in our training. I must not forget to mention the handicaps our horse was supposed to be working under. Never had Bay Chief graduated above the half-mile class. This race was mile heats, the best two out of three, and our hope was to make a haul on the first heat. Right here was where Hunt knew he could and did do his mischief.

" Well, the final day was on, and if there ever gathered a mixed crowd it was right there. It was said that seventy percent of the people of the Pike's Peak country were on the track, all with bags of real gold dust. No small currency was needed. The sun never shone upon a scene more wildly animated than that Frontier race-course. There were no high enclosures, no morose ticket sellers, no insolent gate keepers, no protecting policemen. All was go as you please, where you please, an unending confusion of men and women encircling the track in a weltering chain — the roughest, the kindest, the poorest, the most vile of the border element mingling without distinction. A temporary judges' stand was up and the big retort was hung where everybody could see it.

" Just in front of the starting post a hole in the track had been filled in with dirt from the side of the course, leaving quite a deep ditch, very uneven, from which it was very difficult to get back up on the track without going the whole length of it, about two hundred feet. This Hunt and Miller had decided to use as their safe and certain means of winning the first heat. The rest would be easy. Betting was wild, as high as ten to one on Chief to win the first heat."

When the horses were called up at last, Eugene was amazed to behold on Border Ruffian his friend and playmate young Jim McNassar, for never did he "suspicion that he was to be my opponent." Eugene tried to talk with him, but Jim remained glum and answered no questions.

"Both horses were behaving very badly, seeming to catch the spirit of evil which pervaded the place. For fully an hour the turning and jockeying went on, and much praise did Hunt receive for his masterful way of heading off any unfair start. He certainly did his work well. Father was one of the judges and on several occasions called Hunt to account. But always Hunt's response was that he was on to the tricks of the Miller gang and intended to give Chief a fair start.

"Finally the limit of patience was reached and the judges said they would send the horses off on the first reasonably good score, and they did. But big Tom Hunt failed to hear the word go, at least so he said, and hung on. His two hundred pounds were too much for poor Chief to overcome, with the result that we found ourselves floundering around in the ditch while Ruffian started off under the whip. When I regained the track, Ruffian had the inside track and a start of a good two hundred feet. Fortunately for me, I did not lose my head and abuse Chief, but just let him have his head. Gradually he closed the gap, and I believe I could have regained all the ground lost by the treachery, had I urged him. But for some unknown reason I did not once use the whip, and Ruffian won the heat by several feet."

The track was bedlam. Through the surging crowd came Charley Harrison to Chief's paddock, for he had dismissed whatever sentimental debt he may have owed Border Ruffian and transferred his allegiance to Rocky Mountain Chief for the good reason that the Greers contributed heavily to the profits of his Criterion Saloon. Harrison plied Eugene with questions, confirmed his own suspicions and with drawn revolver marched back to the track to denounce Hunt publicly for his treachery.

"Colonel McNassar, father of Ruffian's rider and a bad man in those days, very ready with the gun, took the lead in championing Hunt's side. This at once brought into action the two most noted gunmen of the day. In the meantime a crowd had gathered about Hunt and gave him thirty minutes in which to gather himself and his possessions and ' git,' not only from the track, but from the town. He went, mostly because of the antagonism of his old pard Harrison. He knew his man too well to risk a later meeting. Well, one can imagine the turmoil."

Back to the paddock came Harrison to talk again with Eugene about their prospects of winning. The boy was most confident, pointing out how well Chief had performed after so poor a start. "All right, young man, but if necessary you whip that horse this time and at least try to win," said Harrison as he departed with the Greers for the betting field in the hope of recouping their heavy losses.

"It was then I saw Bill Greer's woman, known as Moll, go down in her stocking and begin extracting money and some jewelry to start calling the twenty to one odds on Border Ruffian. Soon the crowd was betting mad, and I can still see aged Father Machebeuf hobbling about betting money and ponies, for he had just come in with a bunch of them from his ranch over near the St. Vrain. Harrison in his easy way was calling every offer until he and his friends stood to win back all their losses and more.

" Called to the post again, the horses were soon off to a fair start. I had the outside and from the start Chief held his place close up to Ruffian's neck. Ruffian was being urged harder and harder all the time, but he could not get away, not an inch. I was holding Chief down, never asking him to increase his speed. At the half-mile post, I asked Chief for extra speed and got it. He drew up to a head-to-head place — and that while rounding a curve. It was then that my chum Jim McNassar served me a very ugly trick. He began to use his rawhide whip in the so-called half-wheel style. As our horses were neck and neck, his whip cut my face which bled profusely. Then he tried to hit my horse over the head but failed.

" As we were nearing the last curve into the home stretch, I saw Harrison inside the track mounted on my Father's split-eared Comanche pony, and his words came to me, ' You whip that horse or I'll drop you from his back! ' Well, it didn't take me long to answer that call. Chief came under the wire a full length ahead of Ruffian. Blood was oozing from many severe whip marks on poor Chief, and when it became known that I had been hit by my opponent, more trouble was on in short order.

" The third heat was brief and unexciting, for when Ruffian's backers saw how easily Chief could beat him and how fresh Chief seemed, they failed to show up. Chief was ordered up and sent off alone, with instructions to let him go as he pleased until the half-mile post and then send him in for a record. Just what it was I don't recall, but the judges said it was a record. The ceremony of taking down the big bunch of gold was soon ended, and the remainder of the crowd started for town. Father improvised a band wagon and Alex Benham, superintendent of the stage line, furnished four horses. The boy and his winnings were placed on the band wagon which reached town in time to overtake the big crowd that had gone ahead to arrange a reception."

As the celebration consisted largely of long draughts of whiskey, the boy had no part in it but to come forward to receive in some embarrassment what he vaguely termed a "big sum of money." He thriftily sends most of it home to his mother but does celebrate by indulging himself in a pair of "new white pants with three little gold nuggets as buttons down either leg."

Another effort to give Eugene's education a more academic turn is attempted with the opening of a second school in Auraria. Here a Miss Indiana Sopris labors earnestly to instruct a dozen distracted pupils from a great variety of texts brought from all parts of the country. Eugene is forced to attend, as are his three playmates. One is Jim McNassar, "about as wild and reckless as a boy could be," whom Eugene has forgiven for his treachery. The other two are Jake Hart, butcher's son, and Billy Kehler, son of the Episcopal minister.

"We all pretended to go to school to a Miss or Mrs. Sopris. Her little school building was located in West Denver just about where the County Jail now stands. We really did go to school in the forenoons, and in the afternoons kept out of sight. Our favorite place for lunch was a little saloon and restaurant on Larimer Street. We ate mostly dainties, and depended upon my finding some of the gang in the place to whom I might appeal for help to pay. If not, then we had credit, for the good old Frenchman had made a lot of dollars out of his places on the race track. He had backed Rocky Mountain Chief quite liberally, so of course I had a stand-in. Many times at lunch when my three chums were under the influence of drink, they would try to force me to drink with them, and on several occasions they held me down and tried to force liquor into my mouth. But someone always came to my rescue and saved me. I have always thought that it was Charley Harrison, who having witnessed the frequent dinners of my chums, decided best that my father should know of the temptation. When he called me to task, the matter was easily settled by sending me off to his partner in the mountains where I was allowed to run about the hills looking for gold and getting experience which later served me well. I have on many occasions in later life wondered how I kept from becoming the real thing, but always when temptation was strongest, my mind would go back to my mother's parting words when leaving the farm in Michigan, ' Leave liquor, cards and gambling alone, and you will come out all right.' "

VI. Bummers and Stranglers

" The town, such as it was, was full of gamblers, thieves and cutthroats and by the summer of 1860, soon after our arrival, this element seemed to be running the place."

Blood began to flow along Cherry Creek even before the Larimers' arrival. A gambler named Vincent drifted in from Salt Lake City and a few days later murdered the squaw man Atwell in a quarrel over a game of three-card monte. Vincent fled but was captured and brought back by Arapahoes induced to go in pursuit. Tried before the first People's Court assembled in the territory, he was speedily found guilty and given a horse, rifle, ammunition, provisions for a few days and a command to leave the country instantly. If ever found within a mile of camp, so his sentence ran, he would be shot at sight.

Crime and violence increased with the gold rush which attracted large numbers of irresponsible, vicious and lawless men. Murders became " almost every day occurrences," according to Uncle Dick Wootton, " and stealing was the only occupation of a considerable portion of the population, who would take anything from a pet calf or counterfeit gold dollar up to a sawmill." The first steam sawmill in the gold fields, he declared, was stolen from a flatboat on the Missouri. But Uncle Dick condoned thievery on the ground that disappointed gold-hunters left stranded on Cherry Creek had all suffered cruelly. Many were starving, for " they had little or no money and there was little or nothing for them to do."

Denver City and Auraria contained a " great deal of low scuff from California," and much of the lawlessness was laid upon their shoulders by the gambler Ed Chase. The Californians, he said, " considered themselves a superior class of beings, but the other fellows would not stand for their airs." The Californians were known locally as " the Self-risers." They in turn pleasantly dubbed their enemies " the Pike's Peak Skunks." Clashes between them were frequent and often fatal. Chase identified another particularly lawless group as the stragglers and deserters from the armies which put down the Mormon Rebellion of '57.

Although many men were murdered during the year of the rush, " only fifteen men and women were given notice to leave the country and only two were hanged." While acting as Larimer's personal bodyguard, Captain Peleg Bassett was shot and killed by one Scudder and a desperado named Carrol Wood. Both escaped from custody and fled the country. But so little respect had Wood for the authorities that he returned shortly to defy them with impunity. A negro prizefighter killed a rival and in turn was murdered by the old trader Jim Beckwourth who objected to his attentions to the comely young negress known as " Lady " Beckwourth. The prizefighter in the first instance and Beckwourth in the second were acquitted on the grounds of self-defense.

A young German named Stoefel, who assassinated his brother-in-law to rob him of a few dollars in his pocket, is the first to pay the extreme penalty for murder. He is brought to trial before a People's Court assembled among the cottonwoods in Auraria. Three judges are selected from among the crowd and mount to the bench — a carpenter's bench commandeered for the occasion. A rope stretched from tree to tree keeps the audience from crowding the court too closely. Attornies for the prosecution and the defense are appointed. A jury is selected and seated upon a log to one side. The prisoner sits alone upon a stump to the other. He is quickly found guilty and sentenced to be hanged that very afternoon. Anticipating the verdict, Noisy Tom Pollock the blacksmith has a stout rope at hand and clamors for the job of executioner, finally prevailing.

Stoefel requests a stay of fifteen minutes that he may " arrange his spiritual welfare." General Larimer and the Reverend Fisher, blacksmith-preacher, lead him away to the hall above Wootton's saloon. The crowd follows and is soon demanding its victim. Larimer's head appears at an upper window and after acrimonious debate another fifteen minutes' grace is granted the prisoner. At last Stoefel appears and the crowd marches him off to the gallows, a large cottonwood tree in St. Louis Street. The prisoner is commanded to get up and stand in the wagon always used on such occasions. As Pollock is clumsily fitting the noose, the condemned man begins to speak, for a final address is customary. Stoefel talks of his sins and prays forgiveness in a broken English which moves his audience to roars of laughter. He is forced to stop again and again " to ask the crowd not to make sport of his faulty language." His self-appointed executioner also interferes, commanding him to hold his head higher. Stoefel obeys, stretching out his neck, but continues talking as fast as he can. Now ready, Noisy Tom Pollock jumps down, gives the signal for the wagon to be driven from under the condemned man and stands by critically as Stoefel, still talking, swings out high in the air, choking and shaken with convulsions.

This first public execution affects the community variously. Some remark an improved moral tone. Others remain somewhat skeptical. The hanging not only pleases the Larimers but inspires them to new enterprise. The camp needs another cemetery.

Father and son lay claim to a high sandy hill up Cherry Creek and quickly seize the bodies of both Stoefel and his victim to bury the two together in one grave. The General takes in a prosperous undertaker as partner, but this is a mistake. While Larimer is absent for a brief time, the new partner takes complete possession. And thus, as the younger Larimer complains, neither he nor his father derive " any benefit from this venture, though it is the final resting place of many a body." Tabor, in fact, will one day be laid to rest here in what is later named Mt. Prospect Cemetery, long since neglected and overgrown with weeds.

In earlier days the cemetery is known as " Jack O'Neil's Ranch " from the first prominent citizen to be buried there. A prosperous and popular gambler, O'Neil quarrels over cards with one Rooker, a troublesome desperado, and proposes that they lock themselves in a dark room and settle their differences with bowie knives. As O'Neil is a large man of tremendous strength, Rooker declines but next morning lies in wait behind Wootton's store to shoot O'Neil dead as he comes sauntering innocently down the street. Rooker is acquitted on the usual ground of self-defense.

From month to month murders increase at an alarming rate. Greeley does not greatly exaggerate when in writing of his two weeks' visit he reports " more brawls, more fights, more pistol shots with criminal intent in this log city of one hundred and fifty dwellings, not three fourths of them completed nor two thirds inhabited nor one third fit to be, than in any community of equal numbers on earth."

Moses Young blows his partner to pieces with a shotgun and is hanged. Pocohontas, a Sioux squaw, filled with firewater, kills the French proprietor of the Mountain Boys' Saloon and escapes. The authorities make no effort to apprehend her but belatedly pass an ordinance making it " unlawful for any person to vend or give away to any Indian within the city limits any intoxicating liquor." Marcus Gredler robs and kills his partner and is hanged. For a like offense one Hadley is sentenced to the gallows but escapes. In a row at the St. Charles Saloon a negro slave is killed by " Buckskin Bill " Karl, who is acquitted. A German saloon-keeper stabs a soldier to death and is acquitted. As his final point in an argument over slavery, Postmaster Park McClure fires twice without effect at Professor Goldrick, barricades himself in the post office and forces the authorities to come to terms by holding up the mail. A hunted man, Secretary Dick Whitsitt slinks about town for days during the " Claim-Jumpers' War," provoked when three men building on an unimproved tract claimed by the town company awaken one morning to find not only their cabin torn down but its timbers chopped to pieces by Larimer's agents.

Sporadic and isolated phenomena for a time, crime and violence are soon organized by a gang known as the " Bummers." Cabins are systematically burglarized, clothes are stolen from wash lines. Almost every night raids are made upon wagons and corrals. Eager to force the issue, angry citizens precipitate the " Turkey War " in an unsuccessful effort to rid themselves of their tormentors. Shortly after Christmas, '59, a rustic drives into camp with a wagonload of wild turkeys and in his innocence stops directly in front of the grogshops lining Ferry Street, Auraria. All the Bummers in the saloons turn out to filch a turkey or two whenever the driver busies himself with a sale. When the loss is discovered, the rustic's indignation is exceeded by that of good citizens with mouths watering in prospect of a change from beans and bacon. In their angry disappointment they call a public meeting and appoint a committee to hunt out the guilty. Largely upon the testimony of Sheriff Middaugh the committee names Thomas Clemo, William Harvey, Buckskin Bill Karl, "Chuck-a-Luck" Todd and several others as chiefly responsible. The Bummers in turn marshal their forces and parade the streets heavily armed. They talk drunkenly of burning the town.

Toward evening Sheriff Middaugh is lounging in the doorway of the Vasquez House. A shot rings out. A bullet grazes his hat and crashes through the door, with the Sheriff close behind it. He is shot at again as he passes an open window. An excited crowd collects. The desperado who fired at Middaugh draws a bowie knife on Noisy Tom Pollock who fells him with the butt of his rifle. The desperado's partner whips out his gun but is intimidated by the "ominous clicking of the hammers of a dozen revolvers." Complaints multiply that peaceful citizens are being stopped in the streets by armed ruffians and subjected to indignities and violence. The Jefferson Rangers, a company of recently organized volunteers, are hurriedly called out and patrol the town all night.

Next morning good citizens meet again to proclaim that "Todd, Harvey and Karl must leave the city within five hours under penalty of being hanged if found within the city limits at the expiration of that time or ever afterwards." The desperados, supported by a ruffian crew from Charley Harrison's Criterion Saloon, take their time in obeying the command. Todd and Harvey depart leisurely the next morning. That evening Karl is found hiding in an Indian lodge. When granted another five hours' grace, he decides not to try the community's patience further. The Rangers after a week of day and night patrol are withdrawn.

The Bummers next fall upon the Indians when Cheyennes and Arapahoes come in to trade a few months later, leaving their squaws and papooses encamped a few miles down the Platte. At midnight drunken scoundrels descend upon the lodges to outrage and rape even children, taking horses and mules as they flee. Left Hand and other chiefs threaten war and massacre. An attack is averted only through the mediation of Jim Beckwourth, old Indian trader and once a famous war chief of the Crows. He persuades Left Hand to accept the community's apologies and promises of retribution. But the perpetrators of this outrage are never punished.

Matters go steadily from bad to worse. A prominent rancher has been gambling and drinking all day in Charley Harrison's Criterion Saloon. Finally broke, the rancher commands the bartender to give him a drink on the house. He is refused and begins to curse loudly. Harrison is standing well to the front of the saloon, apparently unheeding the row. Suddenly he spins on his heel, walks up to the intoxicated ranchman and without a word empties his six-shooter into him. The murder creates great excitement because of the prominence of the victim. A motley crowd collects down the street and after a harangue by a friend of the murdered man, moves, some two hundred strong, upon the saloon to lynch Harrison. Advised of events, Sheriff Middaugh drives up to check the mob.

"Give me a few minutes and I will arrest Harrison," pleads the Sheriff and finally gains his point. But the mob insists upon accompanying him.

"No, I don't want any of you to go with me. All the assistance I need can be supplied by this boy here," he declares, indicating his son Asa, a youth of twenty. Together they drive up to the Criterion to find it locked and barred. They knock. Harrison opens the door, shakes hands with the Sheriff and his son and invites them in. There are "fully seventy-five, if not a hundred, cutthroats stationed in the saloon, all armed to the teeth."

"Charley, I have a warrant for you and I want you to submit to arrest and save your own life as well as that of others."

"Will you protect me?" asks Harrison.

"With my life!"

The desperado draws his two revolvers and hands them to the Sheriff. His gang swarms forward about him, ready for any command.

"Boys, put up your guns," Harrison drawls, and all obey. Harrison steps into the buggy and is driven away to jail. The mob disperses slowly.

Harrison's trial proves a farce. A woman of the town, "Ad" Lamont, distributes $5,000 "so discreetly as to bring about a disagreement of the jury after a two days' hearing." This is regarded as an acquittal by the judge who dismisses the jury and releases the prisoner.

Harrison is no sooner free than he himself sits as Judge Lynch. For a purse of $9 a tramp chooses to rob and murder one of the gambler's friends, a rancher named Freeman. The offense is aggravated by the fact that the murdered rancher was Harrison's brother in Masonry while the murderer was a Catholic. Harrison organizes the gamblers as a Vigilante Committee to wreak vengeance. Captured as he flees on a stolen horse, the tramp Pat Waters is brought back to the scene of the murder, forced to confess and indicate where he buried his victim. The body is dug up and the two men, the live and the dead, are placed in a wagon and driven to town. Here the gamblers take entire charge of the proceedings, "with a gambler as judge and a jury composed of gentlemen of the cloth." Found guilty, Waters is sentenced to be hanged that afternoon, but a priest procures a twenty-four hours' stay of execution. Next day a long procession winds its way down the Platte to the McNassar racetrack where a gallows has been erected. Harrison, determined to avoid any mishap, has arranged for a drop of nine feet, " almost sufficient to separate the man's head from his body, but instead of the head coming off, the neck stretched until it was fully eighteen inches long " — the most gruesome sight he ever beheld, according to the young Middaugh, who had a taste for such detail.

The authorities seldom interfere with proceedings of this kind. In the disorganized community a mob is generally accepted as the final authority. Also, as the Sheriff confesses, considerable danger attends an attempt to stop one hundred or more determined men, inflamed with passion and rum. Furthermore, there is little or no money to defray the expenses of more formal trials. Lastly, it is expensive to feed and practically impossible to hold prisoners in the makeshift jail. They must either be summarily dealt with or be allowed to roam at large.

Matters reach a crisis in July, '6o, with another murder by Harrison. One day Eugene Teats and his schoolmates are eating lunch at a restaurant-saloon on Larimer Street. At the next table a game of poker is proceeding " with a big black bullwhacker as its chief victim." Harrison walks out from a back room where he has been having lunch.

" Charley," shouts the negro, rising, " I would like to play you a game of poker, for I know you're honest! These fellows are rascals."

" Who are you to address me as Charley and these gentlemen as rascals? " asks Harrison, coldly eyeing the negro up and down, his Southern pride touched.

" I'll show you who I am. I'll wipe the floor with your carcass."

The negro Stark lunges at Harrison who quickly shakes himself loose and backs off.

" Are you heeled? " snaps the gambler. The negro reaches for his gun. " In a second Mister Nig is on the floor with two bullets in his head, one between the eyes and the second just below his Adam's apple " — " a damn fool and nothing more," adds Eugene. Harrison spies the boy in the excited crowd.

" Get Brigham for me, quick! " he commands Eugene, who runs off to the Corral to bring back his pony. Harrison mounts and rides " out to Bishop Machebeuf's ranch for a few days' outing." Upon his return nothing is said except by his enemy Colonel Miller, owner of Border Ruffian. But he falls silent when Harrison threatens " to riddle his old Secession carcass."

At the same time one Jim Gordon shoots up the town and commits an atrocious murder. A civil engineer, well educated and widely read, industrious and gentle when sober, he lives on a ranch down the Platte with his mother and sisters. But he is a maniac when in his cups. Just after Harrison's murder of the negro Stark, Gordon enters a brothel and in cold blood shoots down the bartender, wounding him seriously. Next day he wanders drunkenly about town shooting at random. He is still at large the next night when he staggers into the Elephant Corral and fires point-blank at Big Phil the Cannibal, missing him twice at close range. Gordon staggers out, " evidently in an ugly mood." In the street he passes a man with a dog at his heels. Without remark Gordon shoots the animal — a most heinous offense in the early West when a dog was more than wife or child. Gordon staggers on to the Louisiana Saloon in the bed of Cherry Creek. Here he amuses himself smashing glasses and destroying furniture until, tiring of the bartender's complaints, he first knocks him out with the butt of his gun, then pulls him to his feet by the hair, holds his limp figure against the bar and at last succeeds "in shooting him through the head, after ineffectually snapping his pistol four times." As no one interferes during or after the pistol-snapping, Gordon reels out into the street again and next day, with Sheriff Middaugh in pursuit, flees the country on a horse provided by the Criterion gang.

The *News* utters a protest against this and the Stark murder. Next forenoon three desperados — Carrol Wood, implicated in the murder of Peleg Bassett; John Rooker, murderer of Jack O'Neil; and George Steele, who has defied two official commands to leave the country — raid the office of the *News,* seize Byers and carry him off to the Criterion with the announced purpose of "stopping his attacks by stopping his breath." Harrison happens to enter in an amiable mood and boldly rushes to Byers' defense, stamping out a threatened rebellion among his followers by sheer audacity. He then smuggles Byers out the back door and personally escorts him back to his office.

Angry and resentful, the desperados send a party to reconnoiter the *News* office. For a time they lie in hiding in a cabin about ten rods distant hoping to get a shot at Byers through the windows. George Steele finally grows impatient, returns to the Criterion, mounts his pony and walks it past the *News.* Suddenly wheeling, he comes galloping back firing volley after volley into the office as he speeds by. Byers drops his pencil and seizes the revolvers "always within easy reach of the editorial desk." Printers jump for the rifles and shotguns always stacked beside their cases. They reply with a fusillade from the upper windows. Steele is shot in the back but not unhorsed.

"At 11 A.M. George S. came down in front of the bank corner on horseback with a revolver in his hand," reads a diary of this day, as tense as any in Denver's history. "Two men on horses after him and hundreds of men on foot." One horseman is Noisy Tom Pollock, armed with a double-barreled shotgun. He pushes his horse up close to the desperado's and with the two racing along together, levels his gun against Steele's head and pulls both triggers. Steele drops into the street fatally wounded although he lingers on till nightfall with an " entire side of his head blown away and his brain freely exposed." But he deserves his fate, remarks Middaugh, as " one of the most desperate men I have ever known."

" Intense excitement," the diary continues. " Orders for all citizens to arm. Several went in pursuit of C. W. [Carrol Wood], R. [Rooker] and others. Wood taken about 1 P.M. Crowd rushed to hang him, but concluded to give him a trial which is to be held tomorrow. W. and R. are guarded by fifty men tonight to prevent a rescue by the gamblers. . . . A large meeting was held tonight to take active measures in regard to the desperados around Denver."

Out of this formidable uprising by the Bummers grows the first organized Vigilante Committee in the gold fields. At first it consists, so a member declares, " of one hundred leading citizens." But among them appears to have been included many a desperado under a fair mask, for proper secrecy is not maintained. The Vigilantes' decisions have a mysterious way of leaking out to warn intended victims. Within the committee there gradually forms a still more secret group of just ten men, arbiters of life and death in the community. " It is an interesting fact that the names of these less than a dozen men who cleaned up Denver and put it on a plane of respectability are entirely unknown," the younger Middaugh once remarked naively at a time when he was the only man alive who could have established their identity.

But he steadfastly refused to name them on the ground that " many have descendants still living and the revelation might be unpleasant to them." The early West showed considerable indifference to the killing of man by man. But it was always somewhat ashamed of its mob murders, no matter what the provocation. They violated its sense of fair play, the very foundation of communal living at a time when all constitutional authority was conspicuously ineffective.

The " Stranglers," as the Vigilantes are known not only to the Bummers but also to many good citizens who object to their arbitrary violence, proceed at once to make Denver " as quiet as any Eastern village." They first send a party to accompany Sheriff Middaugh in pursuit of Gordon. Along the way the Vigilantes seize three men suspected as horse thieves. One escapes, the second is drowned while attempting to swim the Platte under a hail of bullets, while the third is captured, tried, publicly lashed and ordered to leave the country within twenty-four hours. Gordon leads the Vigilantes a long chase, but is at last captured among the Osage Indians in Kansas. After a second and third escape he is finally returned to Denver. Tried and sentenced to be hanged, Gordon fastidiously objects to Noisy Tom Pollock as his executioner because of the latter's brutal killing of Steele.

" If I am to be hanged, I want a decent man to drop the trap. I don't want it done by a murderer." Sheriff Middaugh accepts the responsibility and in the traditional address from the gallows Gordon asks that the Sheriff be forgiven, declaring that he " is only doing his duty and is the best friend I ever had." But the Sheriff is shot down in cold blood a year later by one of Gordon's friends.

The Vigilantes now lay hands upon the mysterious Black Hawk, the second of George Jackson's curious friends, who confesses himself a horse thief and implicates John Shear of the City Council and J. C. Ford, a prominent lawyer and member of the Territorial Legislature. Black Hawk and Shear are lynched two days later. Ford clambers aboard a stage coach to escape. The Vigilantes ride after him and overtake the coach at the head of Cherry Creek. Ford is "taken from the stage, marched across the prairie to a secluded spot and his body riddled with buckshot." But at the moment all that anyone knows of his fate is that a valuable gold watch engraved with his name is recovered in Denver a few days later and "sent to Ford's widow in Iowa."

The Vigilantes soon claim six other victims, the sight of whose dangling bodies sears itself indelibly upon the brain of the boy who discovers them. "At the Elephant Corral we had built up quite a lucrative business," explains Eugene, "and had no opposition in our line, which was mostly that of renting saddle ponies for short mountain trips and of caring for those coming in from the prospecting camps. But soon there appeared on the scene one Jim Latty, who, after carefully surveying the half block just below ours, started to build a barn very much on the order of ours, and announced his purpose of competing with us. Latty was fully six feet tall, with a most beautiful red beard, fine and silky, which reached to his knees when he was sitting. Very often he would take me to the store of Cook and Sears and buy me a new pair of spurs, a lariat or even a revolver or bowie knife—anything I wanted. Then he would catch me up and swing me over his shoulders where I could gather his beard in two lots like reins and drive him down McGaa Street. Oh, how I did like that man.

"But Jim was a gambling fiend, kept a lot of rough-looking fellows about his barn, and often I heard Father, Uncle Phillip and others talking over Jim's doings and his lack of patronage and wondering how he managed to feed his hangers-on. It wasn't long before we began losing some of our herds, mostly cheap ponies whose owners had received from us receipts of high valuation. This was not a very profitable business."

One day Eugene is ordered to deliver a number of horses to his father's ranch on Plum Creek, some twenty miles to the south. He starts early, "knowing the delays likely to beset the long and lonely ride." About halfway he descends into a long hollow and has just reached high ground again when, not twenty feet away, their cold glazed eyes staring at him, he beholds "Jim Latty and five men hanging by their necks in a big cottonwood tree, Jim with his long red beard looking at least twenty feet long."

For a moment Eugene is paralyzed with terror. Then he wheels his pony and abandoning his herd, races back to Denver, giving his pony "no let-up until within shouting distance of friends, giving them the alarm, at least two of them telling me to go home and not be so noisy about it and let the news get out from others." At last he comes galloping into the Corral to report his find. No one seems much interested. Later he understands upon hearing someone grumbling in the barn, "Why did you let the boy start out before they had been discovered and buried?"

The local Vigilantes soon establish espionage relations with those in Montana. The Denver committee sends two men to Helena and receives two in return "for the purpose of identifying newcomers in each place as soon as they arrive." This policy bears fruit immediately. Two men, presumably from Helena, are pointed out to the Denver committee which without delay or investigation seizes them and drags them off to the McNassar racetrack "to string them up without ceremony, on the starting stand." Who the men were or what their offense never transpires.

Crime and violence now become complexly involved with questions of patriotism. The outbreak of the Civil War finds Denver sharply divided, with Unionists in the majority. But Confederates muster considerable strength, one third of the population reputedly, and show themselves more militant under the able leadership of Charley Harrison and one Captain McKee. One morning in April, '61, Denver awakens to find the Rebel flag flying over the warehouse of Wallingford and Murphy on Larimer Street. Knots of armed men gather to demand its removal. The warehousemen, supported by Harrison and his gang from the Criterion Saloon next door, refuse. Bloodshed is imminent when a compromise is arranged. The Rebel flag shall fly till evening never to be raised again.

With the arrival of Colonel William Gilpin, first official governor of the Territory, two volunteer military companies are hurriedly recruited, one in Denver and the other in the Clear Creek camps. The latter is immediately ordered to Denver and quartered opposite the Criterion Saloon, which is publicly regarded as the center of sedition. Several raids are made upon it by the military but to little purpose. Sheer weight of numbers drives Confederate activities underground. Captain McKee now makes an ingenious proposal to render the Unionists' superiority in firearms useless. Confederates quietly begin buying up all percussion caps in the territory.

Now thoroughly alarmed, the authorities order the military and police to disarm the whole populace. This move decides Confederate leaders to quit town in a body. Almost one hundred strong, all heavily armed and well mounted, they move leisurely up Cherry Creek. In the party go Charley Harrison, Postmaster McClure, Mayor John Moore and Captain McKee. The Captain is riding Eugene's beloved Rocky Mountain Chief. The party strikes for the Santa Fe Trail to plunder Government wagon trains there before going on to Texas. When Colonel Leavenworth marshals a force to pursue and capture the Rebels, he finds himself first obliged to send to the Missouri River for percussion caps. By Hinckley's Express, the Flyer of the day, the round trip is accomplished in the almost incredible time of six days. Leavenworth now rides rapidly south to overtake the Rebels who have been loitering along waiting for prey. They are captured and brought back to Denver to be impounded in a stockade as prisoners of war. All soon escape with the connivance of their jailer who flees South with them. With the departure of Harrison and most of his gang good patriotic citizens of Denver feel far more secure.

McKee becomes a colonel of irregulars in Texas. Mayor Moore joins Price's army in Missouri, rises to become an adjutant-general, later campaigns in Mexico with the French Contre-Guérillas and in time returns to Colorado to edit the Pueblo *Press*. Harrison and McClure likewise join Price's army. Both appear to have entertained a notion of stealing back to Denver to enlist guerrilla recruits — an idea cherished by others also. A reconnoitering party of twenty-two Confederate officers slips out of Missouri for the gold fields in '62 but is captured en route by Osage Indians in the pay of the Union. Although nothing is certainly known, there is some evidence that McClure and Charley Harrison were members of this party. If they were, they were killed and scalped with all their brother officers, and the bones of the rather pompous postmaster and the engaging gambler-desperado whom Eugene adored lie scattered somewhere along the Verdigris River, Kansas.

VII. Toward Sand Creek

" Great God! and are we all gone up . . . But no!"

ALTHOUGH drinking, gambling and shooting appear to have occupied a large part of the population of early Denver, the straggling settlement on the Plains had its more serious concerns. A Denver People's Government is formed in October, '60, in a determined effort to suppress lawlessness and improve the condition of camp. A city marshal is appointed and given eight officers. Contributions are solicited " for the purpose of erecting a jail or caboose." Houses of ill fame are declared a nuisance within certain districts of the city. Peddling and huckstering are forbidden on the grounds that they prevent the construction of substantial buildings and fill the streets with wagons, tents and other temporary places of business. A city physician is appointed as well as a special committee to consider the " expediency of establishing as soon as possible, one or more free schools in this city." One is at last established in December, '62, but no public school system worthy of the name is organized till '70. There are constant complaints that school funds have not been properly accounted for or that " my predecessor in office has left no records." In the meantime Father Machebeuf founds St. Mary's Academy. Others organize the Valley Seminary for Young Ladies and Misses, offering instruction in ancient and modern languages, embroidery and calisthenics. In '64 local Methodists incorporate Colorado Seminary, subsequently the University of Denver.

Denver soon has several banks, notably the First National and Kountze Brothers'. The Kountzes ultimately climb to Wall Street to become minor priests there in the financial hierarchy. Tabor will one day buy a half interest in the powerful First National, active management of which early passes into the hands of David Moffat, later multimillionaire and railroad builder. Moffat lays the foundation of his large fortune during these days as a purveyor of paper, envelopes, brushes, playing cards, photograph albums, paper hangings, Masonic textbooks and novels. Another multimillionaire in later years, Walter Cheesman, opens a drugstore for the sale of pure drugs, chemicals, patent medicines, paints, oils, varnishes, brushes, perfumery, soaps, fancy toilet goods, lamps and chimneys, wines, bitters, fine whiskies and brandies. Essentially dull and uninteresting men, both are patiently acquisitive and with their great wealth make their influence felt in the later community. Denver even boasts of a private mint — Clark, Gruber and Company. It strikes off a number of $10 and $20 gold pieces with a rude figure of Pike's Peak on one face and the name of the house on the other. For the most part, gold dust continues as the commonest medium of exchange, although for convenience the merchants and banks issue a large volume of " shinplasters," paper script in denominations of ten, twenty-five and fifty cents, and $1.

The town is not long without a theater. At the height of the gold rush, in fact, " Colonel " C. R. Thorne brings a troupe from Leavenworth to perform the *Maid of Croissey* at Gunnell Hall, sometimes known as Apollo Hall. Situated above a saloon on Larimer Street, it has neither ceiling nor plaster and is lighted dimly by twelve candles. Candles also serve as footlights. The theater will seat any three hundred and fifty willing to pay $1 in gold dust to sit huddled upon its wooden benches. Richardson,

Greeley's colleague, attends the opening night but can hear nothing above the din of clinking glasses, rattling billiard balls and uproarious songs rising from the saloon below.

Colonel Thorne fails and hastily flees his creditors. But "Mademoiselle" Haidee and others of his troupe remain behind to do rather well after discovering a great natural dramatic talent in "inimitable Mike" Dougherty, a miner from Gregory Gulch. Dougherty soon forms a company of his own and is joined by Jack Langrishe, the most famous trouper of his day in the West, who after long wanderings will be summoned one day twenty years later to open the new Tabor Opera House at Leadville. Perhaps Tabor first sees him here to appreciate his talent. Langrishe and Dougherty present, among other plays, *His Last Legs* and a farce *Nature and Philosophy,* in which they captivate their audience "not only with their low comedy but their *Pat Casey, Night Hands* and other popular songs." They enjoy an unprecedentedly long and prosperous season of six months before going on a tour of the Clear Creek camps, playing at the Montana Theater in Central City for six weeks.

Upon their return to Denver, Langrishe and Dougherty decide to build a playhouse of their own. Great ceremony marks the opening of their Platte Valley Theater on G Street. "The new and elegant dramatic institution was filled with a very large, intelligent and respectable audience," it is reported next morning in the *News.* "*The Mistletoe Bough* was placed upon the stage on this occasion in a creditable manner, and the managers and company were welcomed in very flattering style." Perhaps so, but the theater closes its doors three weeks later as Langrishe and Dougherty depart on a longer tour of the mining camps in the mountains. Next year they return heavy with dust to remodel their theater and rename it the Denver. Melodrama and farce do not exclusively hold the stage here. " The great Stereoptican will be exhibited for the first time at the Denver Theater this evening." A few weeks later is advertised a " Grand Vocal and Instrumental Concert by Alexander Sutherland, assisted by Thirty-one Performers, many of them lately arrived from the East." The program announced is as follows:

Anvil Chorus, (Mr. Meyers having kindly loaned six anvils, to render the chorus more effective) .... *Full Chorus*
Cornet Solo .... *Mr. Olmstead*
Overture, the Lone Star, or the Opening of the Battle of Charleston, (The Overture to commence with a Salvo of Artillery, Col. Potter and Capt. Hawley having kindly loaned the use of cannon) .... *Full Chorus*
Cornet Solo .... *Mr. Sutherland*
The St. Louis Serenaders in Quartette will make their first appearance.

Positively the last appearance of
Alexander Sutherland
before his departure for the States.

" The concert Saturday evening was well attended. We have seldom heard the Anvil Chorus performed with better effect, even by the celebrated bands of Boston and New York. Our music-loving citizens are sorry to lose so finished a musician as Mr. Sutherland."

Mike Dougherty soon dies of drink at Central City. Langrishe now establishes a dramatic circuit which each year provides Denver with a six months' theatrical season. Central City has one of three, while the remaining three months are divided variously among other mountain camps — Fairplay, Buckskin Joe and Montgomery in South Park; French Gulch and Delaware Flats on the Blue River; Georgia Gulch and California Gulch on the upper Arkansas. Finally in '71 — having meantime visited Montana to gain additional triumphs there at Helena, Virginia City and Deer Lodge — Langrishe departs for Chicago where at the Globe Theater he stages one of the first performances to be given after the great Chicago fire.

By '61 the Pike's Peak country has a population of perhaps 25,000 and at last Congress creates the Territory of Colorado on a great rectangle of land cut from western Kansas and eastern Utah. The extra-legal government of the Provisional Territory of Jefferson is dissolved. Appointed by President Lincoln as Colorado's first official governor, Colonel William Gilpin arrives in May, '61, to establish himself and staff in the Executive Chambers — a suite of three rooms above a clothing store on Larimer Street. As the Civil War has begun, the Colonel hastens to recruit the First Colorado Cavalry, which with other local units acquits itself well, first at the battles of La Glorieta Pass and Pigeon Ranch in New Mexico, then against General Price's army in Missouri. To arm and equip his " Pet Lambs," as the First Colorado is known, Gilpin issues without authorization $375,000 of sight drafts upon the Federal Treasury. The drafts are accepted in good faith by local merchants and citizens who suffer great embarrassment when the Federal Government refuses for years to recognize them, promptly removing Gilpin from office on their account.

The embarrassment caused by the repudiated drafts greatly aggravates the economic depression from which the town increasingly suffers. Most of the gulch claims in the mountains are washed out. Most of the hard-rock mines are in cap. Quartz mills are everywhere idle. The Civil War not only stops immigration but begins to carry many away. Green Russell and a party of Georgians with $20,000 of dust in their pockets attempt to reach the Confederacy by marching south along the Continental Divide, hoping to slip through New Mexico into Texas. But they are captured in New Mexico and held as prisoners of war. Russell and his friends are released in '63 and return to Denver. But as soon as peace is signed, they at once proceed home to Georgia. Uncle Dick Wootton finds these years " dull years in the mountains generally, and particularly dull in Denver." Convinced that the town will continue to shrink, Uncle Dick closes his store-saloon and departs in '63 for New Mexico to settle down and die upon a huge ranch there. Even the Larimers become discouraged and return to Leavenworth where the General hopes " to spend the remainder of his days in peace and comfort following farming and mercantile pursuits."

Now the town is struck by a series of disasters. Early one morning in April, '63, the fire alarm sounds. A great blaze is crackling in the rear of the Cherokee House on Blake Street. Driven by a strong wind, flames leap across the streets and in an instant eat their way through frame buildings, all dry as tinder. The volunteers of the Hook and Ladder Company and of the two bucket companies do what they can to hold the fire in check, pulling down smaller frame buildings in the path of the flames and dashing water upon those too large for removal. At one time the whole town seems doomed. By dawn the heart of Denver lies a mass of burning timbers. More than seventy business buildings and great piles of provisions have been destroyed. Already high, prices of food mount higher to the great distress of many. But the town is not dismayed. Slowly it builds itself up again with new buildings " of that durable character befitting a city of such importance, and not of that fragile and combustible material distinguishing pioneer buildings."

Then in '64 and again in '65 and '67 comes a plague of grass-hoppers to devour every green thing above ground. " One morn-ing in 1864 when the corn was in milk and the cabbage well-headed, we drove out to look over our farm and rejoiced in the prospect of its yield. While we sat at dinner with the tenant and his wife, the sky grew suddenly black and my husband, thinking a storm imminent, went to bring in the cushions from our buggy. With an exclamation of surprise he called us to the door. The sun was still shining but was veiled with a myriad of grass-hoppers. On our drive home the air for miles was thick with the pests. In a week's time the face of the country was changed from smiling plenty to a desolated waste."

" About the midnight hour of Thursday, the nineteenth in-stant, when almost all the town were knotted in the peace of sleep, deaf to all noise and blind to all danger, snoring in calm security, and seeing visions of remoteness radiant with the rain-bow hues of past associations, or roseate with the gilded hopes of the fanciful future — while the full-faced queen of night shed showers of silver from the starry throne o'er fields of freshness and fertility, garnishing and suffusing sleeping nature with her balmy brightness, fringing the feathery cottonwoods with lustre, enameling the house tops with coats of pearl, bridging the erst placid Platte with beams of radiance, and bathing the arid sands of Cherry Creek with dewy beauty — a frightful phenomenon sounded in the distance and a shocking calamity presently charged upon us . . . Hark! What and where is this? A torrent or a tornado? These were the questions soliloquized and spoken, one to the other. Has creation's God forsaken us, and has chaos come again? Our eyes might bewilder and our ears deceive, but our hearts, all trembling, and our sacred souls soon whispered what it was. Alas, and wonderful to behold! it was the water engine of death dragging its destroying train of maddened waves, that defied the eye to number them. . . . What does this mean? Have the wild waterspouts from all the clouds at once conspired to drain their upper cisterns, and thus drench us here in death? Have the firm foundations of the Almighty's earth given way, and the fountains of the great deep burst forth on fallen men, regardless of that rainbow covenant which spanned in splendor yon arc of sky last evening?" Professor Goldrich is describing in the *News* the great Cherry Creek flood of May, '64.

At two o'clock one morning, as the result of a series of cloudbursts, a great wall of black water twenty feet high came rushing down Cherry Creek which never before had run more than a yellow trickle. It first carried away the Larimer Street Bridge, the Methodist Church and two adjoining buildings. Here one man was "launched asleep and naked on the watery ocean of eternity, to find his final fatal refuge only in the flood-gate port of death. Precipitately and in paroxysms, the tempestuous torrent swept along, bridging bank to bank with billows high as hills piled on hills — with broken buildings, tables, bedsteads, baggage, boulders, mammoth trees, leviathan logs, and human beings buffeting with the billow crests. Next reeled the dear old office of the *Rocky Mountain News* as down it sank, with its Union flag staff, into the maelstrom of the surging waters, soon to appear and disappear between the waves as, wild with starts, in mountains high, they rose and rolled, as if endeavoring to form a dread alliance with the clouds, and thus consummate our general wreck." One of the editors and four employees sleeping in the building narrowly escaped drowning when they plunged from an upper window into the torrent to be rescued at last with the aid of ropes. The *News* lost not only its plant and buildings but even its lot in the treacherous creek bed. Heavy presses were later found two miles down the Platte. The flood next swept away a score of buildings about the Blake Street Bridge, including the City Hall with all its records and the city jail with all its prisoners.

"Great God! and are we all gone up, and is there no power to stem the tide was asked all round. But no! The inundation of the Nile, the Noachian deluge, and that of Prometheus' son, Deucalien, the Noah of the Greeks, were now in danger of being out-deluged by this phenomenon of '64." All in all, almost a score of persons were drowned as well as thousands of head of livestock. Denver estimated its property damage at a half million, a staggering loss for the desperate community.

Almost overwhelmed by the flood, Denver now lies paralyzed with fear of an Indian attack and massacre. Even before the flood there circulated vague reports of Indians suddenly descending upon ranch houses in the vicinity when the men were absent and ordering the women to "cook heap." Now less than a month after the flood Denver is terrified to learn that a wandering party of Cheyennes under Chief Roman Nose have attacked the Hungate ranch some twenty miles distant and killed, scalped and mutilated a whole family — man, wife and small children. The mutilated bodies are brought to town to be publicly exposed. A force of volunteers to serve one hundred days is recruited. Governor Evans orders all stores to close early so that men may be drilled for action. Every evening the street is filled with marching men. Two nights after the Hungate murders a rider on a foaming horse races down Cherry Creek into town.

"The Indians are coming! The Indians are coming to massacre the town!"

In his wake run terrified men, women and children, fleeing

in panic from nearby ranches and the outskirts of the town. Women and children of East Denver seek refuge in the Clark and Gruber Mint, those in West Denver upon the second floor of the brick Commissary Building. Doors are bolted; the iron shutters on both buildings are closed and barred. At the foot of the outside stairs of the Commissary Building stand two men with axes, ready to cut away the stairs at first sight of an Indian.

" In the buildings congregated women in every stage of dress and undress. Some came arrayed in their best, having planned an evening with friends; some came as they sprang from their beds; some carrying clothing in their arms; others carrying valuables, but most had with them whatever was nearest when the alarm was sounded. That night one woman in a nightgown and bare feet carried with her a bandbox with her best bonnet in it. A Titian-haired beauty sought frantically among her neighbors for a handkerchief large enough to conceal her curls, for she had been told that the Indians preferred them of that color."

But no Indians appear. After midnight scouts are sent out to reconnoiter. They fail to find a single savage. But this is thought to be just another ruse of the Indians, until it is discovered that the alarm has been caused by the shouting of Mexicans herding cattle in the dark. But most women refuse to venture forth before daylight. They return to find that in the general panic most of their houses " were left with doors and windows open and lamps burning within, but so general was the belief in a fast-approaching death, or a still worse fate, that no thieving at all was done."

The Indians of the Plains stand convicted of many atrocities, but they have a number of legitimate grievances and in their regard the whites cannot boast of clean and bloodless hands. In the beginning the Arapahoes received the Argonauts peaceably enough. Under Chiefs Little Raven, Little Horse and Eugene's friend Left Hand, the only one in the local tribe speaking English, the Arapahoes remained very friendly until the night the Bummers attacked and outraged their squaws and children encamped below Denver. Nor were the gold-hunters troubled during the first years by the Cheyennes, a brave and fine-looking tribe of Indians, all well dressed and mounted, who for the most part remained out on the Plains far from the settlements.

By treaty in '51, the Arapahoes, Cheyennes and certain tribes of the Sioux were granted all the land between the Platte and the Arkansas. In '61 the head chiefs of the Arapahoes and Cheyennes were persuaded to cede a large part of these lands to the Government and accept a meagre reservation on Sand Creek near Bent's old fort on the Arkansas. A majority in the tribes objected to this bargaining by their chiefs and soon began stealing stock and collecting arms. Many stage stations were robbed during the winter of '62. Cheyennes and Kiowas, a treacherous tribe living along the Arkansas, raided ranches and settlements on Cache la Poudre Creek in '63. Early in '64 detachments of the First Colorado Cavalry collided again and again with the Cheyennes in brisk skirmishes. Then the Hungates were murdered. Soon ranch houses are in flames from Mexico to Canada in the country along the mountains. Fifty or more whites are killed and scalped on the Plains east of Denver during the next few months.

As alarm increases, strong defenses are built about Denver. Every night picket guards are posted. Governor Evans receives authorization to organize the Third Regiment of Volunteer Colorado Cavalry. But in spite of the alarm enlisting appears to have been slow. Evans summons General Larimer from Leavenworth to stimulate recruiting. But Larimer fails to fill the regiment, soon resigns and departs for Kansas never to return. Governor Evans now issues an unfortunate proclamation

Cherry Creek Flood, '64

Lynching at Larimer Street Bridge

in which he promises recruits that they may have for themselves everything captured from the Indians. The proclamation urges all citizens, " whether organized or individually, to go in pursuit of hostiles and to kill and destroy them wherever found, and to capture and hold to their own private use all the [Indian] territory they can take." Even more unfortunately, Evans places in command of the Third Colorado Cavalry his friend John M. Chivington, presiding elder of the Methodist Church in the Territory. Once a blacksmith-preacher in Kansas during the days of the Border War, a giant standing six feet seven inches tall and weighing more than three hundred pounds, Chivington is a " crude but good-natured and well-intentioned Irishman," according to Hal Sayre who serves under him. On the battlefield he proves himself the " very incarnation of war," showing great courage and considerable tactical skill at the battles of La Glorieta Pass and Pigeon Ranch.

Governor Evans now sends scouts among the Indians assembled in the Ridge Country to warn them that the Great Father is very angry and will certainly hunt out and punish the guilty. But as the Great Father wishes to spare the innocent, friendly Arapahoes and Cheyennes are ordered to report to Major Collery, United States Agent at Fort Lyons, Bent's old fort on the Arkansas. Major Collery, so it is promised, " will give them provisions and show them to a place of safety." Through George Bent, whose wife belongs to the tribe, the Cheyennes declare their own and the Arapahoes' willingness to obey if a similar promise is given the Kiowas, Comanches, Apaches and Sioux also on the warpath.

Arapahoe and Cheyenne chiefs are now summoned to a conference at Camp Weld just south of Denver. There is much talk at this powwow but the Indians are allowed to say little, being stopped short whenever they attempt to state their grievances and complaints against the whites, who in many instances have been the aggressors. None is more antagonistic to the Indians or more openly belligerent than the Reverend John M. Chivington, Colonel of the Third Colorado. The Indians quit the conference in a sullen mood, but a large number of Arapahoes and Cheyennes decide nevertheless to come in from the Plains. More than four hundred appear at Fort Lyons and surrender. After a few days they are ordered off to Sand Creek, some forty miles distant, where they may live and hunt without coming into contact with the whites using the Santa Fe Trail. Chief Black Kettle of the Cheyennes and Chief Left Hand of the Arapahoes lead their tribes away as commanded. To their encampment on Sand Creek come several hundred other Arapahoes and Cheyennes from the Plains until at length there are in the encampment more than one hundred lodges containing perhaps eight hundred Indians, including many squaws and children. All settle down peacefully, thinking themselves secure under the protection of the Federal Government. Black Kettle, as head chief of the encampment, immediately proves his good faith by sending a messenger to warn the authorities at Fort Lyons that a large war party of Sioux has just left the headwaters of the Smoky Hill River for a raid along the Santa Fe Trail.

Governor Evans has meanwhile departed for Washington and in his absence Colonel Chivington plans a coup. With two field pieces and six hundred men Chivington sets out quietly for Fort Lyons where he obtains reinforcements and two howitzers. Under cover of night he marches rapidly with almost one thousand mounted men toward the Indian encampment on Sand Creek. The encampment lies in the dry creek bed, to either side of which rise high steep bluffs. In the center of the encampment is Black

Kettle's lodge. To one side stand the tepees of the Cheyennes. Chiefs Left Hand and Yellow Wolf have established their Arapahoes to the other.

Chivington's force arrives just before dawn. It finds the Indians' large herd of ponies on the bluffs and stealthily drives it off. The soldiers move forward in three bodies. Mounted men circle the camp to occupy the high bluff to the east. Another group occupies the lower western bluff. Up the creek bed a large force of men on foot is lead by Colonel Chivington himself, who has ordered that no prisoners are to be taken. There is no hope of escape for the unarmed Indians but through a narrow opening between the bluffs to the north.

Firing begins from the eastern bluff, followed by a fusillade from the two other sides. Taken completely by surprise, the Indians run from their tepees, unable to understand. Many gather about the lodge of Black Kettle who first runs up an American flag. When no respect is paid this, he hoists a white one of surrender. Both flags are riddled with bullets. Old John Smith of Denver, come to trade with the Indians, runs from his tent, is recognized and deliberately shot at by the soldiers who obscenely curse him as a squaw man. As he retreats, a soldier rides out to protect him and is killed. Chief White Antelope, with his hands raised high in surrender, is shot down as he advances toward Chivington. Eugene's friend Chief Left Hand, realizing the truth at last, folds his arms and stands contemptuously facing the whites until he falls dead from many bullets. Old men and women, young girls and small children, run madly here and there in attempts to find shelter behind small ridges of sand, piles of driftwood and scattered clumps of brush. From one side or the other they are maimed or killed. Meantime the howitzers have been booming. Squads of cavalry are dashing along the ridges and ravines cutting down any Indians who may have escaped from the death-trap.

"It may, perhaps, be unnecessary to state that I captured no prisoners," writes Chivington jubilantly in his first report of the massacre, claiming somewhat extravagantly to have killed from five to six hundred Indians and to have seized from four to five hundred ponies. Young Charles Bent, son of Colonel Bent by a Cheyenne mother, is in camp at the time and miraculously escapes alive to estimate the dead more conservatively at two or three hundred, the great majority being women and children. After the "battle" the soldiers tarry to scalp and mutilate the dead most horribly.

"I saw bodies worse mutilated there than I ever saw before," declared old John Smith who had lived his life among the Indians. "The women cut all to pieces; scalped; their brains knocked out; children two and three years old; all ages lying there, from sucking infants up to warriors."

Jack Smith, the old trader's grown son by a Cheyenne mother, is also in camp and survives the general slaughter only to be killed in his father's tent by one of a party of soldiers who come to search it. The shooting may have been accidental, remarks Hal Sayre who was present, "but I know there was no mourning in our ranks over it. As a matter of fact, some of the boys dragged the body out onto the prairie and hauled it about for a considerable time." The whites, it is apparent from this and many another incident, hated the squaw men and their offspring quite as much as the Indians. There happened to be in Smith's tent at the time of the shooting another old Indian trader from Denver, the mulatto Jim Beckwourth, who later testified that young Jack Smith was deliberately murdered. As the Third Colorado marches off down the Arkansas seeking other triumphs, massacred and mutilated Indians are left lying along the creek bed to be devoured by coyotes and vultures, for Colonel Chivington has sworn, according to one of his captains, to hang " any son-of-a-bitch who would bury their bodies or bones."

The Territorial Legislature formally gives thanks to Colonel Chivington for his success in " maintaining the honor of the National Flag."

Jim Beckwourth, known to the Indians as Medicine Calf, follows Chief Black Kettle and some two hundred others who escaped to find them encamped on Box Elder Creek.

" Medicine Calf," they greet him, " what have you come for ? Have you fetched the white man to finish killing our families ? "

The Sand Creek Massacre splits Colorado into two bitter factions. Governor Evans may not have approved but never publicly raises his voice in protest. He remains silent as the local Republican party vitriolically denounces as traitors and renegades any who find fault with the bloodthirsty treacherous Chivington. So deeply disgusted and revolted is a large part of the community that the greatest difficulty is encountered in recruiting additional volunteer companies — such difficulty, in fact, that it is necessary to declare martial law and order the suspension of all business before six volunteer cavalry companies can be filled. Colonel Chivington is subsequently court-martialed. Although acquitted by his brother officers, he is quickly removed from his command to die many years later in Denver as coroner and under-sheriff.

The Sand Creek slaughter drives the Indians to rise in fury and sweep the Plains. They rip up more than one hundred miles of telegraph. Every road East is blocked for months so that Denver's only line of communication with the States is by way of California and Panama. All stage stations along the Platte from Denver to Julesberg are despoiled and burned. Flour rises to $50 a barrel and again many are starving along the mountains. The *News* must print its editions on brown wrapping paper or any other odd bits found about the town. The roads are not again open until '65 and they are periodically closed after that time. In '67 the Sand Creek Reservation is taken from the Arapahoes and Cheyennes who are given lands in Oklahoma. Peace is not fully restored to the Plains till '69, after General Custer at the Wichita has defeated a large force of Cheyennes, Arapahoes and Kiowas under Chief Black Kettle.

In time the Sand Creek affair comes under the eye of a Joint Special Committee of Congress which, after a blasting denunciation of the outrage, recommends the award of a section of land each to Black Kettle and other head chiefs and a half section to every squaw who lost husband or parent at Sand Creek. Congress adopts this recommendation and also undertakes to recompense all those who lost property there by making them annual payments in " goods, provisions, or such other useful articles as may in the discretion of the Secretary of the Interior be deemed best adapted to their respective wants and conditions."

After the Indian uprising Denver enters the most critical period in its history. Mining in the mountains declines year by year. Although farming and ranching have begun in river bottoms and mountain parks and will one day assume first place in the State's economy, they have not yet made any great strides forward. Even the advance of the Union Pacific across the Plains affects Denver adversely for a time. As the railroad chooses a route through Wyoming, Denver loses the advantage it had in the stage-coach era of being on a main road of transcontinental travel. Many move north to Cheyenne to establish themselves on the railroad there.

During these years one catches a last glimpse of many familiar faces. Green Russell returns again from Georgia to settle upon a ranch near the Spanish Peaks below the Arkansas, but does not long remain. With his wife he joins the Cherokees in Indian Territory and soon dies there among her people. Mourning their son killed at Sand Creek, John Smith and his squaw drift away to the farther Frontier. Old Jim Beckwourth also disappears to die soon in the mountains. William McGaa, alias Jack Jones, dies of drink " in the caboose of Denver with none to mourn his sad end." His heart has been broken by the fact that as he grew steadily more disreputable, the name of McGaa Street was changed to Holladay in honor of the stage-coach king of the day. The gambler Ed Chase moves away for a time to Montana. The trouper Jack Langrishe departs for Chicago. Larimer and his son have retraced their steps to Kansas and never return. Although they still own property in Denver, they despair of the town's future. They have little to show for all their enterprise. But before his death some ten years later the General is assured of at least one fortune in the family, for he marries a daughter to a Mellon — a Pittsburgh Mellon. It is said, in fact, that of all the founders of the Denver Town Company only Secretary Dick Whitsitt made even a modest fortune from the enterprise. Robert Teats sells the Elephant Corral before the fire of '63 in which it is destroyed. Taking Eugene with him to Central City, he turns to mining but is not markedly successful in his efforts to solve the problems of smelting the refractory ores of Gregory Gulch. Eugene is soon sent away to the University of Notre Dame. In time he returns to Colorado to become an operator of mines, moves from camp to camp as one after another they rise and fall, later spends many years in the gold fields of Dutch Guiana and finally returns to Denver, dying there in 1929.

As the first days of wild excitement and wilder speculation subside in the Pike's Peak country, an air of premature decay creeps over Denver. A traveler passes in '68 to find it already delapidated. " The old mining excitement has ceased. The old Overland stage has stopped and its business rushes past on a railroad one hundred miles to the north. Business is dull; the town is quiet, almost as an Eastern village. I see scarcely a new house going up, plenty of places *To Let*."

" . . . everything in sight filled with the metal, the pure gold — "

Stagnant and uneventful for the most part, the long years of deflation and depression following the first boom days in the Pike's Peak country are illumined occasionally by bright flashes of gold in the mountains. Strikes are made here and there to set gold-hunters' eyes blazing again with the hope which never quite deserts them. Thousands upon thousands rush desperately from one short-lived camp to another — none more persistently and few with less immediate success than Horace Austin Warner Tabor.

When last seen in '59, Tabor was idling away the winter in Denver upon finding his Clear Creek claim jumped by a treacherous old miner. Augusta was minding her baby, washing and cooking for her boarders. During the winter many rumors circulated of rich strikes in the mountains — now here, now there, in widely separated districts. Tabor at length decides to investigate and knowing as little of one alleged gold field as another, chooses the nearest, having " to sell the cow to buy supplies."

Their battered old wagon is greased and repaired. The two scrawny oxen which have carried them so far are yoked up again, and on a cold blustery February morning Augusta is lifted from a sick bed and driven off by her husband and boarders toward the distant white hood of Pike's Peak. Their slow progress along the base of the mountains Augusta records in her diary:

. . . pitched tent, made a fire. Soon had a dish of hot coffee for supper. . . . Retired for the night at six. The boys made themselves merry singing songs.

March 1st. The sun arose bright and beautiful, not a cloud to be seen. . . . Breakfast of venison ham and sasphras tea. this I call a poor appology for coffee — We camped for noon at the mill. The wind blew very high. I had a walk after dinner. At night we camped on plum creek. The wind blew al night.

March 2. Morning is very windy. Nat [the baby] has a bad cold and is very cross, breakfast of venison ham and coffee. We stopped under a hill to break the wind of and to have dinner. . . . 4 o'clock we camped for the night beside a log cabin in which lived a woman and five raged dirty chuldren Here the prairie caught a fire, and the men worked an hour or so in trying to keep the fire from a small hay stack, but in vain. We retired early as usual, and slept sound until the sun was up on the day.

March 3rd. Windy and cold, I kept the bed al the morning. At noon we stopped at a ranch and built a fire in a cabin but the smoke was so bad we were oblidge to move it out side. The wind is still blowing hard, have kept the bed al the afternoon. . . .
4 Sunday. the wind is still blowing we came near to the mountains and passed some natural monuments, some nearly white as marble and standing thirty or forty feet. We drove into a beautiful valley and halted for noon. There a man overtook us with some cows, and kindly offered us some milk which was thankfully received as we had had no milk for coffee since we had left civilization.

Next morning they pitch camp at the foot of Pike's Peak. For a few days the men prospect the Fontaine qui Bouille and neighboring creeks. They then hire themselves out as laborers on

the toll road building up Ute Pass. When rumors fly of discoveries on the upper Arkansas, they throw up their jobs and
vanish up the Pass, advancing so slowly up the steep grade that
at night Tabor often sees the " smoke sent up by the dying fire
of the camp of the night before." Why Tabor leaves burning
fires behind him to light the forests is another matter. For two
weeks the party toils on over high ridges to find itself one evening suddenly looking down into South Park — a great flat
grassy basin, veined with many silver streams, cupped round with
blue pine-clad mountains rising to sharp glistening points of snow.
Augusta at least is impressed, declaring it " gorgeously beautiful."
That night they camp by a clear stream, have broiled trout for
dinner and later a game of whist in the firelight.

Through the Park they attempt to guide themselves by Fremont's published maps and letters. Four days later they encamp
on Salt Creek to discover its waters too brackish to be drunk by
themselves or cattle. All go thirsty and hungry to bed. All nights
are cold and this one especially — so bitterly cold that a half-wild
burro strays into camp to stand in the fire embers until his fet-
locks are burned off. Augusta adopts him and he proves a great
comfort. Next morning they move on to fresh water and stop.
They are uncertain of the way and can find no exit from the
Park. Someone recalls that a party left Denver for this region
just before their own departure. Tabor and the men shoulder
their rifles to go in search of this party or at least traces of its passing. A rifle shot is to be the signal of discovery. All day Augusta
sits alone in camp listening anxiously. The silence in the lonely
valley grows more and more oppressive. Night comes and the
men have not returned. The little burro wanders into the tent.
Augusta bows her head upon him and weeps " in loneliness of
soul."

Late at night, one by one, the men come in, guided by the fire Augusta keeps blazing, having learned nothing. Next morning they decide to throw a stick into the air and proceed in whatever direction it happens to fall. Providentially it falls pointing southwest. Two days later they descend into the Arkansas valley and after many mishaps ford the icy roaring torrent. They move up the river to Cache Creek where all stake claims. Thick pines are laboriously whip-sawed into sluices and riffle boards. From the creek a long ditch is dug to the sand bank they have chosen to work. Anxiously they clean their sluices every night. They usually find much fine gold, but so mixed with a heavy black sand that it cannot be extricated with the means at hand. Every day they work hard to separate the gold but at night never have more than a few pennyweights of dust.

"For four weeks we worked there," said Augusta later. "Our supplies were almost gone and we felt discouraged. It had been a long year since we had heard of the loved ones at home."

A rumor comes of another strike higher up the valley. The Tabors pack up and are again on the road. Great shoulders of granite force them to cross and recross the swift river. Augusta and her baby are almost lost during one crossing when the wagon slips from a rock ledge into the deepest part of the channel. The wagon bed floats off and goes whirling downstream rapidly filling with water. Augusta clutches at some willows under a steep bank and manages to hold on until she and her child are rescued. The wagon is salvaged and at length, three months after leaving Denver, the Tabors enter California Gulch, where they will suffer many bitter defeats before their ultimate triumph twenty years later.

Here in California Gulch, more than ten thousand feet high,

just a few hundred feet below timber line, Abe Lee and other Georgians from Russell Gulch have just discovered the richest placer diggings ever found in Colorado. They, too, stopped to work Cache Creek with no more success than Tabor. They then joined a passing crowd of Iowans and moved up the Arkansas almost to its source. The Iowans decide to proceed up one gulch, the Georgians up another, both struggling forward through three and four feet of snow. Now and again they dig down to try the frozen sand below. The venture seems hopeless. Abe Lee suggests a last few panfuls. One shows color. Soon they are in rich pay-dirt.

" Why, this is California! " shouts Lee, and so the gulch is named.

The Tabors arrive to find no more than fifty miners working in the snow. Tabor and the boarders stake out claims, then hurriedly throw up a cabin of green logs to shelter Augusta and her child. It has no floor, door or window. Bark and dirt make its roof. The wagon is sawed into furniture — table, shelves and three-legged stools. They have to butcher their lean oxen for food. Augusta takes in additional boarders although she has, she says, " nothing to feed them but poor beef and dried apples."

Here better luck attends Tabor than ever before. By the end of the summer his mine shows a profit of $5,000. But he is not among the richest in camp. Scores do many times as well. Indeed, the claim immediately below Tabor's yields $80,000 of dust, according to Augusta, who personally weighs all of it on her scales, the only pair in camp. For Augusta, in addition to her boarding house, now has charge of the general store and post office established by Tabor. About the store grows up a scattered settlement of log cabins, dugouts in the hillsides and many pine-bough shelters. It is first known as Boughtown. But as it grows, it is more pretentiously named Oro City. Father Machebeuf early arrives to build a log church and almost succumb to mountain fever. Colonel Chivington comes to bless a Methodist chapel. Here gather land and mine speculators, bandits, gamblers, prostitutes and others of their kind to prey upon the miners. Within a few months California Gulch swarms with more than ten thousand fortune-hunters.

Saloons, gambling houses and brothels line the gulch road for miles. The Georgians from the Clear Creek diggings enjoy the reputation of contributing most to their support. But all the miners are " roysterers and spenders, not savers." All pay " their devotions to John Barleycorn, Maude Cyprian and Pasteboard Greencloth." Few in Oro City are unacquainted with " Red Stocking," who within a year departs " with more than $100,000," announcing her intention to reform.

" Money was of no account here then," said Augusta in later years. " Ordinary workmen were paid $6.00 per day in gold. They received their pay every night and the majority spent it before morning. The miners would clean up their boxes, get their gold weighed, go to town (where Leadville now stands), spree all night and return dead broke in the morning to commence again."

Tabor no doubt indulges his passion for poker, for " no old-timer," as one remarks, " has any trouble in associating the name of Tabor with cards — they were one and inseparable." But his games here, necessarily, are yet too modest to be talked of. The bonanza kings of this early camp are Jack Ferguson and Pete Wells, two illiterate old prospectors owning the richest gold pocket in the gulch. Often they take out a " panful of almost pure gold in a day." Every evening they repair to the saloons and before morning return " without a color in their possession." What

Ferguson does not spend for drink, Wells loses at the gambling tables. Preparing to make the rounds one evening, Ferguson invites a miner friend to his cabin which contains nothing but a filthy bunk in one corner and a washstand with a dirty drape in another. But the miner never ceases talking of what else he sees. "Ferguson went to the stand and pushing the cloth aside, revealed a gold washing pan full of nuggets. I would not undertake to say how much yellow stuff there was, but there could not have been less than $10,000. He then produced a bag five or six inches deep, and taking a small spice scoop, filled up the bag. Again I am unable to name the sum, but the bag could not have held less than $800 or $900. . . . Such a bonanza did these two appear to be possessed of, that their gambler friends built a saloon and gambling house on the very brink of their claim so as to make sure of having first access to the wealth these two were taking out and squandering daily."

The camp, too, has its full share of gunplay and horseplay, often in combination. A stranger one day comes galloping through Oro City splashing mud widely. A miner draws his revolver, covers the rider and drawls, " Hold on thar, Stranger! When you go through this yar town, go slow so's folk kin take a look at you! " The stranger proceeds circumspectly up the gulch. On his return he is walking his pony meekly through town when a shot rings out and a bullet whistles by. " Stranger," drawls the now tipsy miner, " when you go through this yar town, go as if you hed business and meant to get somewhar! "

As winter approaches, California Gulch almost empties. Practically all miners decamp for the Plains to return in the spring. Tabor allows Augusta to go home to Maine, following her shortly when he finds he cannot work his frozen claim. They return in the spring with flour and other merchandise. Again the second summer the Tabors prosper. Their profit from mine and store amounts to $15,000, according to Tabor's always generous estimates. But they are nevertheless worried. Although the diggings have already yielded several millions within very few working months, production begins to drop off sharply. Recklessly exploited, the diggings are nearing exhaustion. The camp is obviously doomed.

Miners begin to desert the gulch hurriedly. Some return to the Clear Creek camps or the towns on the Plains. Others push on over the Continental Divide to prospect more distant valleys. A few remain behind to prospect Strayhorse and neighboring gulches. But they find nothing but the same weighty boulders and the same heavy red sand which they so often cursed in California Gulch for impeding their operations there. Not one suspects that these are virtually pure lead and silver in a simple and almost obvious combination. If any could have foreseen the great fortunes built upon them twenty years later, they need have searched no more. As it is, miners rush desperately here and there as rumor beckons. As the gulch slips rapidly to ruin, the last large gambling saloon is torn down by a few stranded miners who from the debris pan $2,000 of dust carelessly spilled by those who once reveled there.

The Tabors, faced with abandoned claims and cabins, again find the future clouded. Their mine has been washed out rather earlier than most. Tabor in his ignorance deliberately staked his claim on a slope above a waterfall, thinking to exploit it more quickly and economically. As he soon discovers, the harder he works, the more pay-dirt he washes over the fall onto the claim below — the very claim which yielded $80,000 the first summer, as Augusta had an additional good reason to remember. The

Robbery of Buckskin Coach

Execution of the Reynolds Gang

Tabor mine, it is evident, will produce no more dust. Nor does a store-post office in a ghost camp hold out any great hopes of fortune.

A report comes of a strike in South Park by that precious pair, Ferguson and Wells, who early left camp penniless upon exhausting their claims. By air line the new Eldorado is but a few miles distant. But by the rough treacherous trail over the high Mosquito Range it is many long hazardous miles. Although it is dangerously late in the season, the Tabors take to the road again in the wake of the gamblers and barkeepers gone in pursuit of Ferguson and Wells. These two have made their strike in a bleak rocky gorge above timber line at the source of the South Platte. Here the camp of Montgomery booms for a day. The camps of Buckskin Joe and Fairplay spring up down the valley as rich strikes are made there.

Buckskin Joe, named for the old prospector who first discovered gold nearby, is to be the Tabor's home for several years. The camp owes its existence to the Phillips Lode, certainly as curious and for its size as rich as any ever discovered. Neither a placer nor a lode mine, properly speaking, it consists of a thick iron-gold deposit at the very grass roots. It is opened up and worked like a stone quarry. It was discovered, according to legend, by a hunter who one day shot at a deer so close that he could scarcely believe his eyes when it bounded off. Certain of having wounded it at least, the hunter went to search for traces of blood. He found these and also the gash ploughed through the grass and sand by the bullet — forgetting the deer instantly in what lay revealed before him.

The hunter, one Harris by name, is soon a rich man. Gold pours from his mine in such profusion that his cabin is filled with it — "everything in sight filled with the metal, the pure gold — pots, pans, baskets, even a pair of old boots stuffed and stowed away under the bed." He takes in one Stancill as a partner and upon the munificence of these two the whole town riots. They provide the camp with three luxurious dance houses and a theater where Stancill at his own expense keeps a negro minstrel company performing almost continuously for his amusement. Soon the town has a newspaper, a bank and several quartz mills. It has every appearance of permanency "with streets regularly laid out and cabins fairly well built." As its hopes and ambitions swell, an attempt is made to change its name to Laurette — a Philistine agitation which fortunately fails.

Tabor upon arrival stakes several claims and purchases some twenty more. All prove worthless. But his general store in Augusta's capable hands keeps the family up to ordinary living standards in such a mining camp. Nothing more than this is known of their life here. In later years neither Tabor nor Augusta talks of the days in Buckskin Joe. Nor can anything be learned from the records of the day. Tabor's name, in fact, is mentioned but once by a contemporary here. When laid up with frosted feet, the Reverend John L. Dyer " sent to H. A. W. Tabor, our storekeeper — now ex-Senator — and paid him sixteen cents a pound to make hominy, . . . a great luxury."

Of all the men in this or any other early camp in Colorado none is more remarkable, none has greater courage or a finer personal integrity, than this same " Father " Dyer, renowned and beloved as the " Snow-shoe Itinerant." Suddenly appearing in Buckskin Joe at the height of the excitement in '61, a gray-haired man almost fifty years old, Dyer builds himself a pine-bough shelter within a few hours and sets out to talk quietly to all who will listen. Every night he preaches on the street corners and not unsuccessfully, he declares, in spite of two balls a week, a dancing school, a one-horse theater and many murders. Dyer knows the ways and speech of the miners, for he has spent many years in Wisconsin and Minnesota both prospecting and preaching. Then he passed as a missionary into the country of the Chippewas before coming to the Pike's Peak country.

As Buckskin Joe does not begin to use up all his abounding energy, Dyer walks several times a week to preach at the neighboring camps of Montgomery and Fairplay, some ten miles distant in opposite directions. Even this does not satisfy his zeal. During the winter he mushes his way on snowshoes over Mosquito Pass to California Gulch, thence over the Continental Divide into the Ute country along the Gunnison, back to California Gulch, down the Arkansas to Cache Creek, again to the Gunnison and back to Buckskin Joe. Within two months he travels by snowshoe more than five hundred miles, carrying a heavy pack with all that he owns, preaching whenever any will listen, frequently having to stop to find work, for collections along the way are everywhere poor, amounting to just $43.

Father Dyer is no sooner in Buckskin Joe than he sets out on foot to attend the Methodist Conference in Denver. As he does not possess $10, he cannot afford the weekly stage. The Conference assigns him Breckenridge and the neighboring camps on the Blue River at a salary of $125 a year. Even Dyer finds this a rather difficult assignment, for board alone costs him almost $10 a week in that far-off district. But he is resolved to tend his flock even though he quarrels with them because they help themselves to his small organ to furnish music for their frequent dances. Only a few realize, exclaims Dyer, " how little regard people have for sacred things and what a preacher has to contend with." Nevertheless he does not despair of Breckenridge and goes to almost incredible lengths to bring it spiritual comfort. He establishes himself again at Buckskin Joe and makes this his invariable Sunday schedule, even in the depths of winter: an early morning service at Fairplay, a walk of ten miles and another service a few hours later at Buckskin Joe, another walk of ten miles and a noon service at Montgomery, and finally an evening service at Breckenridge, more than twenty miles distant over the Continental Divide, here some fourteen thousand feet high. Often he is buffeted for hours in terrific storms during which he keeps his course only by the wind. On one occasion he returns from Breckenridge in a blizzard to find Montgomery completely buried under ten feet of snow.

Now starvation drives good Father Dyer to accept a job at $18 a week carrying mail from Buckskin Joe to Cache Creek by way of California Gulch, a journey of more than forty miles. Over snowdrifts from five to twenty feet deep, carrying a twenty-five-pound mail sack and usually one or more large express packages, Dyer trudges weekly to Cache Creek, often having to travel at night when the crust on the snow is harder. On his day of rest at Cache Creek, Dyer holds services for the miners there. With the approach of Sunday he hastens back under an even heavier load usually containing much gold dust from all the camps on the upper Arkansas. It is Father Dyer, in fact, who delivers most of the dust which is lost when the Buckskin coach is held up and robbed by the Reynolds Gang, whose sudden appearance in South Park in '64 occasions the greatest excitement of all these years.

The leaders of the bandits, John and Jim Reynolds, the latter famed as " Jim the Bold," know the mountain country well. During the boom in California Gulch they both worked as miners there until arrested for their Southern sympathies. They were later taken to Denver to be imprisoned in the compound there along with Charley Harrison, Captain McKee and others. With these they escaped into Texas. There the Reynolds joined McKee's force of irregulars. Early in '64 they approached McKee, now a colonel, with a plan to organize a gang of freebooters to overrun Colorado and even sack Denver as Quantrell's guerrillas ravaged Kansas and sacked Lawrance.

McKee gives them a pass through the lines and the Reynolds with twenty-two men ride rapidly north to the Santa Fe Trail. Here they attack and plunder a large wagon train, obtaining $40,000 in currency and $6,000 in drafts, according to a reasonably measured account of their exploits by City Marshal David Cook of Denver, later Major-General of Militia. The gang immediately quarrels over the booty. More than half desert when Captain Jim appropriates it all on the ground that it is needed to arm and equip the many recruits they hope to gain among the Southerners at the mines.

The Reynolds with eight men cache their plunder on the Spanish Peaks, ride up the Arkansas, cross into South Park and proceed on to California Gulch, traveling in small parties to avoid suspicion. As the gulch is already too decayed to interest them, they quickly return to South Park to fall upon the Buckskin coach, robbing it of $10,000 in dust, most of it delivered by Father Dyer, a much smaller sum than the coach usually carried. The robbers burn the coach and raid a stage station nearby. Here they commit a fatal error in pretending to be the vanguard of a large Confederate force raiding north from Texas. This report spreads rapidly to throw the entire territory into a panic, for no aid can be expected from the East with every line of communication blocked by Indian uprisings on the Plains. Everywhere military companies are organized and drilled daily. Scores of large posses are formed. Troops from Denver guard all coaches through the mountains. As nothing is certainly known of the number or movement of the robbers, alarm increases steadily. With every rumor the danger is magnified.

Wholly unsuspecting the general terror they have inspired, the Reynolds move slowly through the Park waylaying travelers and robbing ranchers, treating all with exceptional consideration. So considerately, in fact, that one robbed rancher warns them of the many large posses converging upon them. The bandits ride up into the heavy timber and leave the Park, dropping down upon the other fork of the Platte to the mouth of Geneva Creek. Here in a grove of trees the remainder of the gang make camp as the two Reynolds ride up the creek to bury their loot. That evening all are sitting around the fire as Captain Jim with a spoon is distributing shares of gold dust. A shot rings out and he falls wounded. A posse of miners from distant Boulder Creek have stumbled upon the camp as much to their own surprise as the bandits'. A terrific fusillade ensues. One bandit is killed. The others break for the brush, abandoning their horses. All but one escape. The miners cut off the head of the slain bandit and carry it in triumph to Fairplay, together with their single prisoner. The head is publicly displayed on a pole for several days and then preserved in a jar of alcohol. Only in recent years has it disappeared.

After a long chase all the bandits are captured but John Reynolds and one Stowe, both to be heard of again. Captain Jim and five others are taken to Denver and given a " sham trial," according to Cook, being sentenced to life imprisonment as there is no proof that they ever took life. As Denver's jail is not thought trustworthy, the prisoners are delivered into the hands of Colonel

Chivington who has just ordered his Third Colorado Cavalry south to Fort Lyons where Reynolds and his men are to be held for safe-keeping. But they never reach their destination. It so happens, rather curiously, that they fall to the immediate charge of Sergeant "Ab" Williamson, driver of the robbed Buckskin coach.

The first two days of the march the prisoners are offered every opportunity to attempt an escape. They cautiously resist temptation, knowing that upon the slightest pretext they will be executed. The third evening a certain Captain Cree is approached and thus questioned by one Sergeant Aston Shaw, according to the latter's daughter.

"How does it happen, Captain, that I have to be with the prisoners all the time?"

"Shaw, I want a man with them that will keep those fellows prisoners and not let them escape."

"Well, I'll tell you this much, Cree, I am not going to herd 'em every night."

"What will you do about it?"

"Go kill the whole bunch."

"That's just what we want done."

Next morning Sergeants Shaw and Williamson gather the prisoners, order a squad of men to follow and march several miles off the road to a deserted cabin. The prisoners are stood up in line and blindfolded. Captain Jim makes a last plea for his own life and his men's, reminding Williamson that his was spared when at their mercy. Argument is vain. The soldiers are ordered back ten paces. Williamson gives the command to fire.

"The sight of six unarmed blindfolded manacled prisoners being stood up in line to be shot down like dogs unnerved the soldiers," according to General Cook, "and at the command to fire they raised their pieces and fired over the heads of the prisoners, so that but one man was killed, Captain Reynolds, and he was at the head of the line opposite Williamson. Williamson remarked that they were mighty poor shots and ordered them to reload. Then several of the men flatly announced that they would not be parties to any such cold-blooded murder and threw down their guns, while two or three fired over their heads again at the second fire, but Williamson killed his second man." Snatching a gun from a soldier, Williamson then shot a third. At this point Shaw offered to help him finish the sickening job. " Suiting action to word, he raised his gun and fired, and the fourth man fell dead. Then he weakened, and Williamson was obliged to finish off the other two with his revolver."

Williamson removes the irons from the prisoners' bodies which are left unburied upon the prairie to be devoured by coyotes. The sergeants then lead their soldiers off to overtake the remainder of Colonel Chivington's command hastening by forced marches to Fort Lyons and the horrible slaughter at Sand Creek.

But one bandit, although seriously wounded, is not killed. He crawls into the deserted cabin and ultimately reaches Denver to recover. He goes in search of John Reynolds and Stowe, finding them at Santa Fe. Reynolds leads them to the treasure buried on the Spanish Peaks. But in robbing ranches for fresh horses all are killed but Reynolds, who soon spends the treasure and comes north again with a desperado named Brown. After many hold-ups along the way Reynolds is at last shot from his horse. Brown rescues him, however, and escapes to an abandoned ranch in a sheltered valley. As he is dying, Reynolds reveals the secret which he alone knows.

" You go up there a little ways [along Geneva Creek] and find where one of our horses mired down in a swamp. On up at the head of the gulch we turned to the right and followed the mountain around a little farther, an' just above the head of Deer Creek we found an old prospect hole at about timber line. There was $40,000 in greenbacks, wrapped in silk oil cloth, an' three cans of gold dust. We filled the mouth of the hole up with stones, an' ten steps below we stuck an old butcher knife in a tree about four feet from the ground, broke the handle off and left it pointing to the mouth of the hole." With a final effort, so the tale runs, Reynolds sketches a rude map on an envelope and expires. Brown buries Reynolds and hastens to Denver. He makes three unsuccessful hunts for the treasure. Disillusioned, he robs a stage coach and flees to perish a few years later in a drunken brawl at Fort Laramie.

" There is no question but that the treasure is still hidden in the mountains," wrote General Cook in 1897 after the map had come into his possession, " and although the topography of the country has been changed somewhat in the last thirty-three years by forest fires, floods and snowslides, someone may yet be fortunate enough to find it." If any have since tried, no one has succeeded.

But disturbing as they are, guerrilla raiders worry Buckskin Joe less than the sudden complete collapse of the boom. Never more than a one-mine camp, it sees the stream of gold from the Phillips Lode cease abruptly. The granite walls definitely bounding the deposit are struck on all sides at once. Montgomery and Fairplay have already declined. Prospecting in the vicinity fails to reveal more treasure. Prosperity departs from the high lonely mountain valley as quickly as it came.

Stancill flees from $40,000 of debts to become a spiritualist in Chicago, ultimately dying in Denver a pauper. The lucky hunter Harris drifts away penniless not to be heard of again. Almost overnight Buckskin Joe is depopulated. Soon it contains less than twenty of the four or five thousand miners who rioted there during the boom. Three years later a prospector passes to find the camp a tumbled ruin.

" There are perhaps forty or fifty houses and cabins still standing — in various degrees of delapidation — not counting the piles of logs which show where houses once stood. Gay signs tell of former billiard halls, barrooms, saloons, etc. — the more modest ones enumerate necessary articles kept for sale. The bank is in ruins, and its books are kept as a curiosity by one of those who remain."

In this bleak deserted camp the Tabors linger on. They are still living here in their small cabin-store when the prospector passes. Why they choose to linger on is a matter of speculation. Perhaps Augusta is tired of the hardships of travel. After all, where are they to go? Back to Kansas and farming? But they have sold their farm. To Maine and stonecutting? They have no money. There is prospecting and mining, of course, but where? All Colorado camps are in cap, and no new Eldorado is discovered to succeed Buckskin Joe, the last boom town in the mountains for almost fifteen years. Tabor, too, is tired and apparently discouraged at last as a miner. At least, he himself never again goes prospecting or mining.

In '68 necessity finally drives the Tabors forth from Buckskin Joe, now entirely deserted. They decide to climb back over the Mosquitos to California Gulch where Fortune once smiled at them. At Oro City, delapidated and decayed, they establish themselves in an abandoned cabin.

A slight flurry of excitement unsettles them immediately. Gold has been discovered on the Printer's Boy lode up the gulch. A small stamp mill is erected nearby. What little there is of Oro City moves up the gulch. The Tabors follow with their store and post office. This new Oro City shelters perhaps fifty miners along one short street containing " several saloons, eating houses and corrals." It never grows larger, indeed it soon declines, for neither the mine nor the mill yields much profit. In Oro City, isolated high in the mountains, the Tabors build a cabin and settle down, content apparently to live here in comparative poverty for the remainder of their lives. Tabor, now forty, is resigned to his lot. He spends his days tending his small store-post office and playing poker. Augusta takes in boarders.

IX. The Carbonate Kings of Leadville

". . . great bodies of carbonates, twenty and thirty and even forty feet deep, milling from one hundred to three hundred ounces of silver a ton, . . . enough to test the credulity of the oldest miner."

THE Tabors at Oro City watch ten long uneventful years pass slowly by. California Gulch, littered with broken sluices and falling cabins, lies almost forgotten in the mountains, apparently another name on the growing list of ghost camps. The gold yield of the gulch, which aggregated millions in '60 and '61, drops steadily until it totals less than $20,000 a year.

During these years the gulch sands are reworked by "Uncle Billy" Stevens, farmhand and iron miner from Minnesota, who in '59 joined the rush to Gregory Gulch, staking a claim and erecting a quartz mill there. Defeated by refractory ores, he drifted away to South Park, worked at Buckskin Joe during its boom days and moved on to California Gulch in the hope of finding some neglected gold pocket there. He finds none but discovers that some profit can be made rewashing abandoned claims so recklessly exploited during the first years. He does reasonably well in spite of profane complaints of weighty boulders in his way and heavy red sands forever clogging up his sluices. Stevens soon takes a partner, A. B. Wood, a trained metallurgist, who is the first apparently with any curiosity to know the exact nature of impeding sands and boulders. That they contain much lead is generally known. Blowpipes have long been used upon them to make bullets.

Wood collects specimens here and there and tests them to discover that some run as high as forty ounces of silver per ton. Wood and Stevens begin a quiet search for the source of the silver sands. They prospect slowly up the gulch and at last in '75 find a surface vein along both sides of the gulch and soon satisfy themselves that they are on the point of making a rich discovery. But they say nothing until they have staked nine claims along the vein — first locating their Rock mine, then the Stone, finally in '76 the noted Iron Silver, which in its day yields twenty millions. Old miners in the gulch with their hopes pinned solely on a gold strike, pay little or no attention to Stevens and Wood until the latter sells his interests for $40,000 to Levi Leiter of Chicago, partner of Marshall Field and posthumously father-in-law to the great nabob Lord Curzon.

California Gulch begins to stir with life again after fifteen years of slow decay. Old miners are genuinely excited and begin to examine the mountain sides with a fresh eye. Only now do they suspect they have been living blindly for years in a treasure house of silver. Three Gallaghers, poor Irish laborers at the Rock Mine, quit their jobs, climb over into Strayhorse Gulch and there start digging a prospect hole. They are down not many feet when provisions run out. When none will advance them money or a grubstake, the brothers return to the Rock mine to work. As soon as a few dollars are saved, they depart again to dig and dig. Once more their provisions are running low. One brother is again sent back to the Rock. The manager hesitates to reemploy him but finally tells him to report for work in the morning. But his brothers climb over Iron Hill late that night and stumble breathlessly into the bunkhouse to whisper the news. All creep silently out to reappear shortly as men of substance and position. The Gallaghers name their mine the Camp Bird and go on to strike the Charleston and Pine. Soon they are hoisting tons of carbonate ore rich in silver. A small furnace to smelt their ore is erected at Malta a few miles away down the valley.

Excitement increases although it still remains almost purely local. Two sawmill hands locate the Carbonate on a spur of Iron Hill, making a clear profit of $70,000 from $87,000 worth of ore mined within a few months. Old Abe Lee returns after wandering far to bring in the Dana on Long and Derry Hill. The Shamrock is found and named by old Tom Wells, king of the gulch in earlier days, whose partner Ferguson is long since dead of drink. Bill Yankee stakes and immediately sells the Yankee Doodle for $50,000. Other poor prospectors locate the Morning Star, Evening Star, Catalpa, Crescent, Adelaide and A. Y.—one of the mines providing the stake upon which the Guggenheims later build their tremendous family fortune.

Prospectors and miners begin to arrive from other camps as rich strikes multiply on Iron and Carbonate hills. An owner of a lunch counter at Fairplay, one George Fryer, abandons his business there, hastens into camp and for a six weeks' grubstake buys a prospect hole on a neglected hill from " Chicken Bill " Lovell, a rascally but competent prospector. Fryer starts earnestly to work, laughed at by practical miners and theoretical experts who pronounce the hill outside the " scientific " limits of the field. For weeks he toils alone sinking his shaft — always painfully slow and laborious work when performed single-handed, one good reason why prospectors usually travel in pairs. Fryer, with nothing more than pick and hand drills, pries loose the " drift " rock, heaps it in the heavy iron bucket, climbs to the shaft head, strains at the small hand windlass as the bucket slowly rises, dumps it, lowers it back down the shaft and descends after it, repeating this clumsy performance scores of times a day. Fryer soon exhausts his supplies and to obtain a grubstake must sign away a half interest in any discoveries made.

Finally at fifty feet Fryer strikes white-green porphyry. Excitedly he hammers his way through this to the iron " cap " usually signifying silver treasure below. He smashes this to come upon a rich body of carbonate ore, the first of the thick " blanket " veins of silver to be found on Fryer Hill, one of the famous names in mining annals. With a wry smile at the " experts " who sneered at him, Fryer names his mine the New Discovery.

Now Dennis Carter, John Taylor, Richard and Pat Dillon, four Irish roustabouts working occasionally and drinking at all times, strike the Little Chief nearby. To Pete Finnerty, a teamster, Carter immediately sells his share in the mine for $2,000, which he spends almost overnight in a drunken carouse. With his dividends Finnerty soon buys out Taylor for $30,000. Within the year, already rich from huge dividends declared each month, Finnerty and the Dillons dispose of the Little Chief for $400,000.

Excitement grows rapidly as rich strikes are made from week to week. Smelting companies rush in to erect sampling works and furnaces at the lower end of California Gulch.

Tabor almost alone among all old miners does no prospecting. He has apparently put mining behind him. Now almost fifty, having lost all faith in his luck, he aspires to no greater fortune than his store and Augusta's boarders are likely to bring him. Oro City now moves back down the gulch to be near the new mines and smelters. The Tabors follow to establish themselves in New Oro City, familiarly known as Slabtown, forming under the smoke and fumes of the smelters. It consists of several dozen slab huts, two saloons, and Tabor's "hotel," a four-room log cabin, larger and more pretentious than any he has yet known. It contains the inevitable store-post office to which is now added a small barroom and a spare chamber to accommodate transients. Here Augusta cooks, sews and washes for her boarders, tending the sick upon occasion — an "angel of mercy," said one, "smoothing the pillow of many an ill, homesick and destitute man." Tabor, too, is kind and a "much better man than in later years he has credit for being." When a trader drives in at this time with a wagonload of eggs, butter and fresh vegetables, Tabor sells them at cost to the miners with the remark that they have lived upon nothing but beans and salt pork through the winter. In leaving camp for the mountains many a prospector entrusts his money and valuables to Tabor, for he is altogether honest according to his lights.

Crude and small as it is, the sprawling new camp with its bustle and vitality seems a very metropolis to old miners in the gulch. It pleases Tabor to see business increase. Customers are now so many that he must assist Augusta in "weighing out sowbelly and flour, selling picks and shovels, assorting and delivering letters and packages." Tabor is pleased as well to observe gambling increase, poker particularly. The first gamblers to swarm into camp boast confidently of owning Tabor's store before the winter is past, but long dull years in the mountains have not been altogether in vain. Tabor more than holds his own.

In January, '78, eighteen miners assemble in a small blacksmith shop for the purpose of merging Slabtown with another small camp forming about Charles Mater's grocery store about a half mile distant up the sandy flat. They wish to have the two incorporated officially as a city. A name is chosen, Leadville, and

Fryer Hill, Leadville, '80

Mine Guards at the Iron Silver

a provisional government established with Tabor as mayor. At the first regular election a few months later Tabor is confirmed as mayor for a term of one year. The combined camp at the time contains perhaps three hundred miners.

A month later two of the strangest prospectors Tabor can ever have seen walk into his store. They come seeking a grubstake. One of this curious pair is George Hook and the other August Rische — " the worst played-out man I ever met," according to one who saw him at the time, " his entire wealth consisting of a pick and a spade and a faithful old dog." Poor German shoemakers, both have been cobbling at Fairplay for some years. Declining business there has at last persuaded them that they can do no worse as prospectors. The two have already asked several in camp for a grubstake. One has been vaguely promised them by Edwin Harrison, president of the St. Louis smelter, but it is long in forthcoming and they are tired of waiting. Tabor also puts them off, but they come back — not once but several times. At last, to be rid of them, Tabor agrees.

" All right, come and get what you want, and don't bother me now."

What Tabor is doing at the moment — whether making a sale in the store or playing poker in the bar — will never be known. In any case, his attention is so engrossed that Hook and Rische in assembling supplies help themselves to a large jug of whiskey, certainly not intended for their grubstake, and hurriedly depart. They select a nearby hill — most mines are on hills — and start climbing. Soon they are winded and less than a mile from camp sit down to rest in the shade of a pine. Tired and thirsty, they open the jug and soon feel restored and more confident. As one part of the mountain looks much like any other, they decide they might just as well start digging here in the shade.

Inspired, they make good progress this day. Having begun, they go on digging the next day and the next. Within the week, at a depth of twenty-five feet, they strike the famous ore body of the Little Pittsburgh mine. They strike it at the " only point on the whole area of the hill where rock in place comes so near the surface," according to the United States Geological Survey in an official report relating the shoemakers' story. A few yards forward or to either side, according to the report, and the prospectors would have struck nothing. A few yards back and their shaft would have had to descend several hundred feet to make contact — a task beyond both the means and patience of the shoemakers. As it is, they have come down directly upon the upper end of a steeply tilted vein running deep into the hillside.

" We've struck it! We've struck it! " cries Rische running into the Tabor store.

" Mr. Rische," remarks Augusta coolly, " when you bring me money instead of rocks, then I'll believe you."

But Augusta is here far too skeptical. Hook and Rische run a thirty-foot " drift " off to the side to find solid ore up to the last foot. All Leadville is excited. Everyone in camp visits the shaft. Every foot of ground nearby is staked. Owning a third part of the mine by reason of his grubstake, Tabor is almost beside himself. Immediately he sells his store. Within two months the Little Pittsburgh is producing $20,000 of ore a week, with hoisting capacity as its only limit. Hook sells his share in the mine to his partners for $100,000, invests his money in Government bonds and departs to visit Germany — one of the few wise men in camp. Now Rische sells his interests to bankers for $265,000, having already received $145,000 in dividends. These mount rapidly to $100,000 a month. Within the year, having already realized a half million from his $17 grubstake, Tabor sells out for a mil-

lion in cash to Denver bankers and speculators, Chaffee and
Moffat, who unite the mine with others under the name of the
Little Pittsburgh Consolidated, a stock-selling concern capitalized
at $20,000,000. Tabor acquires shares in this enterprise and quickly
gains another million as shares soar from $5 to $30 on the New
York Mining Exchange. Tabor is now a millionaire twice over,
Colorado's first great Bonanza King.

Chicken Bill inadvertently gives Tabor his next few millions.
After he had practically given away the shaft which George Fryer
proved as the New Discovery, Chicken Bill moved to the far
side of Fryer Hill to sink a new prospect hole. He has laboriously
dug far down with no favorable indications whatever. Finally
at forty feet he strikes water. All is lost, for he has no money for
costly drainage operations.

Next morning Chicken Bill approaches Tabor to interest him
in buying the prospect hole. He had just struck rich ore, he tells
Tabor, when water came pouring in. Chicken Bill explains that
he can offer only a quarter share in the mine, for he has had to
sign away the remainder to obtain grubstakes. But Tabor may
have his share cheap. If he had capital to help finance draining
the probable bonanza, he would not sell at any price. Tabor decides to investigate and sure enough, as Hook tells the story, finds
much rich ore " in the water at the bottom of the shaft and liberally sprinkled about on the surface." A few miners note its
striking resemblance to Little Pittsburgh ore but offer no comment. Tabor sits down upon the spot, writes a check for $40,000
and hands it to Chicken Bill who all but flies to town to have it
cashed before the banks close.

Next morning when Tabor sends up a force of men to drain
and work the shaft, all Leadville roars with laughter. Now deep

in his cups, Chicken Bill is openly boasting of how the mine was salted with Tabor's own ore, stolen from the Little Pittsburgh dump. In an attempt to brazen his way out of his ridiculous position Tabor keeps the men at work. Within three days they have sunk the shaft eight more feet " to encounter the richest body of ore ever found on Fryer Hill." The mine pays cash dividends of $100,000 a month for more than two years. Tabor also profits handsomely from the incorporation of the Crysolite Mining Company, capitalized at $10,000,000, selling his stock at top prices when it bounds from $5 to $45 a share.

Tabor's apologists have ever tried to discredit this account of the buying of the Crysolite, contending that Tabor knew the mine was salted and bought it because of a certainty of striking silver treasure below. Such apologists appear to have exercised themselves rather needlessly, for the incident never troubled Tabor. One day Hook asked him if he had suspected Chicken Bill's knavery. Tabor at first pretended that he had. But when Hook remained skeptical, for he had been present at the time, Tabor finally laughed and said, " Anyway, I was willing to take a chance on the Crysolite, as Lovell owed me a long overdue $600 bill for provisions, and what I paid him, in addition to cancelling his bill, wasn't much of a speculation, considering the times."

Tabor spoke truly.

An orgy of speculation and frenzied finance develops as Leadville begins definitely to boom. Tabor buys a non-productive mine for $117,000, spends $40,000 in liquidating conflicting claims, sinks tens of thousands more into it against all competent advice and finally proves it as the Matchless, famous alike for its richness and the tragic story of the second Mrs. Tabor who to this day attempts to work it. At a time when it has yet to produce a ton of ore, Tabor buys a third interest in the Vulture for $11,500. Next day he pays $18,000 for another third and offers $20,000 for the remaining third. He refuses to buy when $25,000 is asked, but a few months later pays $250,000 for it. For a half interest in the Maid of Erin, once offered him at $700, he now pays $43,000. George Fryer accepts $50,000 for his half share in the New Discovery which is immediately resold to Tabor and Rische for $162,000. At wits' end to manage the silver stream flooding in upon him, Tabor pours it in varying amounts and not altogether profitably into the Scooper, Dunkin, Union Emma, Denver City, Tam O'Shanter, Henrietta, Empire, Hibernia, May Queen, Elk, Little Willie, Climax and Wheel of Fortune.

The Wheel of Fortune is controlled by George Robinson, a bankrupt banker from Michigan, who drifts into camp to open a small store and make millions from a grubstake. " Judge " Pendery arrives with $2.19, according to tradition, and is soon among the richest men in camp. The Gallaghers sell their claims for $225,000. The Little Chief brings Pete Finnerty and the Dillons $400,000. George Trimble and A. V. Hunter, local bankers, make millions from the Winniemuck and speculations in other mines. Old Abe Lee and Tom Wells sell their strikes for fortunes. Almost any hole in the ground can be sold for thousands. So general is the speculative fever, that a " mining company composed wholly of ladies has been organized in this city," according to the Leadville *Democrat*.

To climax all comes the discovery of the Robert E. Lee to make Leadville in its day the largest producer of bullion in the world. Long an undeveloped claim on the peak of Fryer Hill, the Robert E. Lee is bought for $15,000 by one Jim Dexter who works months sinking a shaft. It is far below one hundred feet without a sign of ore. When offered $30,000 for the prospect hole, Dexter snatches at the opportunity of recompensing himself in part for all his expense and labor.

"Come up, boys! Come up!" he shouts, running to the shaft. The miners below are filling a drill hole with powder and suggest they "shoot" once more.

"No! Come up! I don't want you to work any more. I won't put another damn cent into this hole."

Dexter pays the men off and congratulates himself upon his luck. Next morning the new owners shoot the hole to lay bare a thick vein of almost pure silver. One subsidiary shaft alone produces a half million within three months. During one twenty-four hour period ninety-five tons of ore worth $118,500 are mined and hoisted at a total labor cost of $60. Two men offer their partners $200,000 to be allowed to work twenty men in the mine for thirty-six hours. Another offers $10,000 for permission to work one man one hour upon an area four feet square in one of the tunnels. Both offers are rejected with scorn.

Iron, Carbonate and Fryer hills are soon a tangled patchwork of claims overlapping and running across one another from every point of the compass. Everywhere there is confusion and conflict resulting in endless litigation, brutal murder and private war. So endless and expensive is litigation that Uncle Billy Stevens once declared that lawsuits had consumed seven of the eleven millions produced by the Iron Silver up to that time. "If I ever locate another mine," he said, echoing the feeling of the day, "I'll stand over it with a shotgun and shoot every damn man who comes on it. It is cheaper and safer to defend yourself against murder than to defend your property in the courts."

After a prospector has driven his stakes, he has sixty days within which to start a shaft or tunnel. If he fails in this, anyone can take possession of the claim — that is, it can be legally jumped. But many men jump undeveloped claims without distinction, ripping up all stakes in their way. Once in possession, they are seldom dispossessed but by force. For just this emergency a guidebook of the time advises newcomers " to come provided with a good pair of navy revolvers." Again, a miner upon striking mineral must have his claim officially surveyed and recorded. He may run his survey lines in any direction so long as the discovery shaft stands midway between the sides of the claim. This allows a miner to run his survey squarely over the shafts of neighbors who are near ore but have not yet struck it. These lose all their labor, for absolute title belongs to him who runs the first survey. The race is not only to the swift but to the rich, for many poor miners with good prospect holes have to work elsewhere for wages three or four days a week.

" Men with money and machinery," as one poor miner complains, " have squatted alongside the poor toiler, asserting he has no rights and depending on their cash and power to overreach the start the poor man has made and intends to follow up faithfully. Thus they often strike mineral ahead of him and secure a legal title to hidden treasures which ought justly to have been his reward. Is it any wonder a man should be exasperated at such legal injustice and strive, on first notice, to hold his own ground by force of arms? "

But many make no parade of legality to justify their depredations. A desperado named Williams attempts to jump the Iron Silver. On the claim above he drives a shaft straight down toward the sloping tunnel Stevens and Leiter have driven in following the vein. Deep in the mountain, he cuts the Iron Silver tunnel, erects heavy barricades, mans them with blacklegs and warns

Iron Silver workers off. Stevens and Leiter move quickly and secretly, recruit a larger army and attack in force. There is a furious battle hundreds of feet underground. Driven from the barricades, Williams' forces resist stubbornly, sniping as they retreat along the tunnels. Several are killed and many wounded, but the desperado's army is ultimately routed. Stevens and Leiter then post a guard of thirty men, each armed with two revolvers and a shotgun or Winchester repeating rifle. This guard is retained for years. The Carbonate and other mines adopt like precautions.

Poorer miners and prospectors form two strong organizations to combat claim-jumpers — the Miners' Mutual Protective Association with branches in all the gulches and the Miners' Guard composed, say its founders, of "what is known as low-capital men, or those whose means of defence against mine jumpers lies wholly in bullets." Ten armed men jump the O'Donovan Rossa claim, seize the shaft house and fortify it. Constable Shires approaches and is ordered back. He retreats, ostensibly for reinforcements, but does not return. The dispossessed owners then call upon the Miners' Guard which sends a large party to attack at night. Firing is so brisk and stray bullets so numerous along California Gulch that travelers turn back to spend the night in town. Spectators and reporters watching the battle from afar are "put to ignominious flight by the whistling of the bullets in the neighborhood." At daybreak the Miners' Guard deploys its forces as skirmishers and creeps closer. Their Indian tactics give them a great advantage over those caged in the shaft house, who attract a shower of bullets at the slightest exposure. "The indiscretion of Matt Lynch in peeping over the breastworks, caused him a bullet through the ear and a moment later a Winchester rifle caught him in the right hip. Another of the party stopped a bullet with his shin. . . ." The besieged soon pitch their arms on the dump and crawl out after them to surrender unconditionally. " No arrests have been made, but another batch of suits is likely to follow."

George Robinson hears that his mine is to be jumped. He closes the tunnel with a heavy door and posts behind it a large armed guard instructed not to open under any circumstances. As the Carbonate King hastens away, he remembers something left behind — no one knows what. He returns, bangs on the door and is instantly blown to pieces by his own men.

It is not long before great dumps of gravel and " drift " rock, smaller dumps of pay ore, come creeping down the hillsides, felling all timber in their way. The primitive hand windlass on producing shafts soon gives way to the " whip," a gallows with pulley arrangement by which a mule, driven straight out and back, hoists and lowers the heavy ore buckets. The whip gives way to the " whim," a large wooden drum pulled round by a mule or horse to wind or unwind the bucket rope. Finally the steam engine comes to be enclosed in a shaft house sturdy enough to withstand the assaults not only of fierce mountain storms but of predatory mine-jumpers. Eight hissing engines are soon working full blast over the shafts of the Little Pittsburgh.

From almost inaccessible mines hundreds of heavy ore wagons come lurching perilously down steep rough roads on their way to the smelters which are roaring in the valley, belching forth great clouds of yellow noxious fumes. Here teamsters dump their loads down a large chute into a long dark gallery where the respective lots of ore are shoveled into separate bins to remain until sampled and paid for. Opposite the bins a series of large iron cylinders stands dimly revealed by a lantern or two. Chains of men with wheelbarrows pour ore down the iron mouths of these cylinders from which sound the crunch of the ore-chewers and fierce hoarse rumblings of the white-hot furnaces below. Chewed up in the grinders, the ore reappears in time as molten slag and bullion on the floor below where there is nothing but a hot metal mass covered with soot and dust of arsenic and oxides of lead. Here a sweating worker, stripped to the waist, darts a lance at a sizzling furnace to release Hell itself as, with blinding showers of sparks and long tongues of strange blue and green flames, a stream of white molten rock falls hissing into the slagpots. These are wheeled out boiling and bubbling to be dumped on the lava mole burning its way down the slope. In a small well at the base of the furnace lead and silver come gurgling up to be ladled out into iron molds and allowed to cool into forty-pounds "pigs," with silver seldom exceeding more than one pound of the total. The pigs are shipped to New Jersey to be refined.

Not only ore by the thousands of tons but whole pine forests are consumed by the smelters, which cannot afford coal or coke at $55 a ton. Soon the valley and sidehills are stripped of trees and left a waste of stumps. In the process all brushwood and grass are burned away. Round the smelters spreads a desolate black waste dotted with white cones of charcoal ovens. Through the desolation winds the main road into camp, picking its way uncertainly among the stumps, ovens and scattered log houses of the town. Although Fryer, Carbonate and Iron hills are now brown, bleak and scarred, the hills at a greater distance are still blue with pines, set between the white sawtooth range of the Mosquitos and the long high hogback of Mt. Massive, both shining in the sun. But fortune-hunters have eyes only for black chlorides and "crumbling, ill-smelling brown carbonates" to be found far down cold dripping shafts. What matters is that Leadville is mining more than three hundred tons of silver a year — that no camp in the world is producing more bullion.

As Leadville's fame spreads, the state pays the camp honor through its greatest citizen. Leaders of the dominant Republican machine, eager to turn his wealth to public advantage, wait upon Tabor and offer him a place on the state ticket. Tabor is nominated and in November, '78, elected lieutenant-governor of Colorado. Ex-officio he presides over the State Senate for two years with no very serious lapses. As he must now live for long periods in Denver, Governor Tabor buys a large house there for $40,000. He spends $20,000 more in improving and remodeling it to suit his taste and his requirements as a public figure of great and growing prestige. When he leads Augusta to it, she hesitates to enter. She is still highly skeptical of their sudden riches, perhaps foreseeing the inevitable disaster.

"Tabor," she declares, "I will never go up those steps if you think I will ever have to go down them again."

X. Magic City

"You can't imagine the excitement going on here."

In June, '77, when Charles Mater drew up a half mile above Slabtown to unload a wagonful of groceries and build a cabin there under Carbonate Hill, his small log store stood alone upon the sandy pine flat soon occupied by Leadville. The next year came the fabulously rich strikes on Fryer Hill — the New Discovery, Little Chief, Little Pittsburgh and Crysolite. Within another year the local *Chronicle* in a series of *Midnight Notes* can grow almost lyrical over the rise of the "Magic City":

Leadville never sleeps. The theaters close at three in the morning. The dance houses and liquoring shops are never shut. The highwayman patrols the street in quest of drunken prey. The policeman treads his beat to and fro. The music at the beer halls is grinding low. A party of carousers is reeling through the streets. A mail coach has just arrived. There is a merry party opposite the public school. A sick man is groaning in the agonies of death. Carbonate Hill with her scores of brightly blazing fires is Argus-eyed. Three shots are heard down below the old court house. A woman screams. There is a fight in a State Street casino. The sky is cloudless. A man stands dreaming in front of the Windsor looking at the stars — he is away from home. A barouche holding two men and two women comes rushing up Chestnut Street. Another shot is heard down near the city jail. A big forest fire lights up the mountains at the head of Iowa Gulch.

" Give you the price of a bed, did you say? "

" Yes, I've not seen a bed for a week. Believe me, kind sir, I'm sick and in need of a friend. Help me, stranger, and as true as I live I'll repay your kindness."

The clock on the Grand Hotel points to one. Shots are heard from Carbonate Hill. The roar of revelry is on the increase. The streets are full of drunken carousers taking in the town.

Into the camp in a mounting flood pour miners, gamblers, barkeepers, teamsters, lumberjacks, smelter hands, storekeepers, blacksmiths, carpenters, engineers, lawyers, doctors, preachers, temperance lecturers, quacks of all kinds, variety actors, musicians, school teachers, " fancy " women, plain prostitutes, " pumpkin haulers " from the Middle West, speculators and bankers from the East, pickpockets, footpads and highwaymen — Americans for the most part, but with large numbers of Irish, Germans and Swedes. Many Jews rush in to open stores. There is room for all, the camp decrees — for all but Indians and Chinese. In spite of warnings three Chinese laundrymen cross from Fairplay, are kidnapped the night of their arrival, shot to pieces and thrown down an abandoned prospect hole to be found months later.

Everyone with a store, cabin or lot is on the road to fortune. Food and other necessities are expensive at best, for all supplies must be freighted in from the Plains over more than one hundred miles of steep dangerous roads. At worst, with local storekeepers ruthlessly profiteering, flour and other staples are sold at three or four times their purchase price in Denver. Two small barrels of whiskey return a profit of $2,700 to one who soon swells with aspirations to be governor.

Every foot of ground on the bleak pine flat is hungrily coveted and savagely fought for. Although encouraged in the beginning, squatters are not long tolerated as land rises in price to fantastic heights. Lots bought for $10 soon bring $4,000 and $5,000. On the main thoroughfare, Chestnut Street (there are no chestnuts within eight hundred miles), property sells readily at $250 a front foot. " Rents have reached seemingly outrageous figures. Stores on Chestnut Street and Harrison Avenue rent quickly at $300 to $500 per month," writes a local speculator almost overcome by the multiplying signs of great prosperity. " Rents here are higher than in New York City! "

Upon the basis of a placer mining patent the Starr Company lays claim to almost all the site of Leadville. As such patents ordinarily grant rights only to the minerals in the land, the company's pretensions to absolute title are dubious indeed, although later upheld by the United States Supreme Court. The company divides its claim into tiny lots which are offered at ridiculous prices to miners with cabins already built upon the ground, threatening forcible eviction if they do not quickly pay. The company's offer provokes a prompt and startling reply:

We will notify you to leaf this town in 10 days or less or come to terms if you do not we will hang you in spite of hell we have done the same thing in Montana we hung sons of bitches like you and come out all right now you can do as you pleas come to terms or you will go to hell quicker than lightning you are a dam dirty stink try to monopolize this town but we will wait on you to sure as Christ.

The Starr agent, somewhat alarmed, calls a meeting to arrange a compromise. The miners come away quieted. But the company evidently fails to keep its promises.

*You damn dirty thief told us you would do what was right
at our meeting now you say $50 a front foot you dam son of a
bitch you will and must die for the people will have rest*
                                    Vigulance Committee.

Threats to lynch are repeated at mass meetings of protest
against the "patent tyranny." But nothing avails to check the
company's "long series of outrages such as would disgrace the
wildest Zulu camp of savages," as even the conservative *Chronicle*
protests. "Today a quiet and inoffensive man, who had settled
on a lot long prior to the issuance of the pretended placer claims
and built a humble house, for himself and his family, was beset
by a band of men armed with deadly weapons, in the pay of the
placer patentees or their grantees, had his house torn down over
his head, and his household effects thrown into the streets. We
simply note the plain facts without any stilted invective."

Tabor organizes the Leadville Improvement Company to exploit a large tract bought from the Starr Company. Tabor as
mayor has no difficulty in evicting squatters or in persuading
the City Council to drive a wide street through the property —
Harrison Avenue, soon rivaling Chestnut Street in importance.
With ordinary residence lots along the Avenue soon selling at
$1,000, the Improvement Company proves not the least profitable
of Tabor's speculations.

Chestnut and lower Harrison are soon built up solidly with log
stores and business buildings — with every third or fourth door
opening into a saloon. Nothing but saloons, gambling hells,
dance houses and brothels line State Street, next above Chestnut.
Above State is Main containing the more fashionable bagnios of
Mollie May and Sallie Purple. Behind them runs Carbonate Ave-

nue, the exclusive preserve of the Carbonate Kings, a bleak dusty street with great dumps from the mines at the head of it and a sandy flat waste below. Round about lie cabins, shanties, pine-bough huts, tents and wagons scattered in such confusion that it is impossible to know whether one is walking the public highway or trespassing upon some jealously guarded lot. All trespassing, however innocent, is dangerous with citizens armed to kill instantly anyone suspected as a lot-jumper.

Desperados jump the front part of the lot occupied by the First Avenue Presbyterian Church. For a time the congregation toys with the idea of routing them in battle. Then it considers taking the matter to court, but finally decides to abandon the church and build again elsewhere. Armed ruffians twice attempt to jump and tear down the only hospital in camp, St. Vincent's, founded by seven Sisters of Mercy sent from Denver by old Father Machebeuf, now a bishop. Getting wind of plans for a third attack, Father Robinson musters one hundred men to guard it day and night under instructions "to shoot dead the first man who dares to try to jump the premises." Gangs of ruffians roaming at large then divert their violence upon obscure individuals without means of organized resistance.

Against roughs and criminals the police are almost powerless, numbering only four for many months. Now one of them commits the first murder. City Marshal O'Connor is shot to death in a drunken brawl by Officer Bloodsworth who steals a horse and escapes. In O'Connor's stead Mayor Tabor appoints Mart Duggan, a powerful man of medium height, a notorious bully and killer, boasting openly of seven notches on his gun. Duggan as marshal swaggers about town eager for challenge. Quick with both fist and gun, he terrorizes innocent and guilty alike. Boldly he hunts out the most bloodthirsty desperados to

Lieutenant-Governor H. A. W. Tabor

Mrs. Augusta Tabor, '80

force a duel. Just as boldly he assaults innocent citizens at any or no provocation. One night Rische is drunkenly celebrating his luck when he meets the Marshal and invites him to drink. After a time they quarrel and Duggan decides that the Carbonate King must spend the night in the Pine Street Tombs. When Rische objects and makes some resistance, the Marshal knocks him senseless with the butt of his revolver, drags him off and throws him unceremoniously among the felons in the single small crowded cell at the jail. When Tabor attempts to intervene as friend and mayor, Duggan turns sharply on him, "Close your trap or you'll be run in too." But for all his brutality and lawlessness Duggan retains his position for many years. For it must be said that he is indomitable and absolutely fearless, the one man in camp to intimidate roughs and cutthroats.

"Feed the Miners," cries the *Chronicle* as the rush increases from day to day. "All up and down the mountainsides for miles and miles around Leadville are thousands and thousands of diggers after happiness and homes. It is a fact that many of these industrious delvers are destitute of food this afternoon. They have used their last nickel; they know they will have to go down but ten feet more; they do not like to give up or give away their competence for a few mouthfuls of bread and — well, leave your meal boxes open tonight for but few of these fellows will beg. Neither will they steal anything beyond what is required for the immediate sustenance of life."

Hungry miners walk into restaurants, eat their fill and suggest that the police be called when asked to pay their bill. Many are so arrested, for the authorities take a very serious view of this practice — far more serious than of murder which is committed practically with impunity. A starving prospector enters a store and runs out with a can of peaches. Two clerks pursue, catch and hold him while a third " pounds him over the head with a two-pound weight, inflicting terrible injuries."

The saloons, unfortunately, provide no free lunches. The few making the experiment early abandon it when mobbed by the hungry. Some, however, offer ten-cent lunches. But as these are few, most men must patronize the fifteen-cent eating houses squeezed between the larger buildings along Harrison and Chestnut. Often no more than six feet wide, their walls covered " with muslin calsomined and decorated with cheap prints," these small restaurants contain perhaps a dozen rough pine tables which are always crowded. Miners, teamsters and blackened smelter workers predominate, but here and there appear white-collared clerks, variety actors in " flash " jewelry, drunken women of the town and occasionally a gentleman gambler down on his luck. Everything here smells and tastes of rancid grease. One has a choice of " Mutton, Lamb, Hog and Steak." Potatoes and bread are included for ten cents, but a cup of weak cold coffee costs five cents more.

It is night — a clear cold night early in the spring of '79. The valley lies deep in snow. Drifts are piled high in the gulches down which icy winds race day and night to howl through spectral pines. In this high valley, more than two miles above the sea, there has been no melting temperature since October. For days at a time the thermometer has hovered about zero, dropping occasionally to thirty or forty below. But as early as February the *Chronicle* finds prospectors swarming " thick as bees " in the gulches.

The five stage coach lines now running have brought in a large number over steep tortuous roads hewn out of the mountain sides, full of boulders and bordering on high precipices. Here a slip by one of the horses, a serious break in the harness, a mistake or even a slight hesitation on the part of the driver means disaster. " May God preserve me from such another stage-coach ride," exclaims a frightened tenderfoot. " I will never go over the road traversed in coming here, not even if I have to leave in a balloon." Hazardous as the roads are, serious accidents are surprisingly few. Other men by the thousands, too poor to afford the stages, have walked in over Mosquito Pass, " that high-way of frozen death." Many perish there during these years — how many will never be known.

In a clearing on the sand flat lies the bursting camp of Lead-ville, a ragged black splotch against the snow. Along its lower edge smelters are sizzling and belching forth red flames and yellow smoke. Above them shine two strings of lights joining at a right angle — the lighted windows of stores and saloons along Harrison and Chestnut. Within this angle the larger part of the camp is concentrated. Near its apex is a great blaze of yellow light from hundreds of kerosene flares playing in the wind before the larger sporting houses on State Street. Behind and to both sides looms the sheer black wall of the Continental Divide and the Mosquitos, sharply silhouetted against the white frosty stars.

Along Chestnut, Harrison and State move throngs of rough boisterous men, jostling their way in and out of the bright patches of light cast upon the snow from crowded stores and restaurants and noisy saloons. Many are shouldered from the narrow wooden sidewalks into the streets to stumble along in deep icy ruts cut by heavy ore and freight wagons. A sleigh on business or pleasure bent occasionally jingles by. Although many men are drunk, a surprising number are not. Most are warmly clad in heavy windbreakers or overcoats. But not a few hurry shivering from doorway to doorway, having already pawned or sold their weather coats for a meal ticket or a carouse. It is a good-natured crowd for the most part, innocent enough in its loud camaraderie, but there are those to snarl and fight.

A freighter sits in a crowded saloon with boots and socks off, warming his frosted feet at the stove. A miner staggers in and shouts an offer to set up the house. All must drink, for there is no insult like refusing. The bare-footed freighter asks the stranger to please hand him down his drink.

"No," he bellows, "not by a goddam sight! Any man too lazy to stand up and drink is a sucker and I can whip him." He flashes out his knife, falls upon the freighter, stabs him repeatedly and without interference runs out to disappear in the crowds.

Noisy hilarity steadily increases. But as the hour grows late, all have a common care eating away the heart of their abandon. Where are they to sleep out of the wind and cold? Since early evening the more prudent have been searching for a bed. The City Hotel accommodates eight and has already turned away hundreds. The Tappan, Tontine, St. Nicholas and Windsor are not only expensive but are already filled. A few succeed in finding shelter at last in one of the better lodging houses, "happy to pay $1 to share a bed with another in a small room containing eight or ten others." A few more have luck at the bunkhouses or big tents in the side streets, all dignified as hotels, each with tiers of soiled hard beds occupied continuously day and night. One man crawls out as another crawls in, paying fifty cents for a sleeping turn of eight hours.

Here among the sporting houses on State Street stands a cheaper house, a grimy unpainted frame shanty with a tin sign above the door rattling in the wind, *Lodging* — 25¢. A drunken ruffian staggers up and knocks. His clothes are torn, his hair and beard matted with dirt. One eye is closed and black. He fumbles through his pockets and unblushingly displays three skeleton keys, a gnawed plug of tobacco, a muslin tobacco pouch, a string, a pair of brass knuckles, a short length of iron pipe, a pack of cards, a needle and thread, four ten-cent gambling chips and at last a silver quarter, which he hands to the burly keeper blocking the door. The latter examines the coin, grunts and steps aside to let the man enter the single large room in the shanty. Its walls of rough pine are covered with cheap muslin heavy with cobwebs and dust. A smoking lantern hanging from the ceiling reveals the usual tiers of bunks and in the center of the bare dirty floor a single chair with a broken back.

Now a young man rather too well dressed reels up, knocks and offers a pearl-handled revolver as security, complaining drunkenly that he has just been thrown from a brothel after having his pockets picked. The keeper admits him, approaches a bunk to push the now snoring ruffian against the wall and orders the newcomer to get in there. Again there is knocking. The keeper opens and stands leering at a small frail woman before him. He quickly notes she is no longer young.

" Well, old gal, what do you want? "

" I want a bed to sleep in."

" Well, you can't have it here, see! This layout ain't for no women."

" But I have no place to go and no money — except a quarter. Do you want me to sleep in the streets? "

" Aw, get some fella' to take you to his room tonight," he growls as the door is banged to.

Every night thousands of desperate men fail to find beds and are driven back into the saloons to quarrel and fight for places there. It costs anything from ten to fifty cents to curl up about the stove on hard draughty unswept floors. The sleepers are annoyed by drunken wags amusing themselves by tying them to chairs and blackening their faces. Overhead the rattle of dice goes on till morning. From the bar comes a hum of voices mingled with the monotonous call-song of the gamblers. At last the sleepers doze off only to be startled by the angry shouts of brawlers and be sent scuttling for cover as shots fly wild and fast.

At a time when the camp contains a thousand-odd buildings, a local census reveals " 120 saloons, big and little," certainly sufficient for any traditional purpose but far too few, unfortunately, to house all the homeless thousands. Into stable lofts they creep — into " kennels dug in the side hills and roofed with earth and pine boughs," into packing boxes littering the streets, into hay piles in the alleys, into open sheds and wagons, even into foul outhouses — into anything, in fact, which promises some slight protection from the wind and cold.

The Reverend Doctor Tom Uzzell borrows $6 from an old maid and comes into camp from Fairplay in pursuit of his parishioners who have all joined the rush. With him on the Leadville stage come " Billy Owens, now manager of the Denver Dry Goods Company, a doctor, a tin-horn gambler and two women of the half-world — that bunch and a preacher, can you beat it? " exclaims the doctor rather primly. But he is pleased enough to accept when the tin-horn gambler makes room for him in a large packing case where they live together several days.

Striking with great speed and fatality in the high thin mountain air, pneumonia literally sweeps draughty saloon floors and claims other victims by the score in hay piles, sheds, wagons and kennels. John Duncan, colored, is found dying " in an outhouse on Eighth Street after lying there some time suffering from pneumonia." The authorities, according to the *Chronicle,* are resorting to midnight burials to keep the death rate from public notice, for nothing must be allowed to impair the boom.

" Died Like a Dog," remarks the *Democrat* in describing the tragic end of a middle-aged man found frozen to death in a shanty behind a popular saloon. "The cabin in which he was found is hardly deserving of the name. It is built of rude slabs through which the snow had drifted and covered the floor. In one corner where the body was found was heaped one or two ragged shirts and part of a quilt which had apparently served as a bed. A paper bag or two, containing a little coffee and sugar, and a fragment of sausage and bread were strewn about the floor, and on a rude shelf were some matches and tobacco. There was no stove or cooking utensils. When found yesterday morning he was lying diagonally across the corner with his head against the side of the cabin, his hands clenched and drawn tightly up against his chin and his bare feet projecting from the scant covering. Unknown and friendless, he died like a dog, and when the inquest is held, the verdict will be death from pneumonia and exposure."

Tabor is moved to organize the Leadville Life Insurance Company, with his son Maxcy, now a youth of twenty, as president.

It is morning several months later — a chill morning early in June, for only in July and August are frosts unlikely. Even then they are not unknown. A July snowstorm occurs this very year, in fact.

Long before the sun has mounted over the Mosquitos to warm the valley, the camp begins to stir. Special Officer Donnahune awakens early to find a window open, and upon investigation discovers that his coat with its star is missing and the window pane as well. Finding a drunken stranger asleep in his spare room, Officer Kelly is slapping the intruder to his senses. A tenderfoot in a better lodging house is loudly complaining of having lost both watch and bedfellow. In the big tents and bunkhouses men are being prodded from their beds to make room for others. Thousands are sitting up on saloon floors to stretch stiffly and perhaps discover a corpse in their midst — some poor unfortunate carried off during the night by a powerful combination of cold floors, wet scanty clothing and too much rotgut whiskey. Others by the hundreds come tumbling sleepily out of the most unlikely shelters.

Harrison and Chestnut are soon filled with men, animals and wagons. Prospectors by twos and threes pass by on their way to more distant gulches, belaboring stubborn burros packed high with provisions, blankets and tools. Laborers in leather boots, patched clothes and weather-beaten black slouch hats stride powerfully up the streets toward the mines along California and Strayhorse gulches. In the other direction hurry smelter hands and charcoal-burners in grimy " jeans " once brown or blue. Water peddlers are crying their wares at fifty cents a bucket. A wagonload of deer comes down from the mountains, for with the boom hunting has become a business. At headlong speed through the crowds horsemen gallop to and from the mines. More ceremoniously, a mine manager drives by in a bright new gig. Soon heavy ore wagons come lurching perilously down steep slopes to cross town to the smelters. Astride the nigh-wheeler rides the driver, shouting and cursing, cracking his long whip, guiding four to six yoke by a single rein to the leaders. One wagon bogs down in Harrison Avenue. The " skinner " lashes his sweating teams unmercifully. A struggling leader gets out of harness. The angry driver rushes forward, seizes the excited horse by the bridle and " with the loaded end of his whip beats out its brains. . . . He will be arrested."

From a distance comes the scream of sawmills cutting a million feet of the greenest of green lumber a week without appreciably diminishing the booming camp's demands. When lumber doubles and then triples in price, Tabor organizes the Little Pittsburgh Lumber Company and Tabor, Pierce and Company. Both yield great profits as Leadville " spreads east, west and north like a prairie fire." Every street from old Slabtown below to the new suburb of Poverty Flats above is lined with foundations and skeleton timber frames. Cabins often go up in a day and sometimes vanish as quickly. Now and again a miner returns from work in the evening to find that marauders have left not a board or nail of his new warm cabin.

Substantial brick buildings begin to appear, occupied chiefly by the banks which are " so overrun with deposits that to find places for their money bags vexes the directors sore." Hunter and Trimble of the Winniemuck, Little Pittsburgh Consolidated and other rich properties open the Miners' Exchange Bank on Chestnut Street next door to the Coliseum, a notorious wine theater and dance house. Up the street at the corner of Harrison, in the very center of town, rises Tabor's Bank of Leadville, a " handsome two-story brick with elegantly finished woodwork and beautifully frescoed and painted ceilings."

One small public school is built at last to the apparent satisfaction of all but a few carping critics who protest that it is " inferior in every way to Madame Purdy's House and a disgrace to a city of 20,000 people which boasts of its rich mines and growing trade." It is also unfortunate that the school becomes the center of constant political conflict which on several occasions almost results in bloodshed. Almost every day Dr. Stewart, president of the City Board of Education, either discharges from his post or is himself discharged by one B. F. Jay, " our notorious shilly-shally, wishy-washy, wit-starved expounder of vulgarity, this silly snipe or jay-bird, who calls himself by the name of the County Superintendent of Schools." In one of their endless quarrels over jurisdiction, prestige and spoils, Dr. Stewart, once fined $25 for a murderous assault upon a county commissioner, meets his rival with leveled pistol and a command not to advance another step toward the school building upon pain of death. In time two teachers are hired at $50–60 a month (those " who do janitor work in the rooms are paid $10 extra ") from a number of applicants eager to reach the new Eldorado — one in Illinois expressing a willingness to teach " in Leadville or anywheres else if wages is good," another in New England frankly confessing that he " can teach anything but would rather get to run a sawmill."

The camp in advertising itself also makes much of its seven churches — Presbyterian, Baptist, Methodist, Congregational, Campbellite, Episcopalian and Catholic. Tabor donates $105 toward the Episcopalians' log chapel and a handsome set of crystal chandeliers to the Reverend Tom Uzzell for his new Spruce Street Methodist Church. When the Swedenborgians erect a house of worship, the *Chronicle* is led to comment upon the great variety of religious beliefs in camp. " There are here the Materialists, the Positivists, the Buddhists, the Annihilists, the Infidels and a few believers in what is termed Christianity. All these have but one religion and one God in common: it is the Crucified Carbonate."

Leadville now prides herself upon two large hotels, the Grand and the Clarendon, both famous in the mountains in their day. The Grand, built over and around the old City Hotel on Chestnut, attracts the more sober and respectable. It is kept by Thomas F. Walsh and his wife, a rather refined lady who claps the name of St. Keven's upon well-known Sowbelly Gulch when her husband happens to make a small strike there. Although the Walshes do well enough from roomers and boarders, they do not attain bonanza rank during this boom. But Walsh will one day strike it rich here. He will follow Tabor and other bonanza kings to the United States Senate. He will become a partner of King Leopold of Belgium in developing mines in the Congo, will marry his daughter to one of the McLeans, owners and editors of the Washington *Post,* and ultimately be heralded as grandfather of " the world's richest baby." It is here at the Grand Hotel that Walsh acquires his first stake and polishes his wit and manners which, when circumstances favor, allow him to consort familiarly with senators and kings.

The Clarendon on Harrison Avenue is likewise respectable but with a difference. Less staid and sober, it shines with the well-dressed bejeweled respectability of those who can afford the envious gossip of the vulgar. The Clarendon lobby and bar, in fact, are virtually the club of the Carbonate Kings. Here they discuss their business and personal affairs, conduct their negotiations and plan their coups. As they move from bar to lobby and back again, they are trailed by business satellites, gentlemen gamblers, brokers and promoters, sharpers of all kinds and courtesans almost above reproach. The food at the Clarendon is famous, prepared as it is by Monsieur A. Lapierce from Delmonico's, New York. A three-story frame shell deserted long ago even as a cheap lodging house, the Clarendon still stands forlornly on Harrison Avenue, a crumbling monument to William H. Bush, once almost as well known as Tabor himself.

Originally a teacher of mathematics at Kalamazoo, Bush early came to seek his fortune in the West, settling at Central City in Gregory Gulch. Here he was " running the Teller House, mining some and gambling more when Leadville broke in 1878." Bush arrived in camp with but $10, so it is said, but is soon on the road to fortune. Quick and sharp, the antithesis of Tabor, he soon makes himself indispensable to the Carbonate King, becoming his chief lieutenant and then his partner in rapidly expanding operations. Bosom and almost inseparable friends for a time, one is seldom seen without the other. Extraordinarily proud of his blooded stable, Bush names his prize gelding H. A. W. Tabor, one of a pair of beautiful blacks, his mate in harness being Lily Langtry.

Next door to the Clarendon stands the new house of the Tabors. It is a rather small clapboard cottage, for Augusta remains somewhat suspicious of Fortune's caprices. She refuses to make any great change in their style of living. The five or six small rooms of the cottage are rather simply furnished for the most part, although there is a large marble clock and perhaps more gilt than appeared at Oro City. Augusta is at last free of boarders and is even persuaded to take a maid. She and Tabor, it is noted, are seen less frequently together. Tabor is extremely occupied with private and public affairs, it is true, but perhaps he is beginning to find Augusta rather too stiff and uncompromising for the life of opulent splendor he desires. In any case, as Tabor steps forward to be honored and acclaimed, he is apt to leave Augusta behind him. It becomes increasingly difficult to catch even a glimpse of her behind his large resplendent figure.

But Augusta is not long settled here in her cottage when Tabor for business reasons removes it from Harrison Avenue, wheels it up the street and dumps it down on Carbonate Avenue flush with the sidewalk. There is no lawn, no garden, not a flower or bush about it or any of the more pretentious houses along the barren dusty street. Grass and flowers are grown with difficulty at such an altitude, it is true, but that does not wholly account for their absence. The taste of the Carbonate Kings runs largely to other things — gold watches, diamonds, horses and champagne.

Tabor spends a small fortune to buy for himself a rare diamond reputed to have once adorned Queen Isabella of Spain. Before the window of Brodie's jewelry shop occupying part of the Clarendon, a crowd stands admiring a "novel and very beautiful" piece of jewelry, a gold scarf-pin. "In the top is set a man's head representing the man in the moon. This is of moonstone. Below is a diamond comet with a veritable tail and opposite the comet another diamond framed to represent the planet nearest the moon. All should see this elegant novelty as no description can do it justice." It is immediately reported sold, but to what Carbonate King is unfortunately not disclosed.

One of the Gallagher brothers travels to Denver and as he has never owned a gold watch, buys six of the largest he can find, each with a heavy gold chain. Depositing five with the hotel clerk for safe-keeping, he wanders forth "to promote the circulation of currency, good fellowship and wet goods." On his return the hotel clerk points out that the chain is dangling and the watch missing. Gallagher demands another. As he attempts drunkenly to attach it to the chain, it falls with a crash to the floor. After many unsuccessful attempts to recover it Gallagher demands another and walks out. The fallen watch disappears into the pocket of some lounger in the lobby before the clerk can recover it.

But this is the same Gallagher who upon receiving his share of $225,000 went into the streets of Leadville to buy every poor acquaintance he met a new suit of clothes "of the best quality and highest price." He then took them to the gay and fashionable

Tontine for a great banquet. There was unlimited champagne and the prettiest girls for all. At least one unlucky miner looked back upon this day as the grandest and gayest of his life.

Another of the Gallaghers is at the moment building a mansion on Carbonate Avenue, for Mrs. Gallagher is no longer pleased to live up California Gulch. The Irish up there are not fit for her to associate with, she declares. "We are goin' to move down to Leadville and have a big brick house in the latest style. And be Jasus, it'll have an elbow on it, too!"

Rische has built himself a house on the outskirts of camp almost a mile from his nearest neighbor — whether to escape the camp's thieves or temptations is not clear. Like Tabor he has bought himself a large house in Denver — the mansion of William Byers of the *News,* in fact. He begins paying court to the Tabors' German maid, but the engagement is broken off. Now he visits Chicago and falls in with one Clem Pieriolat, dealer in furs, to whom Rische confesses his desire to be married. Pieriolat takes him to St. Louis and introduces him to a girl in his store there, Minnie Junghuhn. They are married at a fashionable wedding in Chicago. The bride appears with "solitaire diamond earrings, a breast pin containing a cluster of these, a handsome gold watch and chain and massive gold bracelets, each set with a large and superb stone." For the occasion Rische is "not arrayed in exactly the conventional costume, but people of immense wealth can afford to laugh at the conventionalities." Rische and his bride journey on to New York City to spend their honeymoon there taking in the sights.

Down Chestnut Street this June morning there is a great commotion. A stranger has been stopped and asked to explain how he happens to have the horse he is riding — and the silver of the

Grand Hotel in his pockets. A rope is soon up and the suspect swings four feet in the air. He is seized " with the death throes customary on such occasions before being lowered and given a second opportunity to live by confessing where he got the silver and the horse." His answers are not satisfactory, and up he goes again. A burly miner rushes in, striking right and left, scattering the self-appointed execution squad. The dying man falls to earth with a thud, " totally unconscious, and rolls over like any fresh corpse." Revolvers are drawn and there is a great tumult. Several men move to lay hands on the rope. The burly miner steps back and defies the mob, a revolver in each hand.

" The first one to make a move toward this man will die. He's a stranger to me, but by God! he'll have fair play. No damn man, whether he's a horse thief or not, should be hung like a dog without some chance to prove he's innocent." The suspect is hauled off to jail.

John Kane, owner of the popular Catalpa Saloon, staggers home to lunch, beats his wife into insensibility and on his return invades the schoolhouse. He knocks down the clock, kicks it to pieces in sight of the frightened children whose " baby faces would have softened the heart of a Herod," and ends his exploit by firing twice at the terrified children as they flee across the yard. Kane returns unmolested to the Catalpa.

A frightened tenderfoot hastens along inquiring anxiously where he can obtain a permit to carry a gun. When no one proves willing to assume the authority, he consults a lawyer who advises him to arm himself with anything at hand — tent stakes, iron pins, preferably a shotgun — and " never to go out after nightfall without at least one carefully loaded six-shooter in each pocket, and if molested by anyone, to shoot lively."

A shot rings out. A crowd collects before the Little Church

Casino where " Slim Jim " Bruce has just shot " Brownie " Lee to death in a quarrel over spoils from a confidence game. The crowd scatters as the coaches of two rival stage lines come charging dangerously upon it, racing up Chestnut Street with passengers inside and out shrieking curses at one another and firing revolvers wildly. Now men are running to the head of Tiger Alley down which Hattie Garlock and Minnie Pillsbury sprint naked in a spirited race toward a distant bottle of whiskey. A policeman passes with the " first really insane person to be arrested in Leadville," who is charged with spending " all his time in prayer and religious exhortation." Newsboys come crying the *Chronicle* through the streets. *Sickening Accident at the Crysolite. Miner Overcome by Gas and Smoke Falls from Bucket down the Shaft. A miner who ventures to the rescue is also overcome and shares his fate — Smelter Hand Faints and Falls into Boiling Slagpot — Dance Girl Tries to Arsenic her Way from Leadville — Gospel Guide. Where our Local Divines Propose to Hang Out Tomorrow — Perils of the Street. The unknown man who was run over by the stage died at the Sisters' Hospital this morning — Price of Provisions Lower — New Strike in Strayhorse Gulch — Telephone Service Opened. It talks like a charm — Bush Plans a New Newspaper. The* Evening Times *will employ a full corps of mounted reporters all in black uniforms. The horses will all be black and fleet of foot — Wanted: Fifty Waiter Girls! Pay in Gold Promptly Every Week. Must appear in SHORT CLOTHES or no engagement — BULLETS AT THE BON TON. An Attempt to Clean Out the House. N. M. Alexander and Officer Morrissey Shot.*

At the Police Court some thirty men are booked, " with Americans still in the lead." This day a negro gambler is sold into

"En Route to Leadville — Loss of Animals on the Road"

"A Saw-dust Sleep in a Billiard Saloon"

slavery to pay court costs; the successful bidder obtains his services for three months at a price of $2. A few prisoners are fined as much as $50 for indiscriminate use of firearms. Many more pay the usual $10 for being " d.d." — drunk and disorderly. But most receive fines of $5 for being simply " d."

From a room adjoining the solemn court come sounds of great revelry. A grand jury has just finished a fortnight's labors and is frolicking round a barrel of beer. One after another jurors are bound and thrown upon the floor to have the beer " administered through pipes and funnels." Sheriff Tucker has his " nicely starched shirt bosom nicely dyed a nut-brown color." City Treasurer Zollars is " floored and bathed in beer," while County Clerk Wells in protesting as a temperance man has the " limpid liquor poured all over him from the rim of his paper collar down to the soles of his high leather boots."

The police force assembles nearby " to have the Riot Act read to them by Alderman Moore, chairman of the Committee of Police, who made the rounds at a late hour last night, and to his surprise found only two of the eight policemen on their beats." When the alderman has finished, the City Council convenes to wrestle with many serious problems inherited from the Tabor regime, which ended in April, '79.

Tabor's successor is William H. James, a Welsh watchmaker, who came West in the Pike's Peak rush of '59, settling in Nevada Gulch above the Gregory diggings. Here James erected a stamp mill which profited him, he later said, just $13.85. He moved the mill down the gulch without increasing profits, then returned to Nevadaville as a watch repairer only to be wiped out immediately by fire, finally drifting from camp to camp for years as a foreman and superintendent of mines. But here in Leadville he joins the growing ranks of bonanza kings, amassing a large fortune from a sampling works founded in partnership with Edward Eddy, a graduate of the South Kensington School of Mines, London, one of the few trained mining engineers in camp.

Although a far more able and energetic administrator than Tabor, Mayor James achieves no marked success in the almost insuperable task of establishing order. In the first place, the city treasury is empty. Although they owe thousands of dollars in taxes, owners of mines and real estate stubbornly refuse to pay until assured that neighbors are paying their share. This is impossible for the good reason that everyone is evading any and all levies. The police are disaffected, grumbling because salaries ($100 a month) are far in arrears, protesting that it is too much to expect eight officers to patrol the boisterous sprawling camp.

Money or no money, Mayor James makes a desperate effort to remedy the increasingly dangerous condition of the town. The police force is increased to thirteen, with a captain and marshal. Mart Duggan is reappointed to his post. Cabins standing in the middle of streets are removed. Harrison and Chestnut are graded and paved with slag from the smelters to remove the deep bog holes in which several drunken men have had a narrow escape from drowning. A commission " to lay the terrible dust on our streets " is given old Abe Lee, already through his second fortune. In an old wagon drawn by a feeble horse Lee loads several barrels from which he ladles water into the street with a saucepan as he moves slowly forward. Periodically he goes about collecting what he can from householders along his route. The City Fathers establish a free lodging house where penniless fortune-hunters may find food and shelter. A city physician is appointed and arrangements are made with the Sisters' hospital to care for the indigent sick.

Tabor at this time obtains a franchise for his Leadville Water Company. He obtains another for his Leadville Illuminating Gas Company after formal refutation of Alderman Kavanaugh's charge that $35,000 in bribes have been distributed by the several rival bidders. A franchise is also granted the Lake County Street and Horse Railway, a $500,000 concern with Tabor as president and George Fryer as treasurer. It is not a success, for on the steep grades the three large wooden cars prove too heavy for horses.

Against the determined opposition of property owners, hesitant steps are taken for the " removal of the garbage which threatens to depopulate the city." The camp reeks with terrible stenches from filth and dead animals lying in streets and alleys. " At present we can do without water works and gas works," exclaims one citizen as the *Chronicle* applauds, " but we cannot afford any longer to allow the offal and filth of the whole town to accumulate as it is now doing in the rear of dwelling houses and hotels. Today I saw ton after ton of decaying meats and swill collected in the rear of some hotels. Others have dug open holes some eight or ten feet deep to throw offal and filth from the houses into. Owners of property should be compelled within the shortest time possible (what although it does cost highly; they have been reaping the harvest) to have the rear of their premises cleansed and purified. The City Fathers should have this done, no matter what the cost."

Prodded to action by the mounting death rate, the Council decrees that " manure in the rear of stables and barns be not allowed to remain more than a week " and threatens to fine property owners who fail to keep their premises " reasonably clean." It also forbids the manufacture of sausages from diseased or medicated meats. But now citizens in the lower wards complain that the town's garbage is being dumped at night in their front yards. This matter is remedied only to have others complain that the " City Fathers are straining at a gnat and swallowing a camel in allowing the smelting works to remain in our midst. These works poison the atmosphere with deadly gases more deleterious than the heaps of carrion lying on the corners of every street." This the Council cannot even pretend to remedy, for the smelters and mines are Leadville.

In a desperate effort to raise money, the Council instructs the police to give no protection to those who refuse to pay their taxes. There is immediately a great outcry led by the *Chronicle*. " This is the first bill of outlawry ever passed in the United States," it shouts. It gives roughs and criminals a free hand to despoil delinquents. Existing laws are sufficient for the purpose, the *Chronicle* contends, in spite of the admitted fact that the administration after the most strenuous efforts has managed to collect less than $5,000 of the $32,000 owed the treasury. The order is rescinded and a $4 poll tax adopted, exacting as much from the poorest miner and homeless vagabond as from Tabor himself. There is another loud outcry although the *Chronicle* does not join it. " Gentlemen," writes an indignant miner in protesting that the tax equals two days' pay, " have you ever for a moment considered that many, very many, poor men have not a place to lay their heads and are necessarily compelled to sleep in chairs in order to go to work next day to obtain an honest livelihood? "

The poll tax is now abandoned in favor of a system of high licenses not only upon saloons, gambling houses, billiard halls, variety theaters, brewers and brokerage offices but also upon lumber yards, transportation companies, door-to-door peddlers, second-hand stores, restaurants and boarding houses. Brothels and dance houses are not included. Protest waxes louder than ever.

" There are many cheap boarding houses and small restaurants that cannot afford to pay such a senseless and outrageous license. It will close up at least fifty or more places where the miner, laborer, freighter and other transient people may obtain meals at reasonable prices, and throw all custom and profit into the hands and pocket-books of the proprietors of the largest hotels and restaurants. Can the keeper of a modest house or restaurant, who sells meals at twenty-five cents and liquors at a nickel, be expected to pay as large a license as a hotel or restaurant which charges fifty cents, seventy-five or one dollar per meal and fifteen and twenty-five cents for cigars? If city revenue must be raised, for heaven's sake don't raise it *all* from the pockets of the poor man. *Scale* it at least."

But the aldermen are at wits' ends and can think of no substitute devices. The licensing system continues with an abrupt command to the gambling saloons to pay or shut up shop. When none hurry forward, a few are closed by the authorities. But this administrative effort is short-lived. A few months later the *Chronicle* finds that not one fourth of the many saloons are legally licensed. The others continue to ignore the authorities.

Above almost all else, Leadville fears a general conflagration and at the moment is suffering the greatest anxiety. For three weeks a pall of smoke has hung over the valley from a terrific forest fire raging through the timber just behind the camp. White ashes are dropping like snow in the streets. At one time destruction seems almost inevitable. Shooting forth an arm, the fire cuts across upper Harrison Avenue, razing Capitol Hill, blocking all roads but that to Malta. " The only hope for the city is the wind," warns the *Chronicle*. " If it should veer to the north, Leadville will be in ashes before uptown folks have time to eat their suppers." But the wind, fortunately, holds from the west. The fire goes roaring up the gulches, destroying the shaft houses and machinery of the Iron Silver and scores of mines on Carbonate and Iron hills. Now danger threatens again as the fire crosses into Iowa Gulch and sweeps round to the south. The Mayor issues a proclamation ordering all citizens to assemble "whenever an alarm of fire is given by ringing the bell on the Methodist Church." But an immediate cry arises that the whole town dares not answer the call until a force is recruited "to protect property and citizens from the ravages of the army of cutthroats and thieves in our midst while citizens are fighting the flames." A guard is told off for the emergency.

The camp relies entirely upon three volunteer fire companies — the Harrison Hook and Ladder Company, the Tabor Hose Company and the W. H. Bush Hose Company, with young Maxcy Tabor as social president. "The color of the [Bush] officers' hats is straw, with a pink frontpiece. The others have a black frontpiece, red ground and white letters." Tabor has just presented his company with a "four-wheeled, crane-necked, nickel-plated carriage," which upon arrival is pronounced a "perfect beauty."

Even as the City Council sits deliberating, the bell on the Methodist Church begins to toll. In an instant the streets are filled with frightened people. The forest fire has not crept closer, but there is a great blaze on Chestnut Street. From the Coliseum, a large wooden theater and dance house, rises a column of smoke and flame which the wind directs against adjacent frame buildings. Firemen rush for their hats and soon have their apparatus on the street. It proves woefully inadequate. Firemen are greatly hampered by drunken volunteers who must time and again be rescued from the flames. Only one perishes. Nothing can be done but attempt to restrict the fire which several times almost leaps beyond control. A strong wind is scattering sparks and burning ashes over half the town. Suddenly the wind turns upon itself and all but blows the fire out. Three firemen have been seriously injured, but the camp is saved. Fires occur almost daily but never light a general conflagration.

Tabor organizes the Leadville Fire Insurance Company.

Two lady barbers from Chicago have established a shop on Chestnut and are prospering exceedingly. Above them Dr. Mary Barker-Bates is treating nervous disorders in an electric chair equipped with a "$300 Galvanic Faradic battery, a wonderful and very beautiful piece of mechanism." Farther along the street men are crowding into the office of a most versatile quack, Dr. Charles Broadbent — phrenologist, mesmerist, medicine man and temperance lecturer. By examining the head — "Examination $2, and with chart, $3" — he advertises that he "can tell you what kind of a lady or gentleman you should marry, and whether you are long-lived or not." He has Inhaling Balm for catarrh, Dandelion Pills for dyspepsia and biliousness and Nephriticum for kidney and bladder complaints. Nothing equals his Great English Remedy "for Loss of Memory, Lassitude, Nocturnal Emissions, Noises in the Head, Dimness of Vision and Aversion to Society." In an assault upon such quacks the *Chronicle* finds that not one doctor in five in camp is properly licensed.

Up the street is Mr. Needles in his "elegant art photograph shop" which has greatly impressed the Carbonate Kings and their families. "The photographs decorating his parlor, the music from his organ, the brilliantly lighted room, all reminds one of New York City. Miss Needles, talented sister of Mr. Needles, is assisting, and also paints in oil, crayon and water colors, natural as life." But Tabor decides to go East for his art, paying one Fishlin of Chicago $3,000 for an oil portrait, the first of a series ordered painted during these years.

An artist in tattoo a few doors away is not without custom. "Ladies come to me every day to have a monogram or some loved initials inserted into their skin. The habit prevails principally among the fashionable fancy women but also in some good circles of society which follow the fads of London and Paris." For monograms in two colors the charge is $50. For separate initials, $15 for the plain — $25 for the more elaborate. For $200 and up the "Professor" inserts plain or colored mottoes and heraldic devices "on the upper arm, where it may never be detected, or on the knee or side of the thigh, wherever the fancy dictates."

The Grand Central Theater this afternoon is offering one of its occasional matinées. "The bars will be closed and there will be no smoking or drinking in the auditorium," the management has advertised. "All will be conducted with strict propriety so that no feature of the entertainment can be objected to by the most refined society." The play is announced as *I.O.U. or Right at Last*.

For recreation and exercise the fashionable have organized an archery club and a bicycle club. Soon there are many gay roller-skating parties. Now Bill Bush forms the Leadville Trotting and Running Association, which builds just outside the city a half-mile track reputedly the best west of the Mississippi. Here in August occurs the great sporting and social event of the season. From all the surrounding country are brought the fastest horses and ponies to try their speed against the trotters and racers of the Carbonate Kings.

Riding and driving prove most popular with the reputable and disreputable alike. On Harrison Avenue almost every evening one may see the "Mayor and his lady behind their lively stepping blacks; Dr. Square and Miss James behind a pair of mettled bays; Chief of Police Kelley and lady in an open clarence; Rev. Dr. Uzzell, looking as stern and serious as a hard-shelled Baptist, reining his beautiful span of dark browns through the crowded streets with the skill of a Bonner or Henry Ward Beecher." Women of the town drive every evening as well, usually intoxicated and smoking long black cigars.

"Hell on the Road — Fighting All Along the Boulevard," reads the *Democrat* one morning. "Sunday is always an occasion for fast women, rapid men and all the sporting fraternity to air themselves on the beautiful drive. Toward evening these cheerful souls got hilarious. Presently some big double-decked rooster opened the ball by jumping at a small courtesan and smashing her nose. The matinee then began. One female armed herself with a beer bottle and created on the head of a well-known gentleman several bumps not down on his phrenological chart. He retaliated by taking a board and damaging her some. Scarcely was this over when another woman drew a revolver and began scattering galena around in a particularly reckless fashion, and was only induced to stop when her solid man seized her by her false hair and mopped up the boulevard with her. Her yells had barely died away when another circus performance opened. We regret to announce that nobody was killed."

As night falls, men of means begin to take refuge in the hotels where swarm avid speculators and promoters of all kinds. Here many a worthless or salted mine is bought under the influence of champagne. Valuable lots occasionally change hands three or four times during an evening. In a corner of the Clarendon bar "Sheeny Frank" is selling a gold brick to a Denver pawnbroker.

Two other gold bricks, reported to have come from a stage coach robbery in the Black Hills, are bought by young Smith of the banking house of L. C. Smith and Son — bricks which ultimately break the institution to the great distress of many poor depositors.

Here at the Clarendon, Tabor and Bush spend many pleasant evenings together, discussing their business and personal affairs. Tabor has his scores of mines, his real estate, his water company, his gas company, his insurance companies, two lumbering companies and a horse-car company. He has his Leadville Bank. He has meanwhile organized the Pueblo, Canon City and Leadville Railway with George Fryer as treasurer. He has established the Leadville Stock and Mining Exchange with himself as president and Fryer, Bush and Rische as directors. He has founded Tabor City above Leadville on the Ten Mile Road. He has formed the Tabor Milling Company and the Smelters' Supply Company to buy and sell ore, bullion, coke, charcoal and machinery. As all these have done much to satisfy Leadville's more primitive needs, Tabor and Bush now decide that what the camp most wants is an opera house.

XI. Bel Esprits and Bunkosteerers

" Song, Dance and Mirth and Emotional Novelties . . ."

While the Tabor Opera House is building, Leadville does not want either social or intellectual life. It has its fashionable balls and dance houses, its saloons and temperance revivals, its literary societies and beer halls, its theaters and brothels. It has its clubs by the scores — dancing, dining, gambling, musical, literary, religious and political.

" There is much good society in Leadville. Neighbors have hardly had time to get acquainted, but social life is rapidly assuming shape and rendering residence here more agreeable to ladies." Women are so few, in fact, that even women of the town are treated with marked respect. " Long lines of men waiting at the postoffice for letters will fall back from the window as quickly and politely to let a prostitute in ahead of them as a married lady."

Early in '79, at the first fashionable ball in camp, all the youth, beauty and wealth of Leadville assemble " under the coal-oil " at the Grand Hotel. With the arrival of Madame Gallat, French dressmaker, the wives of the richer have cast aside home-made and store clothes, and now appear more fashionably gowned, in black and brown cashmere for the most part. There is also noted an " occasional swallow-tail among the sterner sex, but as a rule a broad-gauge, steel-track, solid-bed mining town can raise but a limited number of such garments, and these of different styles and patterns." Both grace and elegance improve with the coming of Professor G. H. Godat who essays "to teach all the fashionable glide steps of eastern dances, etc., and to introduce to the good people of Leadville all the latest styles of dancing glide quadrilles, contra dances, etc." The Saturday evening "hops" at his academy are always well attended, as are Professor Simon's periodic Soirées Dansantes.

Any number of private dancing clubs flourish, of which the smartest is the Assembly Club, apostrophized in a dull novel written here at the time by Mary Hallock Foote, wife of a local mine manager. More than forty couples attend one of its earliest balls at the Clarendon — with all the gentlemen but one in full evening dress and all the ladies "so gorgeously attired" that the reporter's pen fails him. With increasing prosperity a number of masquerade balls are given by such groups as the German Turnverein, Standard Club, Jefferson Avenue Social Club, Ancient Order of Hibernians, Hebrew Ladies Benevolent Association, Scandinavian Society and Carpe Diem Club. But the climax of the first social season occurs during the Christmas holidays with the Firemen's Ball, described enthusiastically as the largest, most fashionable and elegant affair in the history of the West. It is held on the upper floor of the Central Fire House, "elegantly decorated throughout with the national colors and the hose of the brave fire laddies." Promptly at nine, Chief Engineer Bill Bush steps out to lead the Grand March. Dancing continues almost till dawn. It is a gay and brilliant occasion with the "showing of jewels almost fabulous."

Leadville contains clubs enough to have embraced every lonesome person in camp. Here are Red Men, Woodmen, Masons, Sons of Michigan, Odd Fellows, Knights of Labor, Knights of Robert Emmett and Knights of Pythias "with an elegant lodge

room on Chestnut Street over Herman Brothers' Clothing Store."
There is a New England Society, a Texas Club, a Pacific Coast
Association, the B'nai B'rith and Deutches Casino. Pleasant af-
ternoons of whist and gossip are regularly enjoyed by the Racket
Club ("for ladies only") and the Lady Forget-me-nots. At the
Alhambra Alley Saloon negroes institute a social and political group rather mystifyingly named the Monroe Supporters.
Almost all citizens belong to either the Republican or Democratic
Club. But in protest against machine politics the miners in Big
Evans Gulch form the Elephant Club, which decrees that "any
member caught voting at any city, county, or state election shall
forfeit a keg of beer and be summarily expelled." Among the
more purely social clubs for gentlemen are the Clarendon Club,
the Leadville Club ("to which none of the ignorant bonanza
kings belonged") and the Elk Club, a dining club composed of
younger and more cultivated professional men — engineers, as-
sayers, lawyers and doctors. Now two promoters arrive from the
East to interest Tabor and other Carbonate Kings in a fantastic
scheme to build a Union Club to cost not less than $50,000,000.
"They have been going around among our monied men with
plans and specifications and are meeting with great encouragement. Certainly nothing is more needed in Leadville than a club
house for gentlemen that is thoroughly cosmopolitan in character." Fortunately for all but the promoters, the club remains only
an ideal.

The camp, too, has its more intellectual groups — the Leadville Literary Society and the Bel Esprit Society. The former appears to have been much given to soprano solos although it
boasts of "some of the best literary minds in the country, including one who wrote the most part of Dr. Horace Greeley's
History of the American Conflict." But upon occasion it enjoys

orations, debates, recitations and lectures upon Cleopatra's Needle, the Seven Wonders of the World and the lives of Alexander Hamilton and Robert Raikes. Tabor is one of the " Bel Esprits " who upon one occasion enjoyed this program: " Gray's *Elegy,* a song *Farewell,* a humorous parody *To Dig or Not to Dig,* another parody on *The Boy Stood On the Burning Deck,* a fine vocal solo entitled *Watching,* and a rendition of *The Death of Poor Jo."* Even the bonanza kings at the Carbonate Club occasionally sit through a lecture but more often are pleased to hear Mr. Sullivan sing *Minnehaha* or laugh themselves sick as he and another variety actor parody *Romeo and Juliet.*

A free reading and lounging room is established by the Y. M. C. A., but is little used. Nor can it be said to have received much support from those most vociferously concerned about the camp's moral tone. The superintendent of the Evening Star Mine, one W. S. Ward, contributes to the Central Fire Club yearly subscriptions to *Harper's Monthly* and *Weekly, Lippincott's, Scribner's, Puck, Scientific American* and the *Atlantic,* and to the *New York Daily Herald, New York Weekly World, New York Weekly Times* and the *Chicago Weekly Times.* As he continues these subscriptions from year to year, the volunteer firemen must have made some little use of them. Certainly one of the most interesting documents of the time is the published interview in which a local bookseller declares that a surprisingly large number of miners are among his best customers. " There is no demand for the English classics," he confesses. " The demand for Dickens has fallen off greatly. Miss Braddon sells much better than Dickens. Charlotte Brontë and her sister are out of fashion, too. Another quasi-classic, Ouida, is falling off, considering the fact that some two years ago Ouida was all the rage." Translations from the French sell more than all else — Alphonse Daudet,

Alexandre Dumas and Emile Gaboriau with his great detective, Monsieur Lecoq. "A select and rather superior little circle read Jules Verne." Only less popular than the French are Wilkie Collins, Charles Reade and a certain Farjeon. The bookseller lists as unsaleable Thackeray and Disraeli. Leadville for a time has a publishing house, perhaps the first and certainly the last in Colorado to be devoted exclusively to books. "It is my amusement," explains its founder. "Some men like wine; others take comfort in horses. Others like to play with silver. I am printing books because it is fun." If any volumes were published, no record has been found of them.

Social and spiritual communion is promoted by many church societies. The Ladies Relief Society holds a Martha Washington tea party and the Rector's Aid Society a pancake party to raise funds for the new free hospital to be built upon four lots donated by Uncle Billy Stevens. Now the St. George's Ladies Aid Society holds a memorable bazaar with "fancy" tables, an apron table, a Rector's table, a floral bower, a witch's tent, an ice cream parlor and a gallery of "the richest and rarest works of art." The single event of its kind during these years, the exhibition includes *A True View of Seventy-Six, Horse Fair, Paradise on Earth, Flower of the Family,* and *Five Points of New York.*

Lastly, there are the temperance and similar societies. Many spirited revival meetings are held by the Blue Ribbon Society and the Leadville Temperance Club. A few more earnest women organize a "Praying Orchestra" to parade from dive to dive and, if not forcibly ejected, "offer prayer and song for the salvation of surrounding sinners." The Y. M. C. A. resolves rather ambiguously that "fifteen minutes of each meeting be devoted especially to intemperance." An Anti-Treat Society is founded by the Reverend Mackay of the Episcopal Church. Its members are given pledge cards to carry in their pockets "to protect themselves against the assaults of those with whom they refuse to drink." A Pastors' Union is formed to confer once a week upon the camp's morals and in a laudable desire for knowledge decides to beard the tigers and the harpies in their dens. Often in the saloons it is "nip and tuck between a temperance orator in one room and a gambler in the next to determine which can yell the loudest and attract the biggest crowd," as is remarked by the local press which without exception shows itself most unsympathetic toward the crusading societies.

"Saturday night a party of four distinguished and extremely pious divines made the complete rounds of the camp. They visited the dance dangers, gambling shops, bunko-coolers and May-Minnie unmentionables. It took these pious parsons almost all night to satisfy themselves, and when they walked solemnly into church the next morning, a good many ministerial admirers thought perhaps they had been peeling onions, their eyes were so red and watery. But now they know all about the night side of Leadville. If even a small portion of the stories afloat about town are true, these mournful-faced parsons rather enjoyed some of the wiles of the Wicked Hater of Men.

"'Look here, young woman,' observed a local preacher who was making a night of it recently, 'you possess singular refinement of manners, considering your rude and shameful associations; you have every charm and grace of person which the Lord can endow anybody with — your face tells me that you come from a home of luxury and comfort; perhaps you were educated in some seminary where loving hearts and hands had placed you for your future welfare — why, then, are you here? Think of the

Chestnut Street (east), '78

Chestnut Street (west), '79

opportunities you have wasted, the home you have desolated, the Christian life you might have lead — think of it!'

" 'Look here, old fellow, don't get sentimental, please. You gray-haired old men are the worst, but you can't play me for a sucker. I know what you're after.' "

Too many, unfortunately, prove equally suspicious of and impervious to such moral influence. But if few converts are made, the abstemious enjoy some success in enrolling one another in their several societies, especially when under the emotional intoxication inspired by professional temperance revivalists. "Colonel" Henry Howland comes from Chicago to horrify the more sensitive with a speech which has fortunately been preserved. He first "reviewed the ravages of drunkenness all over the land, in all conditions of society, among all Americans without distinction of age, sex or condition, in Congress and the White House, in all professions — the bench, the bar and the people, and presented a sickening examination of drunkenness in Leadville, ending daily in many deaths from pneumonia, diphtheria and erysipelas, and was heartily applauded by all." The Colonel then concluded, shouting, "Many of you know what drink did to me. I know now that a sainted mother and loving wife never ceased praying for me. And I want to ask — am I the only one here present, who has loving friends thinking of and praying for him in the old eastern home? Are there not firesides in New England and New York, Michigan and Illinois, at which mother, wife and sister are at this moment praying, God protect our loved one from intemperance and vice! When you write, if you will but enclose in the letter one of our pledges, with your name plainly written upon it, it will be to the heart of the dear one far away like a sunburst on a midnight sky, and methinks that quick will come back the answer, in sentiment, if not in these exact words, 'The birds never sang so sweetly as they do this morning, and the flowers never bloomed so lovely.'"

The Colonel is followed by a certain Campbell, "a heavy thick-set man of terrible power, who can convert a drunkard or knock down an ox with equal ease," according to the *Democrat*. "One doesn't hear what he says, but feels it. His words go flying through the hall like red-hot balls of fire. Everybody is excited." So excited, in fact, that six hundred take the pledge. But backsliders are numerous, and the press continues hostile.

"All temperance lecturers take special delight in telling the rising generation how gloriously drunk they used to get," complains the *Chronicle*. "They fill an hour's lecture with anecdotes of how they used to cuff their poor wives about, break the hearts of girls who loved them, dishonor the sacred name of mother and send her sorrowing to her grave. Very often these lecturers will tell how they used to lie, steal, pawn their wife's wedding dress, kick over the kitchen stove, drag their little daughter around by the hair and cut other capers for which, had the law done its duty, they would be serving out a life sentence in some state prison in place of bragging about their crimes before really temperate young men and women."

In camp one day appears a Dr. Gibbons with his wife, both temperance revivalists. But as they have not been officially invited, the temperance societies suspect them of poaching and receive them very coolly indeed. On their last evening in town the doctor and his wife enter a saloon and there obtain permission to speak. "I could speak better after hearing somebody sing," Gibbons begins, "but none of the good temperance people of Leadville are here to sing. I'm all alone with you, boys (cheers). There is no use mincing matters. I'm making this speech without my supper and I don't know where I'll find my breakfast. I had $26.30 when I came here two weeks ago. I have worked hard day and night for the temperance cause, and now am just $26.30 worse off than when I came." Three hundred miners dig down into their pockets and donate sufficient money to satisfy their hunger and start them on their way. No more is heard of them until this headline appears in the *Chronicle* some months later: "THE LORD'S WRATH. Dr. Gibbons, the Great Temperance Apostle, Struck by Lightning. Miraculously Escape Death While Descending Pike's Peak."

When temperance lectures fail, a militant minority attempts strenuously to have the Sunday closing laws enforced. The idea is, remarks a critic, that "all sorts of games, fighting of roosters and dogs, chasing of buttered pigs and highway robbery are to be prohibited within the corporate limits of the town on Sundays; citizens are only to be allowed to buy mines, swap burros, drink lager beer, sing sacred songs and take all rational comfort possible without getting vicious." But the Blue Sunday campaign fails lamentably as well.

" Tis the day of the Lord. The theatres, twirling casinos, concert halls, silver exchanges and A-lafroganzas are all aglow. Down on State Street a female voice is shrieking murder."

Every night, Saturday and Sunday nights especially, pandemonium reigns almost from dark to dawn along State Street, a tumultuous half mile brightly lighted by the great kerosene flares blazing before dance houses, variety theaters, gambling hells, saloons, beer halls and brothels. As it descends from Pop Wyman's Great Saloon at the corner of Harrison, the street grows steadily more disreputable until it ends among the pines on the sand flat in two dark lines of " cribs," notorious Coon Row and still more notorious French Row, a dangerous neighborhood into which many men stray innocently to be seen no more. Behind French Row the *Chronicle* reports three "high joints," opium dens, where it suspects that many another man has been done to death. Above and below State Street run two frightful alleys crowded with dark dens and tenements harboring every sort of vice, depravity and crime. The one above is fittingly named Tiger Alley, while the one below is known as Stillborn Alley from the many evidences of abortion and infanticide found there. "Yesterday morning a small child, or foetus was found in a garbage heap in the alley below State Street. As this sight is not an unusual one in that part of the city, it attracted but little attention."

Above French and Coon rows stand the brothels of Mesdames Frankie Paige, Carrie Linnel, Minnie Purdy, Mollie Price and Sallie Purple. The most fashionable of them, Mollie May's, stands by itself on Main Street. These bagnios are ever in trouble. First and most seriously, wayward girls of thirteen and fourteen are never rejected when they seek admittance here. Several small girls in camp have to be rescued very regularly from a life of sin in these houses. Then, too, patrons complain frequently of being robbed. Also, shootings occur often not only within the houses but between them. One midnight open warfare breaks out between Mollie Price and Sallie Purple. Mollie pours volley after volley into her enemy's house next door. Sallie, her girls and patrons reply with a spirited fusillade. "Both parties are resting on their arms and awaiting daybreak to resume hostilities," reports the *Democrat* next morning. Mollie and Sallie, it appears, had had a bitter argument about the relative merits of Tipperary and Connaught as a birthplace — a dispute in which Mrs. Purple finally triumphed with a particularly obscene remark.

"The music at the beer halls is grinding low." Beer has just been reduced to five cents a schooner, six schooners for a quarter. Leadville now has three breweries which do much to lessen drunkenness, measurably diminishing indulgence in whiskey which alone could be had for a time. No resorts are more popular than the larger beer halls offering simple entertainment. Each has a singer or two to render in a throaty voice to suddenly hushed audiences such old favorites as *Silver Threads Among the Gold, Cottage by the Sea,* and *Papa, Stay Home, Don't Leave Me Tonight.* Frequently homesick miners in sudden outbursts of deep emotion shower a girl with silver after a particularly affecting number, for as one of them later remarked, " these poor despised beer hall singers were a sort of cropped angel after all."

Up the street at the fashionable Tontine are many gay parties. The gayest, perhaps, is the large champagne supper party with George Fryer as host. Fryer soon riotously spends a fortune of half a million and commits suicide. At the Utah saloon nearby miners are being entertained by Professor Joseph Ives, who claims once to have held the chair of astronomy at the University of Oxford. Every evening Ives wanders from saloon to saloon and is given all the drink he can consume by miners pleased with his stories of mythical history, readings from the Greek and Latin poets and snatches from the great masters played upon his old violin. Ives soon drops dead in a Stringtown dive. Monahan's Saloon is attracting custom with Sculley, " the great pedestrian who has walked in Gilmore's Garden, New York, and in London, Philadelphia, Boston, Cincinnati, St. Louis, Chicago and Omaha." Many protest against this craze for " itinerant idiots." Hundreds are crowding in to inspect Bill Nye's new saloon, pronounced the finest in camp. " Behind the bar the cutglass decanters, goblets and so forth are tastefully and skillfully arranged beneath a mirror, the largest and finest in the city. The chandeliers and jets of cut crystal are elaborate, though chaste in their design."

A shot is heard down State Street. Jack Morrissey, a Carbonate King, has been boldly attacked and seriously wounded by two men who escape. It is not robbery as the crowds first surmise. One of his assailants is recognized as the present suitor of the sixteen-year-old girl whom Morrissey seduced and cast aside. The two Dillons come reeling down the street. Both will return to the mines soon and ultimately die in poverty. So, too, will all but one of the Gallaghers after spending their fortunes in saloons and dance houses along the street. Henry Finch, one of the more recent Carbonate Kings, is entertaining at a great feast at Delmonico's "twenty-eight working miners, all of them his former associates in toil." At the Clarendon a smaller party of five, all grown rich from a lease which has just expired, are celebrating with champagne the final division of profits. As cigars are passed round, one suggests that each tell what he proposes to do with his fortune. One intends to buy a home for his mother, a second to pay off the mortgage on his father's farm, a third to buy a herd of cattle, a fourth to try to enlarge his fortune by grubstaking prospectors. Ferdinand Van Zant, a young mining engineer, hesitates to talk of his desire, so the story goes, but finally declares that he intends "to go to London, rent a suite of rooms, get a complete outfit of fashionable clothing, go into society and marry the richest and most attractive girl he can meet." He succeeds, marrying the daughter of Sir John Lubbock, afterward Lord Avebury. But Van Zant, like Fryer, ends with suicide.

"The town is full of old-time sports. There are eight to ten public saloons with all kinds of games, and I think all are making money," writes a gambler as the rush begins. "This is a good place for a small man with money to operate with. It is a gay place and there is plenty of money here. One old sport arrived here with $3 a few months ago and is now owner of a frame house for which he has refused $600 a month rent. Today he received $25,000 for a fourth interest in a mine. You can't imagine the excitement going on here."

Everyone gambles—from the bonanza kings in their private clubs to the little bootblacks who buck the tiger in a shack on Carbonate Hill. "The practice of allowing boys to bet their loose change on various games of chance in this city should be stopped, and we are glad to note that at least one of these gambling houses has shut down on minors." Poker, keeno, chuck-a-luck, Australian poolo, rouge et noir, lansquinette and paddle-wheel are all played, but faro is the general favorite because it less favors the house and is not easily "braced."

But many a tenderfoot foolishly prefers the nut-shell game— the old thimble game of earlier days. The operator employs a simple technique. With three half walnut shells in his fingers he keeps a small pea or rubber ball flying back and forth across the table and then, as if unintentionally, claps down the shells in such a way that the ball is exposed under one. Now he offers to bet $100 that none can "spot" the ball. This bet is a blind and if called, is evaded or withdrawn. Again the ball flies back and forth to vanish suddenly under a shell. At this point the operator usually turns round upon some pretext or other. While his back is turned, a "capper"—an accomplice in the crowd—steps quickly forward, reveals the ball and quickly replaces the shell with a wink at the crowd. Once more the ball flies back and forth and disappears. The capper offers to bet $5. The operator scorns such small bets. "The difficulty is overcome by a green-looking tenderfoot who produces another $5, and the shell is raised—but no ball!" The ingenuous often pay from $50 to $100 to convince themselves beyond all doubt that the hand is quicker than the eye. No player ever wins at this game except when the operator chooses to revive a lagging interest.

Somewhat more sporting is paddle-wheel. This requires a large board with squares numbered from 1 to 100 and an upright wheel bearing the same numbers. "Choose your square! Your money down in time and the wheel goes round!" cries the operator as he spins his machine. With astonishing regularity the wheel stops abruptly short of or passes slowly over the number upon which the largest stakes are piled.

Chuck-a-luck is the most popular of the dice games, played with three dice and a board with squares numbered from 1 to 6. In placing stakes on any square one bets the bank even money that one of the dice will show the number chosen. At the same time the game offers opportunity for the highest kind of play, for one may bet on any of the many possible combinations of numbers, at odds running as high as 180 to 1. Chuck-a-luck operators shake their dice in a "small churn-like affair of metal" —hence the expression, "tin-horn gambler," for the game is rather looked down upon as one for "chubbers" and chuck-a-luck gamblers are never admitted within the aristocratic circle of faro-dealers.

Faro requires a more elaborate lay-out than any of these. It requires, first of all, a large board with thirteen squares representing the respective value of the cards. Every dealer has his indispensable "case"—a small folding box about four inches high, usually silverplated, in which the deck is placed face up. Across the top of the case run thirteen wires strung with four buttons each. A tally of every card played is kept on this abacus—one wire with its four buttons representing, for example, the four kings or four aces. The case is carefully kept to determine odds and protect both player and dealer. The dealer ($5–7.50 a day) usually keeps the case himself, but in more elaborate establishments a second dealer is hired as case-keeper ($3.50–5). Such houses also employ a " lookout " ($3–4), who sits on a high stool overlooking the board to watch for errors by the dealer, particularly when they go against the house. The dealer frequently asks one of these to change places with him when luck runs consistently against him.

The card on top of the deck as play commences is the " soda " and pays nothing. The next card is a loser, the next a winner, and so throughout the deck to the last card, the " hock," which likewise pays nothing. When the dealer has proceeded " from soda to hock," he reshuffles his deck. Cards can be bet either way — if to win, by simply placing chips upon any square on the board; if to lose, by " coppering " the pile of chips with some such token as a Chinese coin or checker. Workers and business men are known professionally as " producers " and usually play " straight up," betting on a single card to win or lose. But professionals " copper the heel " by betting on several cards at once. Although not easily done, faro is sometimes " braced." Tiny holes are punched in the cards so that the dealer may see what is coming and to the bank's advantage pull two cards instead of one, giving the wink to the case-keeper to arrange his part of the swindle.

A faro bank demands, according to the limits placed upon bets, a capital ranging from $100 to $10,000 or more. " Banks in Leadville probably range from $500 to $2,000. The limit with a solid bank is usually placed at $25 a card. But there are banks in Leadville which have no limit, whether $10 or $10,000." In most Leadville houses the minimum bet is a twenty-five cent white chip, sold in stacks of twenty for $5. Ten cent chips, however, are not unknown. In games where stakes run high, a stack of twenty red chips costs $20, of twenty blues $50 and of twenty yellows $100, $200 or even $500. Whether they win or lose, players contribute to the bank, for all winnings are regularly discounted by the house. Faro banks make an average monthly profit of $1,000, according to the *Chronicle,* which estimates that $25,000 changes hands daily over the green cloth. One small faro bank on Chestnut Street reports a profit of $40,000 within four months.

The largest and best of the gambling hells are Jeff Winney's California Concert Hall, the Board of Trade Saloon and the famous Texas House. At Jeff Winney's miners may buck the tiger in the agreeable form of Kitty Crawhurst, lady gambler, who has become a professional woman to spare herself a worse fate. The Board of Trade specializes in stud poker, which in size of stakes is exceeded only by faro. Many men win or lose as much as $10,000 at a sitting here. Until discovered and soundly thrashed, one man wins many thousands here with a " shiner " — a silver dollar with a tiny concave mirror which, when the dollar is placed upon a pile of notes or coin, reveals all cards dealt over it.

On Harrison Avenue just above State Street stands the famous Texas House. It " takes in more money in a day than the Carbonate Bank " to the great profit of Bailey Youngston and " Con " Featherly, both of Galveston. The latter, a " debonnaire little fellow with soft slender hands," is known in the profession as a " mechanic." He can operate the faro box as occasion demands. Youngston is less accomplished, having once been a mural decorator, but by his own efforts he transforms the gambling hell into a " palace of beauty."

A huge saloon with many highly polished bars occupies the

entire ground floor. At a dozen or more tables faro is played continuously from one day to the next. The dealers relieve one another in eight-hour shifts. About the tables at all hours crowd "miners hoping to extend their stay in camp by increasing the remnant of fortune left by last night's debauch; furnace hands and charcoal burners, begrimed with smoke, who have stopped in on their way home from a day or night's work; young men about town with more ease than elegance and more luck than sense, eager to provide for some new depravity in the dens of sin and shame; strangers stranded in their search of a carbonate mine or some other sinecure and seeking means to take themselves hence; visitors endeavoring to learn the mysteries of the tiger's lair at a modest cost; and young clerks who frequently lose more than their salaries." Play goes on quietly and steadily with bets on single cards limited to $25 and on "dubs" (doubles) to $50. Although regarded as penny-ante fellows while working at their jobs, dealers at the Texas earn sensational reputations by their winnings at other houses upon stakes provided by the reckless and gullible.

Mining and merchant kings of the camp are seldom seen in the main gambling saloon downstairs. For them Youngston has provided a separate side entrance leading up a flight of stairs into "three gorgeously furnished apartments, a reception and reading room, a dining room, and a gambling room with a lavishly stocked buffet at which a guest is invited to help himself ad lib." In every room is a piano, "with an experienced musician to play it." Over all presides John Pentland, "round-faced, suave and good natured," a New York gambler who drifts into camp unheralded but quickly gains renown by winning more than $80,000 for the house within a few months. "At one moment he is asking you with an ecclesiastical flourish to join him at the sideboard. One minute he is dealing a $500 card winner with a church-like composure, and the next is looking idly on from the lookout chair and then goes bustling through the apartments to make sure that all accommodations and courtesies are extended to his guests."

Perhaps the greatest social occasion of all these years occurs here when Featherly and Youngston play host to the Carbonate Kings and all richer merchants, bankers, lawyers and judges. Tabor, Bush and Rische are among the selected guests who are said to have represented a capital of $80,000,000. The occasion is a "Parisian banquet for forty men, all in dress suits." There are fourteen courses, half as many wines, cognac and coffee. Brimming toasts are drunk. Speeches are made. There is sporadic conversation but no mention of cards until midnight when the guests insist upon greater excitement. A game of faro begins "with ivory whites at $1.25 and no limit." Deal after deal goes against the house.

"Well, if I don't win again," shouts an excited judge. "$1,000 on the king to win."

"Why of course, bet $10,000 if you wish," replies Pentland with a smile. Play lasts less than an hour. All the guests win, as it was perhaps intended they should. In any case, the loss of the house exceeds $30,000, the largest night's play of the time in Leadville. Shootings at the Texas House are infrequent, but it is here that City Marshal Mart Duggan, then an alderman, is shot down and killed in '88, presumably by a house gambler whose life he had threatened.

Early every evening seven brass bands assemble in crowded State Street before each of the variety theaters. Here they strike up to contend in friendly rivalry for an hour or more. Then one by one they march off with a great roar of brass and pounding of drums to beat up the town, parading it from one end to the other, trailing "boys and banners telling of cancans, female bathers, daring tumblers and other dramatic attractions." An urchin with a "wide-awake" lamp marches at the side of each musician so that he may read his music. At a stop in traffic one evening a small lamp-bearer turns proudly "to tell a newsboy about his father's playing in the band." His lamp swings round against the leader of the band, "catches in the tinsel trappings of his uniform, flashes up through his long curly hair, setting fire to his hat and burning his neck to a blister." The music stops, the lamp drops as the boy darts through the crowd hotly pursued by the maestro, who is blocked and tripped by the miners as they cheer the frightened boy.

After a turn of the town the bands reassemble in State Street to play again till nine o'clock when they repair inside as curtains rise, many not to go down again till three or four in the morning. Here at the top of the street is the Grand Central where Tabor and other Carbonate Kings have their private boxes. A large three-story frame building, only recently risen from the ashes of the old Theatre Comique, the Grand Central advertises itself as the "Largest and Most Elegantly Appointed Theatre West of Chicago." From the boards here has just been taken *Around the World in Eighty Days,* straight from Niblo's Gardens, New York, "with real camels, elephants, etc., in the famous Necropolis funeral procession." But tonight, as announced by large banners and streamers, there will appear before the kerosene footlights *Nana, the Lovely Blonde,* at prices ranging from twenty-five cents to $1, with private boxes at $5.

Song, Dance and Mirth
and
Emotional Novelties

A Host of Talented Artists
and
BEAUTIFUL WOMEN

Four Hours

of Elegant Pleasures, blended with a voluptuous feast without coarseness, concluding with Harry Montague's Spicy, Sensational, Melodramatic Comedy,

entitled

THE

N A N A LOVELY N A N A

BLONDE

Or, the Miser's Pet

Adopted from material selected from Emile Zolos' intensely interesting novel of the same name.

AND terminating with a Quadrille D'Amour (love quadrille) in which Nana and her friends will illustrate

The *Poetry of Motion* a la mode.

At the Grand Central early in '80 appears Charles Algernon Sidney Vivian, an English actor who in '67 founded the Jolly Corks, a society from which in time emerges the Benevolent Protective Order of Elks. Vivian upon arrival in camp ambitiously took over a mammoth tent, a notorious pleasure resort first known as the Great Western Amphitheatre and then as the Buckingham Palace, and converted it into the Vivian Opera House. He there presented *Oliver Twist* and similar plays, but the enterprise soon collapsed. After a period of idleness Vivian does a number of variety turns at the Grand Central until stricken with pneumonia in March, '80. He is first buried in Leadville with funds raised by a benefit performance. Nine years later his body is removed to Elks' Rest in Mt. Hope Cemetery, Boston.

A short distance down the street from the Grand Central stand two other large theaters facing one another, the Gaiety and the New Theater, originally the Athenaeum. The Gaiety offers "Thirty Acts in Lightning Succession — No long waits." These include not only the inevitable *Female Bathers,* but a skit *Shot in the Eye* and an extravaganza *Razulefrom,* so riotously funny that two ladies and a gentleman twice walk more than thirty miles to see it. Across the street James McDaniel, for years one of P. T. Barnum's agents, is presenting "Messrs. Homer and Holly, Emperors of Song and Dance; Miss Lola Cory, Fascinating Serio-Comic Vocalist; Miss Fanny Douglas, Charming and Vivacious Cantatrice; and a Sparkling Olio, including the acts, *The West Point Cadet* and *No One's Darling,* concluding with Lew Spencer's Great Act, *Who Stole Keyser's Dog?* "

"Enter the New Theatre. Admission is free, but you must patronize the bar. We at once hasten upstairs to the first row of curtained boxes. We have barely time to cast a glance at the negro performer on the stage, when the door opens and a girl enters. She is dressed for the stage in a short skirt, short sleeves and low neck. She is decked out in all her war-paint and bedizened out of all reason with beads, flounces, feathers and spangles. She closes the door behind her and trips over to the man nearest her and plants herself upon his lap without the slightest ado. We observe she wears tights.

— Well, ain't you going to say something?

—Say what?

—Why, the drinks."

One must drink copiously here to be welcome. One evening a gentleman entered with a guest, took a box and merely ordered two cocktails. Girls came again and again, and finally two bar-keepers to order them below. The gentleman who was host demurred, declaring he would remain where he was. " But he was mistaken, for he went below so fast that he had a leg broken and his face bruised and battered."

" Within a few minutes our fairy returns with a tray of glasses —beer for us and for herself a cocktail, with slices of pineapple. She raises her glass and nodding pleasantly to each of us, hopes we may live long and prosper. We ask the price and are charged fifty cents a glass for the beer, seventy-five cents for the cocktail.

—God, it's time for me to go, exclaims the dancer, as she trips out and enters the next box to repeat her performance there."

A riot suddenly breaks out below. A drunken ruffian has staggered in to amuse himself by " jerking chairs out from under members of the audience, blowing out lights, pushing over stoves, tearing down benches and taking off doors." A shot rings out, and a bartender falls wounded. The ruffian with smoking revolver runs out and " although hotly pursued by an angry crowd," soon loses himself among the jostling throngs in the street.

At last the Tabor Opera House is nearing completion and Leadville society looks forward expectantly to a gala first night. The Opera House is not merely a theater but an office building and an annex to the Clarendon Hotel which stands next door. On the ground floor are two stores, one occupied by Phil Golding's Cabinet Saloon, the " neatest in the city," where patrons of the drama may enjoy a drink or two or even a hand of poker between the acts. Up a flight of stairs and to the front are two vast apartments, each with a tremendous mahogany desk. Tabor sits at one, Bill Bush at the other, managing their many separate and joint affairs. The third floor is joined to the Clarendon by a bridge and has a number of bedrooms for guests.

Tabor has leased the theater to Bill Bush, who appoints as its manager-director Jack Langrishe of the old Platte Valley Theatre in Denver. Langrishe has traveled far since leaving Denver in '71, having trouped New England, Canada, the Middle West, the Pacific Coast and Mexico. The rush to the Black Hills then attracted him, and he was playing at Deadwood and other camps in the Bad Lands when Bush summoned him to Leadville.

After being many times postponed, the opening night draws near when all Leadville can inspect for itself the " elegant brick Tabor Opera House, the most imposing structure in the city and conceded by all to be the finest theater west of the Mississippi. The theater, which holds 880, is handsomely frescoed and furnished with the celebrated opera chairs manufactured by Andrews and Company of Chicago. All appointments in this temple of amusement are first class in every respect; the scenery, artistic; and under the full flood of gaslight, the cosiest place for lovers of the legitimate drama to throw off the cares of life and yield to the fascinations of music and imagery." The program announced is *The Serious Family,* a comedy, and a farce *Who's Who,* the latter written by Langrishe himself for the occasion.

But the opening night on November 21, '79, is not the gala event anticipated, for just two nights previously the Vigilantes struck, hanging two men from the rafters of the new city jail a few steps up the street. Their lank bodies and the menacing hand of the Vigilantes cast a black shadow over a frightened and suddenly sobered town. Retaliation by roughs and criminals is generally feared. For several weeks all who can remain indoors.

Perhaps this explains in part why Langrishe within little more than a month made trial of a score of melodramas, each followed by a short burlesque or farce: *Naval Engagements, Divorce, The Lady of Lyons, Life and Trials of a Factory Girl, The Dumb Boy of the Pyrenees, Colleen Bawn or The Bride of Garry Owen* (" with new scenery painted expressly for the play, including the famous Water Cave Scene "), *London Assurance* (with "none of the drawbacks incidental to the first presentations "), *Flower Girls of Paris, Self! or The Rich of New York, Ireland As It Was,* (" with Mr. and Mrs. Langrishe in the great characters of Ragged Pat and Judy O'Trot "), *The Obstinate Family* (" given to a half-filled house, for the audiences, we regret to say, have not been as large as expected or such as the company deserves ") and finally the renowned *Two Orphans.* This last is so ill received that the *Chronicle* utters a loud protest against the " ignorant dolts, who, not having the common sense necessary to appreciate the excellent and legitimate performance given by Mr. Langrishe and his most estimable company, must needs disturb others in the house by their senseless interruptions, loud laughter and insulting remarks. It is a matter of sincere regret to all who feel a just pride in the intellectual and moral status of the community that legitimate drama should play nightly to empty benches when amusements questionable in character should draw crowded houses."

During this first season Bush and Langrishe undertake a daring experiment when in March, '80, they offer the camp a program opening with *Othello* and closing with the *Artful Dodger.* " Greeted by one of the largest houses of the season, it is impossible to speak of the performance without indulging in lavish praise," reads the critique in the *Democrat*. "It was a genuine success in all respects. Mrs. Thompson has a very pleasing face and well-rounded form, with a musical voice; her method of delivery is easy and her motions are graceful. As Desdemona she gave entire satisfaction throughout. Mr. Thompson as Iago possesses a fine face and figure, which his neat and elegant costume displayed to advantage. Roche as Othello, although still suffering from a rheumatic ankle, really astonished those who already knew of his talent. His Moorish costume was very picturesque. Mr. Sullivan as Cassio was the recipient of three rounds of applause during his repentance scene in the second act, for his elocutionary efforts. Mr. Norris acted Roderigo very nicely. This gentleman is conscientious in all he does and makes as much of his varied range of impersonations as the author allows. The Gilberts convulsed the audience with laughter in the farce of the *Artful Dodger*, which concluded a pleasant evening's entertainment."

An Othellian near-tragedy almost immediately follows the performance. At two in the morning a boarding house on Main Street is awakened by screams of murder. A woman in nightdress bursts from the door and runs shrieking down the street. In a fit of jealousy the conscientious Mr. Norris has cut his wife's throat with a razor, having observed her seated during the performance beside a " very prominent local gentleman " whose gallant attentions obviously flattered her. The *Democrat* also noted the by-play but added that the " gentleman's character is so entirely above reproach that Mr. Norris' jealous fears are groundless."

With a new Roderigo, Othello is presented a second evening to an audience which fills the lower part of the house but leaves empty the gallery which " was crowded to excess the opening night." Two evenings of Shakespeare are judged sufficient and the company returns to more familiar fields with:

A Romantic Drama in 5 Acts

entitled

the

MARBLE HEART

or

THE SCULPTOR'S DREAM.

Act I — Prologue

The Dream — The Studio of Phidias at Athens — A Reminiscence of Ancient Greece — The Power of Gold Gives Life to Marble.

Act II

The Play — The Artist's Retreat in the Forest of Fontainbleau.

Act III

A Sculptor's Studio in Paris.

Act IV

Fashion's Fortress in the Bois de Boulogne.

Act V

Realization of the Dream.

" False one of the past,

False one of the future,

Woe to him that loves you!

The Gold-bought smiles

Have ever been,

And ever will be,

Ministers of

Ruin, Misery and Death."

Melodrama of this kind holds the stage at the Opera House continuously until the theater is temporarily closed for repairs and remodeling three years later. It is found necessary to add new substantial columns of support throughout the building. Fallen plaster is replaced. "The gallery is being materially improved as well as the ventilation, which has heretofore not been what it ought to be. Improvements are also being made on the stage in regard to scenery, scene-shifting and drop curtains to obviate those ridiculous delays and hitches that have heretofore occurred."

Jay Rial's Ideal Uncle Tom's Cabin Company opens the re-modeled Opera House with an improved version of that classic which is the hit of all these years. "There is more of action and less of dialogue, more of the absurd and comical and less of the commonplace. It ends in a sensible way with the death of Uncle Tom, with the transformation scene added. Ferocious blood-hounds are introduced, but they are not allowed to hurt the audience. Mr. Rial's blood-hounds are the largest and fiercest ever brought upon the stage."

At long last in October, '82, Leadville hears its first opera when Tabor brings from Denver the Emma Abbott English Grand Opera Company. Denied the great social event it had anticipated the evening the theater first opened, the community resolves to make this a most memorable occasion by appearing in full dress to welcome the singers. "Plug hats, heretofore a rarity in this region, suddenly appeared upon the heads of male bipeds. They also brushed their clothes thoroughly and took their pants out of their boots and blacked the latter; a few even ventured to put on kid gloves. The ladies thronged the millinery stores during the past week and came to the opera in full bloom; flashy dresses, white opera hats and colors flying." A society reporter notes a "white satin bonnet with a delicate spray of flowers and two tiny birds in the act of flying, with a trimming of ostrich feathers"—a Gainsborough hat of white beaver with three little tips and one large plume—a handsome little red plush bonnet edged with gold cord—and one "too utterly pretty bonnet of pansies"—and a fashionable "blushing bonnet" or two, equipped with springs pressing so strongly upon the temples that they cause a rush of blood to the face, heightening the complexion. The Lily Langtry coiffure, it is also remarked, has become popular as it requires little or no false hair.

King for a Day, Chimes of Normandy, La Traviata, Martha and *Fra Diavolo* are presented by Miss Abbott who, above all, is English and a lady. She is devoted to the score of *La Traviata* but objects to its libretto as immoral. She herself rewrites it to remove every vestige of amorous passion. It is she who "conceived and executed the idea of singing *Nearer My God to Thee* in the third act of *Faust*, who introduced Siberian blood-hounds in *Lucia di Lammermoor*, interpolated *Swanee River* in *King for a Day*, lugged a real live baby into *La Traviata*, had a trapeze performance in *Romeo and Juliet*, and a trained mule in *Il Trovatore*." Of the operas offered Leadville, *Fra Diavolo* is most appreciated. But the camp confesses to some disappointment even in this. "Only two shots were fired and only one man killed when it fully expected forty flashes of fire and at least half that number of elegant corpses laid out for the benefit of the theatrical undertaker. Then the bed chamber scene in the second act wasn't all it was cracked up to be because of Miss Abbott's prudent and prudish rendition of this little episode." Emma Abbott and her manager are far more critical of Leadville, especially of its want of financial support, and both hurry East vowing never to return.

Certainly the stage at the Tabor Opera House was never trod by a more distinguished and exotic figure than Oscar Wilde who arrives in '82 to talk to the miners on the future of art. Not met and welcomed at the railway station, contrary to the camp's hospitable custom, Wilde slips "quietly into the Clarendon Hotel by the ladies' entrance." A few hours later, reclining upon a couch as he pants for breath in the high altitude, he receives a few of the curious who find him "some six feet tall, with long hair reaching to his shoulders, with a languid far-away look in his eyes and a mouth vying with Soldene's in size." To his visitors' obvious chagrin Wilde is conventionally dressed in tweeds and is without sunflower or lily. Rumor runs that some local wits propose to attend Wilde's lecture in costumes intended to cast ridicule upon the speaker, leading the newspapers to protest that the miners should not prove themselves such boors as the students at Harvard. "Whatever may be the value of Wilde's peculiar views, it is certain that he is a gentleman and as such is entitled to ordinary courtesy." Whatever Leadville's faults, Wilde is not insulted here as he was by fatuous wags throughout the East.

"I went to the theatre to lecture and I was informed that just before I went there, two men had been seized for committing a murder and in the theatre had been brought on the stage at eight o'clock in the evening, and then and there tried and executed before a crowded audience," said Wilde later in a series of stupid and almost incredibly naive lectures to English audiences upon his American visit. "They [the people of Leadville] are miners —men working in metals, so I lectured to them on the *Ethics of Art*. I read them passages from the autobiography of Benvenuto Cellini and they seemed much delighted."

A surprising number indeed attend Wilde's lecture on *The Practical Application of the Aesthetic Theory to Exterior and In-*

terior House Decoration, with Observations on Dress and Personal Ornament. The majority no doubt have been attracted more by curiosity about Wilde himself than by any great interest in his practical aesthetics. For the reception of the "apostle of Beauty," Bill Bush has had the stage at the Opera House "laid in a balcony scene and prettily adorned with bric-a-brac."

"Wilde stumbled on with a stride more becoming a giant backwoodsman than an aesthete, dressed in a suit of very elegant black velvet, which included a cut-away coat cut in circular form, knee breeches, low shoes and black stockings. At his neck was a Byron collar with a flossy white neck-handkerchief, while from his snow-white shirt front glittered a single cluster of diamonds. His hair was very straight and very long, falling in a dark mass over his shoulders, and was parted directly at the equator. Without much introduction he proceeded at once to business, pitching his voice at about middle C and inflecting only when tired nature asserted itself and compelled a rising inflection by a long-drawn breath. There was not a comma or a period in the whole hour save when he came to a stop to take an unaesthetic drink."

Scant attention was paid to Wilde's address — and deservedly, if, as seems evident, his observations were fairly reported. He talked at great length of Beauty, nebulous and bizarre, and "said nothing but what has been better said by Ruskin and scores of others," as the *Democrat* remarked. "What he did say was in a dull heavy and uninteresting manner, in a monotonous voice, very much like a school boy reciting his lessons. As a lecturer Oscar Wilde proved a conspicuous failure."

But Wilde is pronounced a "Prince of good fellows" by the miners who are pleased to discover "no piousness in his nature." He in turn finds them "very charming and not at all rough."

During his stay Wilde is invited to inspect Tabor's famous Matchless mine. He is dropped down the dripping shaft in a rickety iron bucket in which, so he said, it was "impossible to be graceful." At the bottom of the shaft his party is met by a dozen miners, each with a bottle. By invariable Western custom every bottle must make the rounds. Within a few minutes all have had twelve "snorters." The miners without exception are rather dizzy, but Wilde remains cool, steady and collected. He is cheered loudly and "voted a perfect gentleman."

After his lecture Wilde is entertained by being shown the town. When he is led into Pop Wyman's Great Saloon, the largest and most popular of its day, his velvet coat and silk stockings cause some agitation among minors unread in art. But Wilde is soon drinking with them and the evening passes quietly.

Wyman's Great Saloon is a complete pleasure resort — saloon, gambling hell, dance house and variety theater, with luxurious rooms on the second and third floors for private parties of every kind. A short powerful man, florid of face and jovial, quiet in voice and manner, Wyman rules his house with a firm but gentle hand. No drunken man is ever served at the bar and no married man allowed to play at the gambling tables, rules of the house strictly enforced by several special policemen. In his dance hall Wyman will have none but young and pretty girls possessed of some manners. These he protects and treats well as a "Pop" (every keeper of a dance house is "Pap" or "Pop" to his girls). Orderly and well run, the resort witnesses few brawls and causes no public scandals. Perhaps no man in camp is more popular than Wyman with rich and poor alike, for he is kindly, affable to all and genuinely good-natured, which can be said of few of his kind.

Come to Pop Wyman's Tonight!
Free Roll at 7:30
Everything Wide Open
Bible Reading by
T. Dewitt Talmadge of New York.

An " ecclesiastical yellow-back, a sort of religious Bowery Boy,"
as the newspapers stigmatize him for his passion for notoriety,
Talmadge is delighted to read from the large Bible which Wyman
keeps chained to a mahogany pulpit just inside the swinging
doors. All guests from Paddy Ryan to Oscar Wilde remark upon
this pulpit as well as the sign painted across the face of the clock
above, *Please Don't Swear!* In the dance hall behind the saloon
Wyman has painted another sign just above the heads of the
orchestra, *Don't Shoot the Pianist — He's Doing His Damnedest!*
Wyman, too, has a flair for publicity of a kind and carries his
small change in a purse fashioned from a human scrotum.

Wyman, some say, started life as a preacher, but the story is
apocryphal. At one time or another he has been, in fact, almost
all but that. He began his career in Massachusetts as a friendly
rival of Jim Fisk, Lord of Erie. Both peddled wares about the
neighborhood from small wagons. Wyman became shoemaker,
mechanic, farmer and auctioneer before coming West to the
Clear Creek camps to establish himself as a grocer. A lone horseman buffeting the snow, he rode into Leadville late in '77 as
local agent of the Colorado State Lottery. This advertised itself
as the " Grand Two Dollar Scheme," offering a first prize of
$30,000. But the winner of this prize, curiously, could never be
found. Such was the announcement in '78. When a similar announcement was made the next year, the *Chronicle* counseled
the wisdom of finding the winner at all costs. " The public has

an aversion to being hum-bugged twice in succession by the same party." Even before the Postmaster General suppressed this swindle, which by charter paid five per cent of all its earnings to the State, Wyman opened a small saloon which grew rapidly into one of the largest and most elaborate resorts in the West.

The Great Saloon profits him $45,000 a year, Wyman confesses, in spite of high wages to a large staff of barkeepers ($100–150 a month), gamblers ($5–8.50 a day), actors ($25–75 a week) musicians ($25–35), cooks ($15–50), waiters ($7–10) and dance house girls. Such girls receive a wage never exceeding $10 a week and a small commission on all drinks sold to their partners. With only the rarest exceptions all have other sources of income ($10–25), which in the first days of the boom made many relatively rich.

Almost a lone monument to old State Street in the days of its shameless glory, Pop Wyman's Great Saloon still stands at the corner of Harrison and State, now a cheap rooming house, all warped and bent by sun and rain.

" The clock on the Grand Hotel points to one. Shots are heard from Carbonate Hill. The roar of revelry is on the increase. The streets are full of drunken carousers taking in the town."

So crowded are the gambling hells that tables are overturned and games interrupted. There is none but standing room in the wine theaters, many having to send out to rouse the nearest grocer for more baskets of champagne. One cannot squeeze into the beer hells. But as the hour grows late, the throngs are greatest in the dance houses — Little Casino, Silver Thread, Dillon's, Tudor, Bon Ton, Red Light and Odeon, among others. The last two stand side by side facing the Grand Central, lighted by its flares. The Odeon especially is notorious for its " forty-rod vitriol, its hat-rack females, its cheap faro brace and general odor of degradation, attracting a case-hardened pugilistic crowd fit for treason, strategem and spoils, particularly spoils."

Along one entire side of the Odeon runs a bar against which lean a number of drunken men spoiling for a fight. Along the other wall are ranged a half-dozen tables devoted to poker, faro, chuck-a-luck, rolling mustang, twenty-one, keeno and paddle-wheel. Here grim silent unsmiling men " stake their all in the hope of bribing fortune for enough to buy a good night slug of whiskey, a twenty-five cent bed and a meagre breakfast in the morning." A few men win a little something perhaps, but most slink away penniless into the night, some to drift down the street to the more disreputable dives below, the more desperate to prowl the back streets in search of drunken prey.

At the far end of the Odeon is a small open space for dancing. On a dais here play three musicians. The fiddler is very drunk. The banjo player has difficulty picking his strings. The cornetist at the moment is carrying the tune. Several miners, either dead drunk or bucked to death by the tiger, lie snoring in far corners.

" Gentlemen, get your partners for the next dance," shouts a tall powerful figure in shirt sleeves and red vest, edging his way through the crowd. He singles out a well-dressed tenderfoot and urges him to dance. The stranger hesitates, pleading that he has not been introduced. The " rustler " seizes him by the arm, leads him through the crowd and all but hurls him into the arms of the nearest dance girl.

" Partner for you," he shouts and turns away. The dance is scarcely begun before it ends abruptly. The rustler collects fifty cents from every man on the floor and hands each girl a pasteboard check. The girls lead their partners to the bar to present their tickets, for a drink of bad whiskey for both is included in the bargain. One short dance succeeds another till dawn.

"Checks," calls the head barkeeper sleepily when the house has emptied. The girls hand in their tickets. Usually a little tipsy, the barkeeper slowly and methodically counts the checks of each, concentrating upon his task with a rather painful effort.

"You done good tonight, Em," he remarks at last, handing the girl $2.

XII. Reign of the Footpads and Vigilantes

" Footpads may rob a man in broad daylight on the most public streets, and there is no civil power in Colorado that can give the robbed redress."

Relatively quiet in '78, Leadville becomes steadily more boisterous and lawless as the boom rises toward its height during '79. Among thousands of adventurers of all kinds the new Eldorado attracts a large number of hardened ruffians from all of the older mining camps in the West. Violence and crime rise rapidly to such alarming proportions that local newspapers soon style the period the " Reign of the Footpads." Early in the year the *Chronicle* remarks that " of late depredations have been committed almost nightly." Others complain loudly of the playful promiscuous shooting in the streets. " It is getting to be a nuisance, this indiscriminate pistol practice from ten P.M. to daylight." The police, numbering only eight at the time, can do little as matters drift from bad to worse.

Much criminal violence must be attributed to hunger and necessity. In March, in fact, several minor bread riots occur. Local newspapers suppress the fact, but Governor Pitkin hears of it and promptly writes Tabor to make a number of confidential and highly disingenuous proposals. " The presence of so many people in Leadville, some of whom are idle and destitute, is undoubtedly an element of danger, and even a slight trouble, if not promptly checked, might soon become a serious matter." It might involve

" not only the lives of good citizens but their property, including merchandise in the stores and money in the vaults of your banks." The Governor suggests that " leading citizens take steps quietly to organize a military company with membership limited to those only in whom the utmost confidence can be placed." He promises arms for a full company.

The Governor's allusion to the banks impresses Mayor Tabor, who next morning summons a select few to a secret meeting. Among others, he invites Bill Bush, August Rische, George Trimble of the Miners' Exchange Bank, Phil Golding of the Cabinet Saloon and City Marshal Duggan. Mart Duggan at the moment is suspended from the force upon the complaint of a barkeeper at the Tontine. When he made the usual discount on a " trade " dollar offered him by Duggan, so the bartender testifies, the Marshal "became violent and abusive, drew his revolver and threatening my life, came behind the bar, knocked me down, called me all kinds of bad and dirty names and denounced the owners of the Tontine as thieves and robbers." Duggan is exonerated at a hearing before Mayor Tabor a few days later.

So nervous are richer and more respectable citizens that they recruit not one but many military companies. All are ostensibly organized to suppress any outbreak of the Utes, long ago driven far over the Continental Divide. In reality, the companies constitute the private armies of the Carbonate Kings who arm and equip the several companies — the Leadville Guards, Carbonate Rifles, Wolf Tone Guards and Tabor Highland Guards. Tabor's company musters sixty-four men handsomely accoutered in " black doublets with royal blue and red cord and facings, kilt of royal Stuart style, and stockings dashed with red and green." Each also wears a " sporan of white goat's hair with silver tassels and mountings, a Prince Charlie bonnet ornamented with silver buckle and plume, a royal Stuart shoulder plaid with silver buckles and *cairn gorn* jewels, and every man carries a *skein dhu* in his stocking."

But his Highland Guards neither quiet Tabor's fears nor satisfy his growing need of splendor. Soon the Tabor Light Cavalry is beautifully mounted and comes clattering along the crowded streets in red trousers, blue coats and shiny brass helmets very like the German *Pickelhaube*. The company musters fifty fighting men, commanded by three line and five staff officers. " The staff officers, including General Tabor, wear black felt hats with a black plume and gold cord, and flashing steel scabbards on belts mounted with gold and having gold buckles with the monogram of the company. The General's belt is of Russian leather, embroidered in gold by hand. The price of this article is $50. The sword is a straight one. The blade bears on one side the inscription, *General H. A. W. Tabor, C.N.A.,* and on the other, *Tabor Light Cavalry.* The General's epaulets are mounted with a silver star and ornamented with three-ply genuine gold fringe. The spurs of the privates are plainly formed of brass with steel wheels, while those of the officers are plated with gold. The uniforms of the officers are blue broadcloth trimmed with gold. Their pants are of light cloth with broad gold stripes running down the legs."

Tabor provides the squadron with stables, club rooms and an armory, which is dedicated with a grand ball. The hussars wear " their tasteful uniforms to a man, with General Tabor in the full attire of commander as the central figure." In one of her few public appearances Augusta attends " in an elegant black silk with white lace and magnificent diamond jewelry." Altogether it is a brilliant affair with the wives of the Carbonate Kings in " expensive white and wine-colored satins, light blue brocades,

Leadville Gambling Saloon

Dance House in the "Wonderful Mining Town of Leadville"

black velvets with white bunting, black silks with carmine bows and lace."

It costs Tabor $10,000 to become a general and immediately he leads his men in an impressive demonstration to awe the lawless and hungry. The military companies in full regimentals, the police in their new uniforms, the Harrison and the Bush fire brigades, the Tabor Hose boys with their nickel-plated carriage —all parade up and down the town, looking their most martial when passing the vicious dives along State Street. But footpads, burglars, highwaymen, counterfeiters, lot-jumpers, mine-jumpers, road-jumpers, bunkosteerers and ruffians in general—none appear to have taken General Tabor very seriously.

" HELL LET LOOSE," reads the *Chronicle* a few days later, " Bloodiest Night on Leadville's Calendar — Murderous Attack upon a Kokomo Freighter — Assault and Robbery on Harrison Avenue — A Tenderfoot Garrotted on Capitol Hill — Daring Robbery of a Man at the Comique — Arrest of a Notorious Confidence Man."

Two murders are committed by " Big Ed " Burns, leader of the roughs and bunkos. He is indicted for one but is promptly discharged " for want of evidence." A member of his gang, one " Keeno Bill," wanted for murder, returns boldly to town, precipitates a drunken row, shoots twice at an officer who attempts to interfere, furrowing his scalp, and again escapes — only to return shortly. " Slim Jim " Bruce, another of the gang, first shoots down a " greenie " who objects to being swindled in a confidence game and then kills " Brownie " Lee in a quarrel over the spoils. Officer Townsend is shot to death by a prominent young lawyer in a quarrel over constable's fees amounting to ten or fifteen cents. City Clerk Murphy, removed from office for drunkenness and many gross abuses, openly threatens the life of Alderman Kavanaugh who on two occasions barely escapes assassination. The owner of a dance house murders a miner for slapping one of his girls.

Desperados jump the Ten Mile Road and erect toll stations to levy tribute upon travelers. Several attempts to jump the Malta Road, the main highway, are forcibly repulsed. Lot-jumpers continue their assaults upon isolated individuals. In quick succession mine-jumpers attack the Buckeye Bell, Black Prince, Panhandle, Grand View and Highland Chief, with several killed. The attack on the Highland Chief is led by City Marshal Duggan and Edward Frodsham, who post a guard of sixty blacklegs to repulse any counter attack. Warrants are issued, but only Frodsham is arrested to be dealt with shortly by the Vigilantes. When the Park mine is jumped, it is stormed and recaptured by the Miners' Guard which then placards the town with a warning to all mine-jumpers "not to repeat the performance upon pain of having their necks stretched."

New crimes make their appearance as the rush increases. Pickpockets ply their skill profitably in all public places of resort, finding their fattest wallets in the crowded lobby of the Clarendon. Rich ore is stolen in daring raids upon shaft houses and dumps. To "ore agents" are added others specializing in horses, stoves, shoes and groceries; the bold thefts of a clever "oyster-champagne agent" cause much concern. The school is raided time and again by sneak thieves who steal all the children's apparel from the cloakrooms. Timber thieves are cutting their way through the claims of others in the mountains; many a brisk skirmish is fought among the pines. Ghouls are robbing the dead not only of jewelry but coffins. The armory of the Pitkin Light Cavalry is looted of arms and ammunition. Coffee Joe's, largest of the negro gambling saloons, and the house of Judge Pendery, a Carbonate King, are dynamited. In a drunken fury Kate Armstead, Sioux-African queen of the quarter, fires and destroys Coon Row. At least two attempts are made to burn the town in hope of plunder during the excitement. " A person would naturally suppose that real silver is found in sufficient quantities about Leadville to make it unnecessary to make spurious articles or import them from abroad. However the supposition may stand, the facts show that a considerable amount of counterfeit halves and quarters are afloat in the city." " There is a gang of ruffians living in a frame shanty on Fifth Street who are constantly on the watch for unprotected females, whom they insult with foul propositions and filthy epithets. . . . The police should keep an eye on this gang." " Last night about eight o'clock five men armed with revolvers and shotguns came bursting into the Long Branch Saloon on the Big Evans road in great excitement. They said they were looking for the man who had attempted to outrage the daughter of Mr. Welsh who keeps a saloon in the neighborhood. The little girl is only three years old."

Every night men are assaulted by footpads not only in the lonely dark side streets but on the principal thoroughfares. Many a jaw is broken and many a skull fractured in murderous attacks with sandbags, metal pipe, clubs, stones, iron wagon pins, hatchets and axes. So many known footpads and bandits openly walk the streets and prowl the surrounding highways that stage companies practically refuse to transport coin and bullion by raising their rates to prohibitive heights. Again and again the *Chronicle* gives warning of twelve " road agents " hiding in California Gulch from which they plan to swoop down upon the stage coaches and raid the banks some noontime. The *Chronicle* has made the most alarming discovery but does not yet dare specify.

Many men disappear never to be seen or heard of again. It is no doubt true that in the restless chaotic camp many are reported missing who merely drifted away unnoticed. But it is also true that a number were secretly done to death — crimes rendered practically impossible to detect, according to the *Herald,* because " victims could be buried in the cemetery without a certificate from the coroner or even from a physician." Three well-to-do visitors, the *Chronicle* announces in June, have been missing several weeks. " They were taking in the sights, got separated from their friends and have been seen no more. Their friends know these men were murdered. They were hustled in some dark alley — every alley is dark — or into one of the five hundred dark dens in these dark alleys, killed, robbed, put into a box and perhaps taken to the City Cemetery and buried in an unmarked grave."

Yet hired pamphleteers and local boosters can attempt at this very time to represent that Leadville is as orderly and almost as quiet as the " most Puritanic town in New England." Reports of crime and violence, they assert, are grossly and maliciously exaggerated. Certainly that is not the opinion of the local press which frankly admits that the reports are " false " in a different sense — that the reality is far blacker than they paint it.

" Not one-twentieth part of the depredations committed by the several scores of well-known bunko thieves and highway robbers in the city ever find their way into print. None of the local papers desire to deter capital and enterprise from seeking this camp. They report only the most glaring crimes that are publicly known."

Although good citizens are clearly in a majority during even the worst of the Reign of the Footpads, they are disorganized and powerless. Nor can they place any great reliance upon the police for protection. In fact, the police themselves become increasingly suspect — and with good reason. Riddled with politics, the force is notoriously inefficient. "A man with influence gets himself appointed, is numbered and branded with a star and turned loose. From this time on, he runs wild as it were. He has no instructions what to do and what not to do. He makes arrests when he feels like it, and sometimes tries and discharges his own prisoners. There are citizens who, owing to the murmurings of an approaching Vigilante storm, would be glad to see this matter changed."

In the second place, the police from Mart Duggan down are as violently lawless as any desperado. On duty one evening Officer O'Connor entered a saloon and offered to set up the house. The negro porter asked if he was included. "For reply O'Connor knocked him down and kicked him in the head and groin." O'Connor was arrested. A party of seventy-five men soon collected near the jail, "all armed both with shotguns and six-shooters, the latter being frequently discharged." Led by ex-Officer Kelly, a desperate character constantly in trouble, the gang demanded O'Connor's release. A magistrate was awakened and hurried to the jail to free O'Connor on bail. "After the release the crowd quietly dispersed and returned to its State Street headquarters."

Lastly and worst of all, many of the police appear to have been in league with criminals and bunkos. When honest men complain of being robbed and assaulted, they themselves are arrested and long held in custody, ostensibly to assure their presence as witnesses in the event, always remote, that their assailants will be brought to trial. One naive citizen, still bleeding from a savage attack, points out a notorious desperado as the offender, is himself arrested and thrown into the single small cell of the jail. At the moment it contains forty-four hardened criminals, including the offending footpad and many of his confederates. These pounce upon the robbed citizen and beat him almost to death. When he screams to the jailer for help, the latter growls, " Oh, hell, let them give it to you. Who cares? "

" There is a general feeling," remarks the *Chronicle* in reporting this incident, " that every man must be his own bodyguard and be prepared to shoot down anyone who attempts to invade his personal or property rights " — dangerous doctrine no doubt, but inevitable under the circumstances. Robbed on State Street in broad daylight, a miner gathered witnesses and followed the culprit as he walked boldly up the street. Upon meeting a policeman all identify the thief and demand his arrest. " The thief conversed with the officer for a short time and then handed back to Mr. Devins his two $20 bills. The officer and the thief smiled, and Mr. Devins, the man robbed, fortunately escaped being locked in a felon's cell."

As the summer of '79 advances, considerable activity among both good and bad citizens becomes apparent. " The respectables are busily organizing a Vigilance Association to hang the bunkos by the neck till they are dry. The bunkos, who complain of dull trade on account of the opposition of the respectables, are actively engaged in preparing to hang all those who have or may hereafter interfere with their profession. They consider themselves sufficiently strong to take charge of the city, choose their own mayor and city magistrate, and appoint their police force. There is a third party consisting of highway practitioners, road agents, put-hands-up and stand-and-deliver professions. An attempted fusion between this last party and the bunkos has fallen through. With these three parties in full operation, about every man in Leadville can make arrangements to pull hemp about four days after the ball opens."

But first a preliminary skirmish under legal auspices occurs between the bunkos and respectables. Caught red-handed, a desperado is indicted and brought to trial. All his confederates turn out in force to intimidate the court and swear mightily to the prisoner's preposterous alibi. With the explanation that "men look so near alike in Leadville that it is difficult to tell one from another," the jury acquits the cutthroat. "The bunkos positively, unequivocally and without the least reservation of mind or matter, have things all their own way in Leadville," so the *Chronicle* concludes from the trial. "Footpads may rob a man in broad daylight on the most public streets, and there is no civil power in Colorado that can give the robbed redress."

Matters come to such a pass that Alderman Kavanaugh seriously offers a resolution that the mayor "be empowered to discharge the entire Police Force, Fire Warden, City Jailer, Street Commissioner, Deputy Clerk and City Engineer." Mayor James speaks in favor of the motion. As every ordinance is flaunted and juries refuse to convict on the clearest evidence, there is "no use wasting time, paper, ink and light in discussing and passing ordinances for the good government of the city," he declares, adding ominously, "I have lived under no law and am prepared to do so again."

The motion is lost after long debate and the usual formal processes of government continue to function feebly as the camp drifts slowly under the arbitrary law of Judge Lynch. In a last desperate effort to strengthen the forces of law and order, Mayor

James appoints a private detective under his immediate command to spy less upon criminals than upon the police whose lawlessness and neglect of duty become daily more flagrant.

Storekeepers unite to organize and support a private police force of eight men to stand duty from sunset to daylight. They are " to try doors, watch for burglars and other bad characters, convey messages, collect letters, answer calls and make themselves useful to the public generally." The manifold activities of the Merchants' Police are reflected in their report for December, '79. Altogether they answer more than five hundred calls. They pick up thirteen starved or inebriated men lying in the streets and rescue them from freezing. They discover and help extinguish three fires — one from a lamp explosion, the other two bearing every mark of incendiary origin. They make fourteen arrests themselves and assist the " Metropolitan " police to make sixteen more. They escort seventy helpless or frightened citizens to their homes and help quell twenty bloody brawls and riots in the streets.

With the rush continuing from day to day matters move rapidly toward a crisis during September and October as cold, hunger and crime increase together. The *Chronicle* announces that it is " keeping a list of those robbed every night until the Vigilance Committee starts giving hanging bees." Again next day the editors return to the subject. " It is not generally known that there is a Vigilance Committee in this city in full working order. A large proportion of their number is so eager to begin operations that they are out every night watching for prey. It is the determination of the Committee, many of whose members have been compelled to hold up their hands and deliver, to burn the first highwayman they catch over a slow fire until he is dead." But threats of Vigilante violence impress bunkos and bandits as little as militia and fire companies upon parade.

" THEY'VE COME. First Appearance of Road Agents in Leadville. They Bounce a Coach within Sight of the City." Alarm knows no bounds next day when the *Chronicle* lets slip what it has long known — that California Gulch harbors none other than the almost legendary Jesse James himself. With him are the two Ford brothers, Charlie and Bob, the latter of whom treacherously shoots James through the back three years later. Although they are living quietly and working hard on a claim in the gulch, James and his followers are plainly suspected of the robbery. But no one dares move against them. A few weeks later when two other coaches are held up almost on Chestnut Street, a great howl of indignation sweeps the helpless baffled city. Jesse James is again suspected most unjustly, for all three robberies are soon laid at the door of one John Fraser, Captain of Police.

Lynch! Lynch! Lynch! cries the press. Lynch! echo the judges, one declaring most naively that " every policeman in the city is anxious to have a hanging." An organized mob is now ready to move, but no one quite dares take the lead. It remains for a little German barber to precipitate the crisis. Held up on State Street one November midnight, Carl Bockhouse shoots one footpad dead and wounds the other who escapes. Several hours later a youth of twenty is found bleeding and freezing to death in a doorway nearby. Suspected as the wounded robber, he is arrested but stoutly denies his guilt, protesting he was wounded in a saloon brawl, as he might well have been. No one ever charges the youth with being a professional footpad, and he convinces many of his innocence. But whether innocent or not, a question never to be determined, he can have been only the clumsiest kind of an amateur in crime as proved by the disastrous holdup itself. At worst, he is no more than one of many poor unfortunates driven to robbery by hunger and cold.

But the populace is not interested in extenuating circumstances or nice questions of evidence. It is rejoiced beyond measure that someone at last has dared resist criminal violence. Next morning Bockhouse in his barber's chair is raised on the shoulders of the mob and paraded in triumph through the streets, " with the wildest cheers and waving of banners." The celebration ends at a jeweler's where the barber's admirers present him " with a gold watch and chain costing $250 to acknowledge his valor and courage."

The morale of the respectables markedly improves until on November 19th, a few nights later, the Vigilantes strike under cover of dark. City Jailer Caldwell, so he testifies later, is relieved of duty early and sent home. A heavily armed mob collects on the outskirts of camp, descends upon the jail about midnight, overpowers the turnkey with a show of force, unlocks the single cell, chooses its victims and drags them forth. Somehow word of the proceedings has leaked out. All respectables but those in the mob remain apprehensively at home. All bunkos and bandits go into hiding. The streets are strangely quiet and deserted, remaining so throughout the night.

Those abroad early next morning discover two lank black forms dangling from the rafters of the new City Hall under construction on Harrison Avenue. There, for all to see, they hang many hours before they are cut down. Upon their backs the Vigilantes have pinned lists naming some eighty undesirables who are to leave town before sunset. Below appears a warning that the Vigilantes have their eyes upon many more whose names they do not happen to know.

The lynched are readily identified as Stewart, the boy suspected of robbery, and Charles Frodsham, arrested with Mart Duggan for an attack on the Highland Chief mine. The coroner returns a verdict of death "at the hands of parties unknown." But the coroner is alone in his ignorance, if real and not feigned, for all in camp know the facts. There are indeed two active Vigilante committees in town. One consists of "Gentlemen Vigs organized among the more wealthy portion of the community." As their ultimate aims are already rather suspect, another committee has been recruited "among the mining and laboring element." The *Chronicle* has good reason to know that "the city is indebted to the former association for the work done at the jail a few mornings since."

Why the Gentlemen Vigs chose only Stewart and Frodsham when any number of known murderers and notorious ruffians were roaming at large, notably Big Ed Burns and his gang of desperados, is rather difficult to understand. Perhaps they were restrained by the same fear of reprisal which so long held the *Chronicle* from specifically naming Jesse James as an object of suspicion. Stewart was not to be feared, for he was alone and without confederates. Frodsham commanded a crew of lot-jumpers, but they were really not desperate characters. Neither Stewart nor Frodsham had taken life. To many the choice of the Gentlemen Vigs seemed so partial and ominous that poorer people generally, led by working miners, promptly organized themselves into an armed body seven hundred strong.

For weeks after the lynchings a cloud of gloomy apprehension hangs over a subdued and strangely sober camp. Who will strike next and where? Business is virtually abandoned. The military companies are mustered to patrol the streets day and night. Roughs and criminals go into hiding or withdraw. Big Ed Burns leads his gang down the canyon to Buena Vista, the terminus at the time of the Denver and Rio Grande Railway pushing on hurriedly toward Leadville. Burns and his ruffians take the town by storm and terrorize it for several weeks. But the freighters and workers there rise in force, " select a stout piece of rope " and set out to overpower the desperados. Unused to such open and spirited opposition, the bunkos flee in all directions. Leadville breathes a sigh of relief when word comes at length that Big Ed has been lynched in Arizona for murdering a deputy sheriff.

During all this time Jesse James and his followers, although suspected of many villainies, live quietly and unmolested in California Gulch. A year later when he departs, one of his gang confesses that their exemplary conduct has not been as innocent as might appear. Upon carefully looking over the ground they decided against action, he declared, because the roads of escape were too few. If true, Jesse James feared and respected local authorities far more than almost anonymous hundreds whose brazen deeds, far from spreading their fame over the earth, earned them no more than a passing notoriety in an evanescent boom town.

Gradually alarm subsides. The town begins to talk of other things than the lynchings. Business is resumed. By Christmas time some note " evidence that a feeling of confidence is returning to the city, for simple drunks are again approaching their former average." But unhappily, as confidence returns, so do the bad men. Again on the streets are seen the familiar faces of bunkos, footpads and murderers. All set to work with a vengeance, until in October, '80, crimes of violence reach almost incredible totals for even the most turbulent camp of 30,000 people. Within this single month five are arrested for assault and battery, twenty-eight for assault with deadly weapons and forty for murder — ten times the homicide rate in Chicago in 1929. Another hanging occurs in Leadville in March, '81, but under legal auspices. Gilbert and Rosencrantz are executed publicly in the streets for several particularly brutal slayings. Of the many hundreds of murderers in jail or at large in camp during the boom these two alone pay the extreme penalty for their crimes.

But if the Gentlemen Vigs have little success in suppressing crime, they succeed rather better in breaking a strike which is regarded apparently as a more serious crime than murder. As early as June, '79, miners talk of organizing a union. At the time there are eight thousand of them working twelve-hour shifts at an average wage of $3 a day, a high money wage but during the inflation of the boom a low real wage. The authorities and Carbonate Kings both frown upon the proposed union as dangerous and revolutionary. As the miners themselves prove lukewarm, each hoping yet to strike it rich and become a bonanza king, the union is not effected.

The first labor difficulties in camp occur at the Malta Smelter where furnace-keepers ($3.50 a day) and their helpers ($3) strike for an eight-hour day and the installation of a few fundamental safety devices. Within two weeks three men die of frightful wounds at this one smelter. Growing faint from the terrific heat and fumes of the furnace, they stagger back against boiling slagpots to be burned alive under a flood of white lava. All are forced to work twelve hours a day and frequently long periods of overtime, which " in the poisonous atmosphere of the tanks is enough to kill a horse," as even the conservative *Chronicle* protests. Supported by almost the entire community, the smelter strikers obtain concessions.

Late in '79, encouraged by this successful strike, the miners begin to agitate for an increase of wages to $3.75 a day. They complain, too, of unnecessarily dangerous working conditions. Many mines, the Little Pittsburgh and Crysolite conspicuously, are paying such huge dividends monthly that no money remains for safe or even economical development, resulting in great ultimate loss to investors. More seriously, it causes the death of many miners from falling rock in shafts and tunnels inadequately timbered. Many a miner breaks his neck in falling from battered iron ore buckets when these strike the rock wall of shafts and tip over. Premature explosions of blasting powder result in more than a dozen serious accidents, almost half of them fatal, within a period of four months. The very nature of the ore results in so much serious sickness that an attempt is made to establish a hospital to treat miners for lead poisoning. Miners die by the scores of pneumonia contracted during long exhausting hours in cold wet unventilated mines. But agitation among the miners at this time is checked when Gentlemen Vigs, fresh from hanging Stewart and Frodsham, accuse the miners' leaders of being " Molly Macguires " and forcibly escort them from camp with a warning not to return.

Late in May, '80, the miners strike. The immediate cause is an order issued at the Crysolite that anyone found talking or smoking underground is to be discharged instantly. Rather than carry out this order the shift bosses resign, declaring the men work hard enough as it is. The Crysolite miners select one Michael Mooney as their spokesman and under his leadership march from mine to mine. All men walk out and by afternoon only a few carpenters and timber-haulers are working at the shafts.

Next morning the miners at a great mass meeting on Carbonate Hill formulate their demands — eight-hour shifts and a wage increase from $3 to $4 a day. Then, some four thousand strong, drawn up four abreast, led by Mooney on horseback and a band, the miners march through town to Fryer Hill. They march in perfect silence and the community is awed. There is not a drunken man among them and the best of feeling prevails, according to the *Democrat*. A committee is appointed to confer with the mine managers. But as these have been instructed by their companies to concede nothing, they walk out of the conference and throw heavy guards about the mines. The Crysolite and Little Chief in particular resemble established military camps with pickets, outposts and breastworks. At another mass meeting on Fryer Hill the miners first pledge themselves to refrain from destroying property and then send an embassy to ask that the armed guards be withdrawn. The embassy returns to report failure.

" Stop the damned pumps," roars the crowd. But Mooney advises peace and order, and turns the energies of the meeting to the organization of a Miners' Cooperative Union. A hat is passed to raise funds but less than $10 is collected. Altogether, remarks the *Chronicle,* the meeting was " as orderly as could be expected with the thermometer nearly at zero and with flakes of snow cutting the faces of the audience."

Shopkeepers feeling the pinch call a combined meeting of business men, mine owners, mine managers and strikers. The Reverend Mackay enters the lists with a hysterical appeal to the miners: " Look across the ocean to poor starving Ireland, to the working men of England, to the down-trodden of Russia; and I ask you, are you justified in the course you have taken? " Business men talk compromise and seem on the point of triumph when George Daly, Superintendent of the Little Chief and mouthpiece of the mine owners, makes a most unconciliatory speech. Prophesying violence and bloodshed, he walks out. After a week of inactivity Daly resolves to open the mines and resume work at all hazards. The miners make no announcement, but it is rightly suspected that they will resist. Now the county commissioners, the Sheriff and the editor of the *Chronicle* issue a proclamation calling upon all good citizens to stand behind the authorities in the assault they plan upon the miners. Such pressure is brought to bear that Mooney feels compelled to sign a pledge that the strikers will not interfere with miners desiring to return to work. " From the moment Mr. Mooney relinquished the right to prevent men from working for less than $4, the strike became harmless. . . . Thus ended the great strike at Leadville," the *Chronicle* complacently announces.

But that night and throughout the next day there is rapid and continuous firing all up and down the gulches, with the Little Chief and the Little Pittsburgh as the chief targets. Miners returning to work are roughly handled. The Sheriff musters the Carbonate Rifles to disperse the strikers, several of whom are shot and wounded when they resist. The Union Veterans stand ready to respond instantly to three bugle blasts. Two companies of militia are dispatched from Denver. Meanwhile, those rushing in to steal the miners' jobs prove most inefficient and in their ignorance of mining so destructive that most managers drop all pretense of operating. They are infuriated at their inability to hire trained workers, asserting that most of these are being intimidated by a few dozen strikers. " The authorities and managers are using every means to ferret out the men who are doing this work and giving them warnings, with the commendable idea of making short work of them and setting an example that will have a salutary effect upon all offenders of this class." But nothing is accomplished and matters drift along for another two weeks, with beggary and robbery on the increase, with Strayhorse and Big Evans gulches echoing every night with rifle fire.

"Road Agents near Leadville—Searching a Commercial Traveler"

Harrison Avenue, with Tabor Opera House at the left

The Carbonate Kings now frighten the community by threatening to close down the mines for six months. This threat appears to have been part of a calculated attack upon the City Treasury. Abetted by the local press which daily shrieks commands at the miners to return to work as the strike is hurting business, the Mine Owners' Association intimates through the *Chronicle* that citizens have signally failed in their duty and that the least the City can now do is assume full responsibility for the armed thugs at the mines, including payment of their salaries at $10 a day. This is an especially brazen piece of business, for the mines have violently and successfully resisted every effort to tax them on anything more than surface improvements. One mine owner carries out the threat, ordering his superintendent to stop operations until November, remarking that it will then be possible to get " all the labor we want at $2 a day."

The threat fails, however, for the authorities dare not manifest their partisanship so openly. Increasingly angry, Carbonate Kings and shopkeepers now meet in Tabor's vast apartment at the Opera House to organize a Committee of Safety " patterned after the famous San Francisco Vigilance Committee." Pinkerton detectives are hired to watch the strikers. Arms for additional military companies are ordered. Next morning every store closes at ten o'clock as shopkeepers, leading their clerks, march to the police station to enroll their names in the several military organizations. These are now organized as a regiment with Editor-owner C. C. Davis of the *Chronicle* as commander-in-chief. A demonstration in force is decided upon. Together with a large number of mine guards, the regiment marches through town armed with revolvers, shotguns, repeating rifles, clubs, axe handles and other weapons. Tabor makes a martial address from the balcony of the Opera House. It shocks the *Chronicle* to report

that the regiment has been greeted with hoots and catcalls by the
street crowds which seem to be largely in sympathy with the
strikers. It displeases Editor and Commander-in-Chief Davis
even more to note that the miners remain "exasperatingly quiet."

Five days later the Carbonate Kings petition Governor Pitkin
to proclaim martial law. The Governor agrees and Sheriff Tucker
forthwith issues a remarkable proclamation commanding the
miners to dissolve their unlawful organization and go back to
work. A ten o'clock curfew law is established. Saloons are ordered to remain closed day and night. All without means of support are to be arrested as vagrants and made liable to a fine not
exceeding $100. More than four hundred, including a number
of strike leaders, are so arrested.

Fortunately for the honor of Leadville and Colorado, which
is thus spared an earlier Cripple Creek and Ludlow, Pitkin entrusts the high command to David J. Cook, the terror of all outlaws since the days of the Reynolds gang. From City Marshall of
Denver he has risen to become Major-General of Militia. Cook
arrives, according to his own report, to find a fatal collision imminent. He discovers mine owners, business men and property-
holders arrayed against the miners, with a large lawless element
playing one side against the other in the hope of plunder during
the conflict and confusion. Dispossessing General Tabor and establishing himself in his private apartment at the Opera House,
Cook immediately sends reliable men among the crowds to learn
what is afoot, especially on the part of the Committee of Safety.
He quickly learns that the Committee is plotting to arrest
Mooney and five other leaders, deliver them into the hands of
military organizations friendly to the Committee to be spirited
away and lynched. Cook early discovers that the local military
companies which he must use are not to be trusted to preserve

order. From their ranks he carefully selects three hundred men whom he sends out to report any suspicious gatherings and arrest all defying the curfew order. At midnight he learns that a mob has collected and is only awaiting his retirement for the night to seize the miners' leaders and hustle them away to their death.

Cook meets the challenge decisively with his usual fine instinct for fair play. "I sent for Captain Murphy and Lieutenant Mart Duggan of the Tabor Tigers, a company formed principally of sporting men, who were opposed to hanging on general principles, arguing that it was something that might happen to anybody. On being questioned as to whether their men could be trusted to round up 'stranglers' or not, Murphy replied: 'Now you're shoutin'. If there's anything in the world these boys are dead sore on, it's stranglers.'" By squads the Tigers are sent out to patrol the streets with orders to arrest any group of three or more, whether militiamen or civilians. Several arrests are sufficient to avert the storm. By daylight all is quiet.

Two days later the saloons are allowed to reopen. Next day the Governor decides to end the reign of martial law, but a large part of the camp protests. "We request you to leave the matter of military law in this county in the hands of Major-General Cook. It is for the best interests of all," telegraph the miners. A few days later the strikers declare their willingness to return to work at their former wages but insist upon eight-hour shifts. But mine owners and managers refuse even to consider this, serving formal notice "that their right to regulate the affairs of their mines is absolute and that they will not submit to any dictation as to hours of labor or rates of wages from any person or association." Exhausted by hunger, the miners capitulate and three nights later the victors celebrate with a grand military ball at the Clarendon. In the view of the "Radical bonanza kings of the Carbonate Camp," as even the conservative *Rocky Mountain News* of Denver protests, "laborers have no rights. If they assert any, they ought to be hung by the Vigilance Committee."

But if the Carbonate Kings win the strike, their triumph also marks the end of the boom, for it brings to light the fact that Leadville's largest and richest mines are nearing exhaustion from hasty reckless exploitation. The Crysolite has actually been borrowing money to maintain high dividends. When this is discovered, the price of its shares falls sharply from $46 to $3.75. A similar state of affairs exists in the Little Pittsburgh and Little Chief. The stock of both drops from many dollars to a few cents a share. The Little Chief should never have paid dividends of more than $50,000 a month, according to the mining engineer George Daly, leader of the Carbonate Kings' forces during the strike. Instead, it continued to pay double that amount up to the day of its premature collapse. There were charges that the stock in all these mines had been manipulated by insiders, with the result that Eastern investors began to look askance at the Leadville field.

"The year of '80 has been one of mingled prosperity and melancholy, of gladness and vicissitudes. The wild and reckless career of unchecked prosperity, the great boom with which 1880 opened, received a violent set-back early in the Spring," as the *Democrat* declared late in the year, "and from that time on, all through the summer and Fall, it was an incessant struggle with adversity, with widespread distrust, with undeserved obloquy and loss of confidence."

Although the peak of production is reached in '82, when the mines produce more than $17,000,000 of bullion, the camp in other respects begins slowly to decline. In '81 it is remarked that the variety theaters and sporting houses are much less crowded and prosperous than a year or two before. Much less champagne flows. Millions have been spent in these resorts and " yet not one manager can be pointed out today as the possessor of a handsome independence," remarks the *Chronicle* at the time.

One after another the banks fail, impoverishing many. The Grant smelter burns and is rebuilt in Denver. Fires break out with startling regularity. The Windsor Hotel and the Palace of Fashion, the camp's largest department store, burn and are not replaced. Many fires, obviously, are of incendiary origin, although but one merchant is convicted of arson committed to obtain insurance on his stock and building. Tabor definitely abandons Leadville in favor of Denver in '81, and is followed by other Carbonate Kings. The decline of Leadville is not rapid during the next decade but continues steadily from year to year.

" The Leadville of '79 is now a thing of the past," writes one who knew it then and comes to revisit it in '89. " The omnipresent six-shooters that used to outnumber the men of the mining camp ten years ago are rarely seen here in public. If men carry pistols, it is in their pockets, and the shoot-the-lights-out ruffianism of the old frontier days rarely shows even a symptom of revival."

XIII. Dies Faustus

" Lightning has struck Tabor again; he has made more money in four years than a man ever made."

By '81, as the Leadville boom subsides, Denver has established itself beyond challenge as the capital of all the surrounding plain and mountain country. It is no longer the wild bleak straggling settlement it was when last seen in the 'Sixties. The railroads have come to make it an important distributing center. Increasing tribute is paid it by farmers along rich river bottoms and cattlemen who have carved out great ranches on the Plains and in the mountain parks. Denver is already favorably known as a health resort. It has profited, too, from the great silver flood from Fryer, Carbonate and Iron hills. It draws revenue as well from the Clear Creek camps which are enjoying a renascence. Senator Hill has built one large smelter here and now Grant comes from Leadville to build another. As the Magic City begins slowly to decline, it is Denver, " Queen City of the Plains," which attracts Tabor and other Carbonate Kings with the hope that they may here increase their fortunes and perhaps enjoy a few amenities of life.

In comparison with Leadville, Denver is almost sedate. Already it has the veneer of civilization which it has never since lost. While not remarkable for either convenience or design, its buildings begin to be less obviously makeshift. It has a number of large houses surrounded with lawns and trees. " The dis-

tinguishing charm of Denver architecture," so a contemporary remarks, "is its endless variety. Almost every citizen is laudably
ambitious to build a house unlike that of his neighbor, and is
more desirous that it shall have some novel feature than that it
shall be surpassingly beautiful."

In '82 Denver holds a Great Mining and Industrial Exposition.
Tabor takes the lead in building a large fair building south of
the city to exhibit Colorado's products and resources — ores of all
kinds, grains, vegetables, fruits, factory goods, and art. Gold
and silver medals are awarded to the best exhibits of each kind,
together with "a handsomely engraved certificate suitable for
hanging." Any number of special prizes are offered — a plush
piano stool for the best display of silk-worm eggs and cocoons,
an accordion for the best portrait in crayon. Tabor and Bush
offer cash prizes for artistic floral designs and the best collections
of dried Colorado flowers. The art gallery at the Exposition is
especially remarked by the press, with the comment that "it is
high time for our gentlemen of wealth to begin to encourage
taste and show it in their homes."

As Denver grows larger and more circumspect, there is a smell
of moral reform in the air. The Denver Citizens' Protective Association is formed to prevent "ladies from killing themselves
with tight lacing." The police close all brothels except on Holladay (formerly McGaa, later Market) Street. "Cigarette smoking
is rapidly becoming a national curse," declare other agitators.
"No person can smoke them habitually without serious injury
to health." Women of the town are forbidden to use the Exposition Road on Sundays. A Law and Order Association directs
its energies largely to closing stores and saloons on Sundays. Led
by Dean Hart of St. John's Cathedral, parsons thunder against
the gambling house of Bat Masterson, old gun-fighter, and espe-

cially against the Palace, famous gambling saloon and variety theater kept by Ed Chase, owner of the Progressive of earlier days. Dean Hart pronounces it a " death-trap to young men, a foul den of vice and corruption." But the popularity of the Palace is little affected. Among his " almost nightly visitors " at this time, Chase entertains Tabor, Edward Wolcott and Tom Bowen, all soon to be Senators. " I always took good care of them," said Chase later. " All of them liked to josh the girls and some of them would play strong, especially Wolcott and Bowen. Wolcott was at the same time the finest gentleman and the biggest loafer I ever saw." Chase is soon devoted to a new and most charming client, Eugene Field, just arrived to become city editor of the local *Tribune*. Sensing the beginning of a moral crusade, Field begins to promote the cause in his own way in occasional paragraphs later collected and published as the *First Primer*:

This is a Bottle. What is in Bottle? Very bad whisky. It has been sent to the Local Editor. He did not buy it. If he had Bought it, the Whisky would have been Poorer than it is. Little Children, you Must never Drink Bad Whisky.

What is this Nasty looking Object? It is a Chew of Tobacco. Oh, how Naughty it is to Use the Filthy Weed. It makes the teeth black and Spoils the Parlor Carpet. Go quick and Throw the horrid Stuff away. Put it in the Ice Cream Freezer or in the Coffee Pot where Nobody can See it. Little girls, you Should never Chew Tobacco.

Tabor, approaching the zenith of his career, is the man of the hour. His enterprise is the talk of Denver and all Colorado. He establishes his son Maxcy as partner of Bill Bush at the new

Windsor Hotel with its charming Ladies' Ordinary, Grand Banquet Room and Russian and Turkish baths. " These oriental ablutionary parlors," they advertise, " are elegantly fitted up and handsomely furnished throughout in white marble." Tabor talks of building himself a hotel — " such a one as Denver never heard of or even dreamed of," he writes Bush. On Larimer Street he spends $325,000 to build the Tabor Block, " something new in Colorado architecture." As Colorado granite will not do, stone is imported from Ohio, even that for the sidewalks. " Each stone was chiselled and fitted ready for its place. Thus was reared, like Solomon's Temple, a magnificent six-story building, with brownstone front, ornate but tasteful. Over the front arch are engraved the words *Dies Faustus.*"

Lucky day indeed for Denver, which is now given its Tabor Opera House. It is to be as impressive as money can make it. With Frank Edbrooke, local architect, Tabor goes East to make notes upon all larger and handsomer theaters. Edbrooke is sent on to Europe to continue his studies there. But in the end Tabor is " practically his own architect " in designing " that matchless specimen of modern architecture, the Tabor Opera House, with its perfect plan and arrangement of detail, the auditorium with its graceful curves, its grand columns, exquisite carvings and luxurious appointments, the stores opening upon the streets, and the furnace, pumps and artesian wells in the basement." A five-story office building of red pressed brick with white stone trim, " an oddity of architectural originality," the general style of the Opera House is perhaps most justly described as " modified Egyptian Moresque " — a phrase coined for it by Eugene Field. No one will ever amuse Field as much as Tabor does during the next few years.

The theater proper, so Tabor announces, is " designed upon

the selected features of the Covent Garden Theater, London, and the Academy of Music, Paris, and combines the beauties and excellencies of both." It is finished entirely in cherry brought from Japan. Marble comes from Italy for pilasters, wainscoting and lintels. It is a large theater, seating fifteen hundred in parquet, dress circle, balcony and gallery. The beamed ceiling has at its center a large dome of cathedral glass. From the top of it depends a huge chandelier of cut crystals partially concealing many hundreds of gas jets. The red cherry is everywhere richly carved and upholstered. Heavy silk fabrics brought from Lyons at $50 a yard line each of the boxes, rising in three tiers. Over them rare Italian tapestries are stretched as canopies. Two massive cherry columns support the proscenium arch, above which appears a painting of Hector quitting Andromache for battle. "The handiwork of many artists is apparent in frescoes throughout the house."

The stage itself is large and well equipped, with an elaborately invested Green Room and many large dressing rooms below. Tabor spends a "small fortune on the curtain alone," giving the commission to a Robert Hopkin of Detroit who is recommended to him as "essentially an artist in temperament, and as an executant, especially strong and effective in marine compositions." But the Tabor Grand's curtain, renowned in the West from that day to this, presents no seascape but an old Roman city, its former grandeur departed. Beautiful temples and proud palaces of marble are seen tumbling to the ground on every hand. Only a few broken columns remain standing. Fierce lions and other beasts of prey lurk in the shattered ruins soon to vanish under a tangled mat of grass, trees and vines. Below this scene of melancholy desolation there appear these lines of Kingsley's, their irony growing more bitter with the years:

> *So fleet the works of man*
> *Back to the earth again,*
> *Ancient and holy things*
> *Fade like a dream,*
> *And the hand of the master is dust.*

As the opening night approaches, a heated and acrimonious debate rages upon the question of whether it will be a " full-dress swallow-tail affair " or not. Both the *News* and the *Tribune* devote many long editorials to the issue. Tabor insists upon the proper formality and is roundly abused. This, as the *Tribune* protests, " does not furnish good grounds for an assault. The wearing of a dress coat has never been regarded as a crime, even in Colorado. A man who will not wear a dress coat on a dress occasion is a snob. . . . When Tabor is before the public as a politician, he is legitimate subject for criticism. When he is before it as an enterprising citizen, he is not."

Tabor has installed Bill Bush as manager of the theater, and for the opening the latter secures the Emma Abbott English Grand Opera Company, which explains Miss Abbott's visit to Leadville. For the occasion programs are printed on gorgeous silk. The railways offer low excursion rates from all points within several hundred miles.

On September 5, 1881, an evening long remembered, the Tabor Grand is opened with *Lucia*. A drizzle is falling, unfortunately, as the fashionable and the curious depart for the theater. There is an annoying scarcity of hacks. Regardless of the rain, a large crowd has collected in the street to see the more eminent drive smartly up and alight under the bright marquee. A red plush carpet crosses the sidewalk and ascends the steps into the lobby. Here to one side is a luxurious reception room where the ladies doff their " cloaks of snowy plush " and arrange their jewels and costly gowns — " heavily-embroidered silken crapes and exquisite combinations of cashmere and swan's down, satin-lined." The gentlemen improve the interval in the large bright saloon to the other side.

There are cheers in the street as Tabor himself arrives to push into the brilliant animated lobby. He is pleased with all he sees there but a portrait on the wall. He calls Bill Bush aside and pointing to it, inquires, so the story goes:

" Who's that? "

" That's Shakespeare."

" Who the hell is he? "

" Why, the greatest author of plays who ever lived."

" Well, what has he ever done for Colorado? Take it down and put my picture up there."

As Denver society slowly jostles its way inside the theater, it finds it everywhere garlanded and festooned with flowers, with any number of floral pieces designed to spell " Tabor." It is a gay scene. Tabor's private box, lined with white satin and elaborately furnished, is wholly filled by a great horseshoe of flowers.

In time the lights grow dim and conversation drops to excited whispers as the curtain rises slowly to reveal Bill Bush, bowing and smiling, who is pleased to announce that Miss Abbott will now sing the mad scene from *Lucia*. It is received with thunderous applause, and " honest Little Emma " is called back to receive a floral harp. She will sing no more this evening as other rites are to be performed.

An unknown gentleman appears upon the stage to ask Governor Tabor, if he is in the house, to please come forward. After a few moments Tabor appears from the wings, obviously nervous and flustered. With his stumbling gait more pronounced than usual he crosses the stage to great cheering and clapping. The audience now rises to its feet to cheer him again and again. This, unquestionably, is the high moment of his life, although Tabor himself may have more highly prized an evening two years later at Washington. But this evening of popular acclaim deeply moves him. It takes all bitterness from those long lean years of obscurity in the mountains. His present position of splendor and honor is brighter because of them. The audience rejoices with him and for the most part bears him only good will. But many ask about Augusta, who is conspicuously absent.

The gentleman upon the stage at last makes himself heard and at the conclusion of a long eulogy asks Tabor to accept an album autographed by all the workers, artists and contractors who had a part in building the theater under his direction. Then in behalf of the citizens of Denver another speaker presents him with a gold watch and a gold fob " engraved with the milestones on his road to wealth and fame." Genuinely and modestly moved by the ovation, Tabor can only mutter a few words of acknowledgment which drop unheard and are forever lost as the audience rises to its feet to cheer him again.

A large audience, although not in evening dress, attends the second night and all through the two weeks that Emma Abbott remains. At her last performance she receives many handsome presents — a huge star of tuberoses and geraniums from Tabor. A great reception follows to which Tabor brings an autograph album. Miss Abbott inscribes her name under " Conquer or Die."

The Tabor Grand then enjoys a week of Gilbert and Sullivan. Lawrence Barrett comes to play *Hamlet, Othello* and *Julius Caesar*. The Madison Square Players offer *Hazel Kirke,* which is " doubtless better known to theater-goers than *Hamlet*." Rafael

Joseffy, Hungarian pianist, fails " to draw even a moderately full house." At the conclusion of the season Bill Bush announces that the undoubted favorites were Emma Abbott, Leavitt's Minstrels and Hasenwinkle's Ideal Dramatic Company in *Uncle Tom's Cabin*.

Early the next year Oscar Wilde arrives. Field makes a plea that he be received politely, " if not as a lecturer, then as one who may yet rank among the strong English poets, for his first volume certainly holds out such hope." Denver is somewhat more impressed with Wilde than Leadville. " He has taught no bad doctrine and advanced no startling innovations. He has simply said that the gentle and beautiful are pleasant in life and worthy of consideration. If aesthetes are fools, it is because they have a higher opinion of our powers of intellectual evolution than they should have." But Denver, like Leadville, finds that Wilde as a lecturer " never stirs his audience but in the direction of the door." After the lecture Wilde returns to dine late in his suite at the Windsor. Many visitors come pounding upon the door, including Tabor, who gives Wilde a pass allowing him to visit the Matchless mine while in Leadville. " Mr. Wilde expresses himself delighted, saying that of all things, that which he desired most was to visit a mine."

This same year the great Modjeska, Christine Nilsson and young Minnie Maddern appear at the Tabor Grand. " Miss Maddern is bright, talented and earnest, and it seems a great pity that her youth, beauty and talents should be handicapped and hampered by such a conglomeration of dramatic rot as *Fogg's Ferry,*" writes Field with fine critical appreciation. " A successor to Maggie Mitchell is demanded. Miss Maddern seems qualified to answer that demand." In later years she returns as Mrs. Fiske to surpass Field's first estimates of her singular gifts. Up to 1900 the stage at the Tabor Grand is trod by Booth, the

Salvinis, Irving, Jefferson, Drew, Mansfield, Forbes-Robertson, Mary Anderson, Clara Morris, Lily Langtry, Ada Rehan and many another famous player. After some years of cheap melodrama and cheaper vaudeville the Tabor Grand is transformed into a movie palace.

Although profits are relatively small, amounting to a mere $31,000 the first year, Tabor is delighted with the popularity of the opera house which is usually well filled. Now he begins to dream of building opera houses throughout the country. When certain of his mines in New Mexico begin to promise more than any of his Colorado strikes, it is " openly stated that if they pan out, the Governor will enter upon the erection of opera houses in New York, Chicago, Kansas City and San Francisco. Tabor has long had this scheme in view — in fact, his intimates say it is his pet ambition. He has divulged it to Eastern managers and they have encouraged him in it. All are to rival the Tabor Grand in splendor, the New York edifice to cost $2,000,000."

But Tabor, now at the zenith of his career, is too occupied elsewhere to realize his dream. His millions multiply from year to year. His income from his mines alone at this time cannot have been less than $4,000,000 annually, according to Hook. The crash of the Little Pittsburgh Consolidated and the Crysolite has not affected his fortune, for he disposed of his stock in both before the collapse. The Matchless continues to pay him $2,000 a day, and scores of other mines help swell his purse. His milling, lumbering, real estate, insurance, gas and water companies are still profitable. Now he strikes it again in the Tam O'Shanter and the Henrietta, the latter valued at $1,000,000.

From day to day Tabor expands his operations. As old mines play out, he buys new ones — in Colorado, New Mexico, Arizona and Texas. He buys the Colorado Fire Insurance Company to merge with his own. He buys patent rights to the cyanide process of extracting gold and spends $100,000 to erect a large mill in West Denver. He buys almost a half interest in the prosperous First National Bank of Denver controlled by Chaffee and Moffat. He plots with others to corner the wheat market. He speculates in corn as well. For $1,200,000 he buys a controlling interest in the Calumet and Chicago Canal and Dock Company, which owns a stretch of ground on Lake Michigan some ten miles south of the Chicago River. Tabor plans a great harbor and manufacturing center to rival Chicago itself. Finally he organizes the Tabor Investment Company, with agencies in New York, London, Amsterdam and Paris, " to buy and sell mines and fill orders for capitalists in all parts of the world." The company buys more mines — in Utah, California, Mexico and South America. It buys a great empire of 460,000 acres in southern Colorado. And by a master stroke gains a concession in Honduras of almost four hundred square miles, a vast empire rich in minerals and mahogany.

" In fine," remarks an Eastern financial journal after this coup, " the combined interests, mining and otherwise of Mr. Tabor, will make him the richest man in America in ten years. It is almost staggering to hear him talk of millions as glibly and unconcernedly as other men talk of hundreds. Mr. Tabor is far from being visionary. He does not look like a man whose head would be easily turned if the course of events should lift him to the highest pinnacle of fame in the councils of the nation or make him the greatest moneyed king of his day."

Tabor, in fact, has long had his eye upon the United States Senate. As lieutenant-governor he had hoped to advance a step nearer his goal by succeeding to the governor's chair. But he abandoned his aspirations as premature, realizing that more preparations were necessary to become a statesman. He has been ingratiating himself with the leaders of his party. At the most casual hint his purse flies open to forward the Republican cause. " Tabor is going to have the senatorship or know the reason why money has lost its potency. He has more of that excellent senatorial qualification than any one or two of the balance of the Republican crowd," as is remarked by the Denver *Tribune,* itself a Republican organ. But it adds, " Tom Bowen's gold is a very nightmare to other aspirants."

Tabor has every reason to fear Bowen, another bonanza king, once a carpetbagger in Arkansas where he ultimately rose to the Supreme Court Bench. He then became governor of Idaho Territory during Grant's administration. Returning to Arkansas, he ran for the Senate and was defeated. As native Arkansans were obviously coming into their own, Bowen chose Colorado as a new field of endeavor. For a time he drifted from town to town, practising law, gambling heavily, running deeper and deeper into debt. At last he succeeded in having himself elected a district judge in the San Juan Valley in a far corner of the state. There he struck the Little Ida, a rich gold mine, which soon yields him several millions. Bowen is more suave than Tabor and an even better poker player.

A seat in the Senate falls vacant in '82 when Senator Henry Teller is made Secretary of the Interior by President Arthur. There is a great flurry in local Republican circles. Bowen announces his candidacy and Tabor his. As a " moral man," according to the *Tribune,* Governor Pitkin objects to them both, and the power of making the temporary appointment to the seat lies in his hands.

Tabor annoys the prim Governor further by publicly boasting, upon being told that Pitkin is cold to his pretensions, " H'm, I've started for it, and you bet I'll get there."

All Leadville unites to boom Tabor. All the San Juan camps unite behind Bowen. Leadville supporters obtain five thousand signatures on a petition asking Tabor's appointment. The San Juan camps present one almost as long. At a great mass meeting in Leadville, Tabor announces he " will use only fair means to obtain the seat." Next day a large number of prominent citizens, both Democrats and Republicans, journey to Denver in a body to urge Tabor's qualifications. Within the week Pitkin announces the appointment of George M. Chilcott, lawyer and Congressional representative, " certainly not brilliant but generally regarded as an eminently respectable politician."

Both Tabor and Bowen are hurt and indignant. One obstacle to Tabor's appointment is said to have been that he refused to give his promise not to run for the seat at the next election. Bowen blurts out, " Pitkin knows I am not such a scalawag as some fellows try to make me appear." Both Tabor and Bowen plot revenge, for Pitkin himself aspires to the Senate.

Tabor allies himself with the notorious Jerome Napoleon Chaffee, banker and speculator, charged with much sharp practice, to say the least of it — charged particularly with the crash of the Little Pittsburgh. Chaffee has served in the Senate and is suspected by all but Tabor of seeking to serve again. Eugene Field remarks the curious alliance:

> *Chaffee had a little lamb*
> *Who wore a fierce moustache,*
> *And people wondered how that lamb*
> *On Chaffee made a mash.*

> *What makes this Chaffee love the lamb?*
> *Incessantly they cried.*
> *The lamb has got a golden fleece,*
> *The knowing ones replied.*

Even friendly critics pronounce Tabor's ambition rather pathetic. " He must know that he is not the man for the office and that his supporters will rest under suspicion." By all he is pronounced a dupe. " It will be worth a great deal of money to Mr. Tabor to tumble to himself, even if it is necessary for the opera house to fall on him to bring about the desired result." But Tabor entertains no apprehensions, announcing confidently to the Associated Press that he is certain of election. When the *Tribune* remarks that " this method of doing it costs very little but is unsatisfactory, because not lasting," Tabor takes the rebuke to heart and, according to Field, this colloquy ensues:

> *Are you pretty well up on geography, asked H. A. W.*
> *Waal, ya-as, said Chaffee*
> *The reason I ask is because I am curious to know where in hell Phillipi is. . . . You see I met Governor Pitkin this afternoon and says I to him, in a humorous way, Fred, says I, what do you think of my campaign now? Aren't me and Chaffee agoin' to scoop in the Legislature next winter as easy as rollin' off'n a log? Never mind, says he, we will meet at Phillipi.*
> *Maybe it's some little town down in the San Juan Valley, you know Pitkin is powerful strong down there.*
> *No, there's no such town in Colorado. . . . We must investigate this Phillipi affair.*
> *Of course we must and if Phillipi hasn't been fixed, you'll have to draw a check and I'll see that it's solid at the proper time.*

In January, '83, the State Legislature meets in Denver to elect two senators — one for a full term of six years, one for a term of only thirty days to fill the seat temporarily occupied by Chilcott. Not only is Tabor himself confident of winning the long term, but the public in general and the gamblers in particular share his opinion. The latter offer bets of $1,000 on Tabor against the field but find no takers, for it is almost officially stated that Tabor in his campaign has more or less judiciously distributed $200,000. Not altogether sure of Chaffee, he has also made a deal with Bowen, who is to throw his support to Tabor on the first six ballots. If not then elected, Tabor is to support him on the next six.

On the first ballot for the long term Pitkin receives twenty-one votes, Tabor ten, and Bowen five in the Republican caucus. Day after day the balloting continues with Tabor still the favorite. Once Tabor receives twenty-four votes on a ballot on which Bowen receives three — just enough to have given Tabor a majority if Bowen's men had supported him. Tabor is furious, tossing a note to the leader of his henchmen, " Bowen in bad faith. Adjoin." Bowen now arises in joint legislative session frankly to confess the deal and deliver counter charges of treachery. Charges of chicanery and treachery fly so thick that a motion is passed that votes in caucus be cast *viva voce* so that all may see how each man votes. " This probably prevented Tabor's nomination," according to the *Tribune,* " for Pitkin's followers were open to seduction." Finally, on the ninety-seventh ballot, Pitkin's men swing to Bowen and the prize is his. Republican leaders now wait upon Tabor to offer him the thirty-day term unanimously. Tabor does not immediately reply but finally accepts. " It is not always that one who goes in for a big prize is put off with one seventy-second part of it as I have been," he tells the Legislature, " yet I am thankful and satisfied."

At the Windsor Hotel that night occurs a " regular old Wild Western celebration." Bowen's four-room suite is packed with men. A half dozen bellboys are " kept busy opening the best brands of champagne." In the center of the crowd stands Bowen, " shaking hands and being hauled about pretty much as if at a dance in a mining camp." Tabor comes in from his suite opposite but soon withdraws. Later that night he departs alone for Washington. Augusta is not with him. Indeed, they have just been divorced.

Late in '79, Augusta went home to Maine for a long visit. After her return she and Tabor were seldom seen together. This caused no particular comment, for Tabor had long been accustomed to taking his pleasures without her. But day by day relations between them became increasingly strained. Augusta had developed a sharp tongue and may have become somewhat cantankerous with the years. When many gentlemen of the cloth descend upon her to argue the merits and comforts of their several churches, Augusta remarks caustically, " I suppose Mr. Tabor's soul and mine are of more value now than they were a year ago." Angular and spare, certainly she is no beauty in the blue glasses she now must wear before her nearsighted eyes. But what moves Tabor to anger and disgust is Augusta's stubborn refusal to set up as a grand lady. She refuses to entertain as lavishly as Tabor thinks fitting. She frankly dislikes his parasitical friends and takes no pains to conceal her contempt. She insists upon inviting the servants in to hear music, no matter what bonanza kings are present. She insists upon dressing simply and in good taste. Tabor feels thwarted and frustrated by her want of any adequate idea of splendor.

Although few knew it, Tabor had deserted Augusta in January, '81, which explains Augusta's absence at the opening of the Tabor Grand. A few months after Tabor's triumph on that occasion, all Colorado is scandalized when Augusta files a suit of complaint against Tabor with the charge that he has contributed nothing to her support in spite of the fact that his " income amounts to more than $100,000 per month in money." She has been supporting herself " by renting rooms in her place of abode and by keeping boarders."

In her suit Augusta asks for house and lands worth $100,000 and $50,000 a year for her support. Tabor has the suit quashed on the grounds that the Denver court does not have jurisdiction. But little more than a year later Tabor actually forces Augusta to obtain a divorce, for he is in a delicate position — just how delicate only he knows. The trial occurs in January, '83, at just the time the Legislature assembles for the senatorial election and not three weeks before Tabor departs for Washington. The trial proceeds smoothly and speedily in spite of the most startling evidence of fraud and perjury on Tabor's part. His counsel admits that some months previously Tabor journeyed to Durango, a small town in a far corner of the state, and there fraudulently obtained a divorce without Augusta's knowledge, for no papers were served on her. Then, to keep the matter secret, Tabor found means to persuade the clerk to paste together the incriminating leaves of the record. But an election soon occurred and the new clerk, curious about the strange state of the record, unpasted the leaves and notified Augusta who protested vigorously.

But Augusta is finally persuaded to accept the inevitable. Tabor announces that the settlement exceeds $1,000,000. The court record more conservatively places it at $250,000–$300,000, including the Tabor house. At the conclusion of the trial, when presented with papers to sign, Augusta turns toward the judge and asks somewhat hysterically, " What is my name? "

" Your name is Tabor, ma'am. Keep the name; it is yours by right."

" I will; it is mine till I die. It was good enough for me to take. It is good enough for me to keep. Judge, I ought to thank you for what you have done, but I cannot. I am not thankful. But it was the only thing left for me to do. But, Judge, I wish you would put in the record, *Not willingly asked for.*"

Augusta rises to leave the court, striving to control herself. But before reaching the door, she breaks down in tears, sobbing to herself, " Oh, God! Not willingly, not willingly! "

Tabor arrives in Washington preceded by a story which, true or false, makes him an object of ridicule throughout the country, for the newspapers circulate it widely. Tabor is becoming a national figure for a day. On the train to Washington, according to the story, Tabor ordered the porter to make up his berth early. " A gorgeous velvet cap, elaborately decorated, was first produced and hung on a hook for all to see. Next followed a magnificent ruffled nightshirt, half smothered with costly point lace of the finest quality, which the Senator said was worth $250."

Sworn in on February 3, '83, Tabor comes forward to take the oath of office dressed in black with an immense diamond solitaire on either hand and large square cuff buttons of diamonds and onyx in checker-board arrangement flashing above them. One Senator is heard to exclaim, " G-r-e-a-t God! " But the general impression is that he " will do at least as well as Chilcott who won golden opinions by his silence and promptitude in voting as directed by his party. But he must shoot that diamond ring. If any burlesque actress should happen round, it might get him into trouble. It did once before as will be remembered."

Tabor, it must be said, takes his honors easily and attempts to adapt himself to Washington society "by relinquishing some of the splendid diamonds which, not out of place among the further western peoples, made him unnecessarily conspicuous here." But Tabor as the "Wild Western Senator" is considered fair game by every scribe at Washington and they make the most of their opportunity — not very amusingly. But their raillery stings the Leadville *Herald* and other local newspapers to reply hotly that the "people of Colorado do not feel that they have any reason to be commiserated on their representative in the present Senate."

But the scowls of local patriots cannot silence Eugene Field who relentlessly goads poor Tabor. Almost every day the *Tribune* carries a fictitious account of the Senator's activities, many containing just enough fact to make them not altogether fanciful. Tabor is reported to have said of his first day in the Senate that already "he had set in with the boys on the tariff game and proposed to stick it out until either the pot was gone or other hands were drawn." He is next introducing a bill for the suspension of gold coinage: "Tabor, having obtained the floor, kept the whole Senate at bay for three hours, delivering the most powerful address heard in the Senate since the great French Arms debate. He analyzed the bill to the dregs and was at times ferociously satirical." Now President Arthur has asked him to join the Cabinet in its deliberations and it becomes "definitely understood that the Administration will hold up all appointments until Senator Tabor gives the word to go ahead." Now he raises a question of privilege. "He said his attention had been called to a late copy of the *Wet Mountain Pilot* in which occurred a paragraph designating him (Tabor) as an anomaly. He had determined when he started out on his political career to pay no heed to the utterances of his enemies. . . . But here was an instance where the libel was so unprovoked, so wanton, the slander so malicious and the charge so appalling that he felt impelled to notice it. How and at what time had he committed the offense? Who was his accessory to the deed? Honorable Senators would observe absolutely no specifications; why had his slanderers neglected to draw up a bill of particulars? He would tell the Senators why; the charge was unqualifiedly and ignominiously false (Applause)."

During his thirty days in the Senate, Tabor makes no address, seconds one motion and introduces two bills of his own. One asks an appropriation of $100,000 to establish a military post in Colorado. The other asks a similar sum for the preservation of forests in the West, for Tabor confesses he " don't see where railroad ties will come from unless something of this kind is done." But Tabor is not always at his desk or in his study. Chilcott returns with the news that Tabor has been warmly received at Washington and is finding all the poker he desires. " But he thinks he was played low down and feels quite sore over the result." Eugene Field gives Tabor many a pleasant evening in the highest society. " Tabor spent Sunday in New York as the guest of the Honorable Roscoe Conkling. ' Tabor,' remarked Conkling to a New York Herald reporter last evening, ' is a charming fellow. He is full of anecdote and *bon mots,* and quicker at repartee than any man I know. As we sat at table this afternoon, Vanderbilt, who is something of a wag, was inclined to banter Tabor for cracking nuts between his teeth instead of using the silver implements provided for the purpose. What have become of your crackers, Horace, said he. Quick as a flash, Tabor retorted, I ate them in my soup an hour ago! Ha, ha, ha! a merry fellow — full of jest and song and mirth when occasion demands.'"

But Tabor actually has his social triumphs, one of which is the talk of Washington for many days. On March 1, '83, less than two months after his divorce from Augusta, Tabor is married at the Willard Hotel, "amid a fairyland of flowers," to Elizabeth Bonduel McCourt of Oshkosh, Wisconsin. The bride is just turned twenty-two, golden-haired and blue-eyed, "a blonde of rare personal attractions, with a full fine figure and of charming manner, with vivacious and entertaining conversational powers." Tabor's gift to her is a $90,000 diamond necklace.

Miss or Mrs. McCourt, as she is called at this time, is not unknown in Colorado as "Baby" Doe, divorced wife of Harvey Doe, son of a rich Oshkosh lumberman. After their marriage they came West to live at Central City for a time. Not much more than a year later Mrs. Doe obtained a divorce on the grounds of non-support. Where Tabor first met his bride cannot be definitely stated. Bill Bush later declared that they first met in New York City in '82, publicly and specifically denying that Tabor "had fitted up a magnificent suite for her at the Windsor."

In her own handwriting the bride has addressed the invitations, each with its quarter-inch silver margins and its engraved superscription, also in silver. President Chester Arthur has received one. So, too, have Secretary and Mrs. Teller, Senator and Mrs. Hill, Senators Sawyer and Chaffee, General Charles Adams, Bill Bush, Tom Bowen, young Maxcy Tabor and all of the bride's family. The McCourts are numerous, as Tabor soon learns. There are fourteen of them in all, "Lizzie" being the fourth daughter. Born in Ireland, old Peter McCourt had once prospered at Oshkosh as a clothier but was living in greatly reduced circumstances as a small tailor until aided by his new son-in-law. Tabor is said to have generously provided him with a comfortable house and a fortune of $150,000.

At nine o'clock in the evening the wedding party assembles at the Willard. The bride is gowned in heavily brocaded white satin. She wears long white gloves and carries a bouquet of white roses. She is attended by her father and mother, two sisters, two brothers and two brothers-in-law. As they are in mourning for the recent death of another brother-in-law, all are in black, although the ladies' black silks are "relieved by ornaments of diamond and onyx." Tabor appears with Bill Bush and Tom Bowen. It is the latter, so it is said, who persuades the President to attend.

In one of the larger hotel parlors the bride and groom now stand before a table richly draped in cardinal, bearing a "candelabrum with ten tapers shedding a subdued light over all." The ceremony, an abbreviated nuptial mass, is performed by the Reverend P. L. Chappelle, D.D., of St. Matthew's. Upon its conclusion the bride is "fittingly congratulated by the President, her husband and family, and attending friends."

Now the party proceeds "through the folding doors to the collation chambers," profusely and beautifully decorated for the occasion. In the center, standing six feet high upon a great basin of blossoms, rises a "massive wedding bell of white roses, surmounted by a Cupid's bow, with an arrow on the string, tipped with a heart of violets, the rest being composed of various hued roses." At either end of the long table extending the entire length of the parlor, appears a "colossal four-leaf clover in red and white roses and carnations." A canopy of flowers with trailing foliage stands above the separate table required to support the wedding cake, "chaste in design." Everywhere there are sweet-smelling violets. Flowers encompass every guest's place at the board. Beside each plate is a boutonnière. Flowers appear upon " each dish of dainty viands," and even are garlanded about the champagne buckets.

" The collation ended, the party engaged in general conversation, the President paying particular attention to the bride. Just before he left he expressed a wish for a rose from her bouquet, which she quickly chose and handed to him. At 10:45, President Arthur took his departure. He was followed by the other guests, and by midnight the gay reception room was deserted."

XIV. Back to the Earth Again

" Trusting in God that something will be done for me."

Tabor is elated by his social triumph and is at no pains to conceal his pride. Nor is he less obviously proud of his young and beautiful bride. On his last day in the Senate, as he goes from desk to desk with an autograph album, he points her out to his colleagues as she sits prominently in one of the galleries. None can deny her striking elegance and beauty.

"Special advices from Washington agree that yesterday was the most exciting day ever witnessed in the United States Senate," Eugene Field romanticizes. "It terminated the Honorable H. A. W. Tabor's career in that august body. . . . Early in the day the streets were alive with people hurrying to the Capitol. Flags were hung at half-mast. . . . The galleries were filled to overflowing with the most beautiful and accomplished ladies of the Republic and the floor of the Senate was crowded with eminent persons. When Senator Tabor entered the room bearing a new patent-leather grip-sack and wearing a superb trousseau of broadcloth and diamonds, the vast crowd was as hushed as the grave. Senator Sherman submitted a series of resolutions lamenting Tabor's departure. It was unanimously adopted, Senator Tabor maintaining his characteristic modesty to the last and abstaining from voting. The Senator rose to speak. As he proceeded to recount his services, love of country and devotion to the public weal, men groaned in speechless agony and whole platoons of police were kept busy carrying insensible ladies from the galleries. . . . At night there was a torchlight parade in ex-Senator Tabor's honor. It was an imposing affair, numbering 12,000 persons in line and the entire American Navy on wheels, and was gorgeously illuminated. The crowning feature of the procession was a huge papier-mache yacht, representing the Ship of State, and manned by forty-one beautiful young girls, representing the States and Territories, from Oshkosh."

But the Tabors provide an authentic sensation this day. Father Chappelle who officiated at the wedding publicly announces that he has been imposed upon and returns the $200 fee given him by Tabor. Had he known that both Tabor and his bride had been divorced, he would never have married them against the canon of the Catholic Church. Father Chappelle adds that he took every reasonable precaution to satisfy himself of the eligibility of the couple to receive the marriage sacrament. When the bride's father was asked if he knew of any impediment to the marriage, " he clearly answered that he did not," the priest complains. " To say all in a few words, I was shamefully deceived by the McCourt family." To this Tabor replies through the press that " Father Chappelle did not ask either himself or Miss McCourt whether either had been divorced or not." The priest threatens to have the marriage declared illicit by carrying the question to the highest authorities in the Church, but nothing more is heard of the matter.

Next day a greater sensation occurs when the news is published that the Senator and his bride had been secretly married at St. Louis six months previously — three months indeed before Tabor's final, legitimate divorce from Augusta. Next day another shudder runs through Washington, according to the correspondent of the New York *Tribune,* when Tabor announces that he likes the Capital and proposes to build himself a large house there in which to spend his winters. "There has been nothing so picturesquely vulgar as this gorgeous hotel wedding of a pair married months already," as several exclaim. But others are inclined to look upon the Carbonate King's exploits rather more tolerantly. "If he wants to marry a wife, and Mrs. Teller and Mrs. Belford refuse to come to the wedding, he can get on just the same. Still, it is sure to be mentioned. When a man steps out into the public square and has a band play behind him, he must expect people to look and listen. The man who insists upon Tabor's sort of a good time must take it and be content without honors or office."

Tabor and his bride return to Denver in April to establish themselves in a large suite of rooms at the Windsor. Few come to welcome the Tabors but the members of two German Athletic Societies who serenade them upon their arrival at the Windsor and then carry them off to a banquet at which the Senator is honored as one of the first Americans to identify himself with a movement which " aims to educate our youth, not only in physical, but also in moral development." Tabor and his bride visit Leadville to be received by the Tabor Light Cavalry and the Tabor Hose Company which escort them to the apartment prepared in their honor.

Now a most scandalous public quarrel occurs when Bill Bush resigns as manager of the Tabor Grand to be supplanted by the bride's brother, Peter McCourt. Tabor brings suit against Bush on a charge of embezzling $2,000. Bush is acquitted and replies with a terrific blast in the form of a deposition placed before the Supreme Court, claiming that Tabor owes him $100,000 for various curious services rendered. He demands $5,000 for time and influence employed in helping Tabor "emerge from the obscurity of California Gulch into the realms of statesmanship." He asks the sum of $10,000 for securing testimony and witnesses for Tabor's divorce at Durango and for persuading Augusta at last to bring suit. He asks a larger sum for "aiding him in effecting a marriage with the said Mrs. Doe, commonly called Baby Doe." He asks $1,547 for bribes paid to legislators during the senatorial election, in sums ranging from $5 to $475. The court strikes Bush's complaint from the record as indecent and irrelevant. The quarrel between Tabor and Bush is never mended. But Bush remains a friend and partner of young Maxcy who sides with Augusta after her divorce. With her financial aid the two lease the large Brown Palace Hotel, perhaps still the finest in Denver, upon its completion in '91. Augusta loses most of her investment during the panic of '93 and two years later suddenly dies while on a visit to California, having lived virtually as a recluse since the day of the divorce.

The sight of Tabor and Bush quarreling publicly and scandalously alienates many of the Senator's friends and delights his enemies. The smelter king Senator N. P. Hill, his most outspoken enemy within the Republican party, seizes the occasion to deliver Tabor what he hopes is a death-blow. Even the once friendly *Tribune* scathingly attacks the Carbonate King. "Tabor is an utter disgrace to the State; he disgraced it in private life; he disgraced it as a public officer; he made it the jeer of the country during his brief but petty career in the Senate. Essentially a vulgarian of doubtful antecedents, he strove to buy his way into political position. To a small extent he succeeded. He bought the cheap creatures of the Legislature for the first place in its gift, but did not buy them in sufficient number, and when this failed, he begged his way into the second position. Society in

Denver gave its verdict on his course when it recognized the kindly old lady whom, in his gulch ignorance, he put aside. He is a social and political outcast in all senses of the word." Even the Leadville *Democrat* protests against this savage editorial. But no one rushes forward to defend Tabor by attempting to justify his course.

Tabor buys a whole city block in Denver's fashionable quarter and there for his bride erects a large Italian villa. It impresses all with its great lawn about it where sport iron dogs and deer. He presents his wife with a magnificent carriage in black and pale blue enamel, upholstered in azure satin. Four black horses richly caparisoned draw it through the streets with two negros in scarlet liveries perched solemnly behind. Tabor showers his wife with diamonds and jewelry of all kinds, and of a painter named Heyde orders five oil portraits of her, each in a different pose and costume. And for her he relines his private box at the Opera House in white satin.

Two daughters are born to the Tabors. The first is named Elizabeth Bonduel Lillie and begins to attend the theater regularly from the time she is six weeks old. She is seldom left at home with her nurse but " usually accompanies her parents when they go out." The baby seldom cries at the theater and as she grows older, amuses herself " by capering all through the play in her father's box." She is the most photographed baby in the world, it is said at the time, and " always poses herself without assistance."

" Baby Tabor is now two and a half years old. She is the child of her father's later years, and of course his idol. . . . When three months old Baby Tabor was taken to Oshkosh to be christened in the old church which Mrs. Tabor's father had built. . . .

The robes in which she was christened were marvelously fine, being of the most costly point lace, the two flounces on the robe costing $500 apiece. They were covered with a cloak of white embroidered velvet trimmed with point lace and marabou feathers. Her tiny French felt hat was heavy with marabou tips, each one of which cost not less than $10. The baby's wardrobe at the present time consists of fifty lace robes and dainty velvet gowns of the richest description. She has a profusion of jewels of rare and unique designs and of great value, presented by her father and by friends everywhere, even from Europe; and every pin placed in her clothes is garnished with a diamond."

In '89 a second daughter is born and named Rose Mary Echo Silver Dollar Tabor. She, too, enjoys her triumph in an $800 christening robe, but she is not to know many years of splendor.

Tabor, little affected by sharp and general criticism, still has hopes of being returned to high office. Politically, he is only half ostracized, as it were. His party is not unwilling to accept his contributions to its funds but persistently denies him any customary reward. Tabor seeks to be governor in '84. He spends $75,000 on his own campaign, donating an additional $40,000 to the party's coffers. But another receives the nomination in spite of all promises given Tabor by local leaders. Two years later he pours out money to obtain the Senatorial nomination and is defeated. Again in '88 he unsuccessfully attempts to secure nomination as governor. It is an interesting speculation how long Tabor would have continued spending his money for the ultimate benefit of rivals and enemies within his own party, had he not now begun to lose battles on the main front.

Investing injudiciously and speculating wildly, Tabor is in financial difficulties as early as '86. Indeed, when Tabor was

making his only successful campaign for the Senate in '82, one
responsible newspaper attacked him solely on the grounds of
insolvency. The attack was, no doubt, premature, but certainly
Tabor is soon hopelessly involved. One by one his mines " peter
out." He buys others only to spend hundreds of thousands in
unsuccessful attempts to make them profitable. Not only does
his income from the mines cease, but his capital funds begin to
diminish rapidly. He loses a half million on the Calumet Dock
project on Lake Michigan and another half million in speculating in the grain pits. His copper lands in Texas prove valueless.
His realty, lumber, gas and water companies at Leadville pay
smaller dividends and then become a liability as the camp slowly
declines. His life and fire insurance companies are early dissolved. He has literally spent millions in politics without recompense, tangible or intangible. Although he has long been an excellent poker player, now sharpers lie in wait for him. Stories
of his heavy losings are too many and circumstantial to be altogether ignored.

Pressed for money, Tabor first mortgages the famous Matchless mine, the single one of his Leadville shafts which continues
to run a trickle of silver. Soon Tabor has little income but from
his Denver properties. Now he has to mortgage these, one after
another — finally, the Opera House. At this time Tabor might
easily have liquidated his unprofitable enterprises, according to
friends, and have secured himself in possession of a considerable
fortune. But he is determined to hold all, still having faith in
" Tabor Luck " at which he himself used to smile. Unfortunately,
he delays too long in attempting to salvage something from the
inevitable catastrophe. He cherishes illusory hopes not only of
restoring but of increasing his fortune up to the very day the
great panic of '93 strikes the West to close twelve strong banks

in Denver within three days. The panic here and in the mountains is intensified by the repeal of the Sherman Law. The Government suddenly stops buying for coinage 4,500,000 ounces of silver a month. Throughout the world the price of silver drops sharply. What little activity remains in the silver camps abruptly ceases.

Tabor strives desperately to hold on. He buys what seem to be two good prospects on Boulder Creek. In charge of them he places a poor carpenter, Winfield Scott Stratton. The prospects do not develop. Now Stratton strikes it rich in the new Cripple Creek gold field behind Pike's Peak. Tabor, too, hopes to make a strike here. With the last of his capital, increased by a loan from Stratton, he obtains an option on the Phil Sheridan and Free Coinage groups of mines in the field. But his stake is soon used up and he must relinquish them at a loss. When the mines begin almost immediately to yield millions to their new owners, Tabor realizes at last that his luck has changed and abandons all hope of striking a new Little Pittsburgh or Crysolite. In a frantic effort to save at least the Opera House, Tabor writes Senator Henry Teller a most naive and moving letter:

SENATOR TELLER
   My Dear friend
To fully let you know the status of affairs relative to the blocks,
I will tell you what Mrs. Smith told me this week. She told me
a party told her he had the money in hand to loan her to pay off
the North Western [Insurance Company] but that he would not
talk to her about it until she was in possession. I today tried to
get a thirty days option from her and she flatly told me she would
not take less than four hundred thousand dollars, but of course

if we can establish it as a mortgage in the upper Court she will have to accept three hundred and thirty thousand dollars ($330,-000) the amount at which she bid it in at. She was very hard on me this morning and was very determined to get this buildings. If she gets possession it will cost me many thousands of dollars on account of her management, therefore we must leave nothing undone to defeat the same. On account of my being such a strong advocate of Free Coinage *it is at this time impossible for me to make a loan. I feel that the Judges of this silver state should protect me until after the elections for then there will be no trouble to make a loan. But now Senator you know that it is exactly the same as in a time of actual war and the Judges have power to issue any order that will protect their own and I feel that I belong to them for my funds were always freely used for the good of the party and country. and if I have it again it will be the same and all I want is to keep what belongs to me and lead a quiet home life. And I feel that if you will go now to the supreme court or court of appeals and ask them to issue an order to Judge Johnson restraining him from giving her possession until my time expires for redemption with the North Western which would leave her three months to secure a loan if I failed she being a Judgement creditor I feel senator that the judges will not refuse you but that they will recognize that there is an actual war. It will not only save me but it will help our silver cause and such an act will be admired by the toiling masses. Senator I believe if you ask Judge Johnson to make an order that the assignees stay in possession for both parties the full time of my redemption with the North Western giving Mrs Smith all the money over and above running expenses because the assignees are economical and trustworthy that he will do it for you and the silver cause But I feel*

*sure that the upper court will do it for you alone. The case comes
up before Judge Johnson at ten on Monday next. Trusting in God
that something will be done for me I remain*

Very sincerely your friend

H. A. W. Tabor

Senator Teller fails, if indeed he tries, to persuade the United
States Supreme Court to declare a state of war in Tabor's behalf.
Now the Tabor Grand passes from his hands and Colorado's first
great Bonanza King is, in fact, destitute. His carriage and stables,
his Italian villa, his and his wife's and daughters' diamonds —
all have been sold over the block. An old man approaching seventy, utterly crushed and bewildered, Tabor sets out alone into
the mountains to go prospecting, working futilely for many
months at the old Eclipse mine on South Boulder Creek.

In January, '98, after a year of hardship, Tabor confesses himself " stunned at the information " that his former generosity to
his party has at last been recognized and rewarded. Experience
gained during the long lean years in California Gulch now stand
him in good stead. Senators Wolcott and Teller use their influence to have Tabor appointed postmaster of Denver at a salary
sufficient " to rescue him from penury." In the curiously complete
cycle of his life Tabor is back where he began.

A year passes. Tabor and his family live in one small room at
the Windsor. He has abandoned all hope of regaining fortune.
He is again as quiet and resigned as on that day when those two
strange prospectors, Hook and Rische, entered his store at Slabtown. What he thinks or dreams of during this year, what
memories of triumph he has and what regrets, will never be
known. On the morning of April 10, 1899, after a week's illness,
Tabor passes quietly away at the Windsor. His wife and daugh-

ters are at his bedside. Shortly before the end Maxcy Tabor is
sent for, although he has been estranged from his father for years.
But he does not arrive until Tabor has sunk into the coma from
which he never awakens. In a grave marked by a small granite
stone bearing only his name, Tabor is buried with simple ceremony in the presence of a few mourners at Mt. Prospect Cemetery, Jack O'Neil's Ranch of earlier days, long since a neglected
patch of brambles and weeds.

In its personal aspects Tabor's tragedy had its roots less in his
vices than his virtues, for he was " confiding, charitable, generous
and merciful to an extreme," as even his enemies testified. " These
attributes proved his financial undoing. No man ever went to
him for a favor when he had money and came away empty-
handed. No man ever forgave his enemies quite so cheerfully or
testified so willingly to the sincerity of his forgiveness by afterwards aiding them. . . . He made many mistakes during the
days of his prominence and prosperity but, his surroundings and
opportunities considered, carried himself as well as any of his
contemporaries."

But in larger part Tabor's tragedy must be attributed to his
misfortune in outliving his era. Business men and financiers with
their studied methods of systematic exploitation had already won
the West. Tabor and others of his kind had nothing to oppose to
their refined techniques and fell an easy prey to them. Bluff and
usually straightforward even at his worst, Tabor boldly blun-
dered ahead where shrewder and more sophisticated men of fun-
damentally less integrity felt their way along cautiously and cun-
ningly toward success. His sudden complete loss of fortune is
inexplicable unless, as seems likely, he really never understood
the forces he strove to master. His ways were the simple and

naive ways of the Frontier which had already passed before his death—"in the Southwest with the capture of Geronimo in 1886–8, in the Dakotas among the Sioux with the totally needless murder of hundreds of women and children at Wounded Knee in 1891–2, and throughout the whole West in 1893 when the world panic of that year enabled the eastern money-lender to foreclose on the overborrowed West and pull the frontiersman—now gray-haired—from his saddle," as many an old pioneer bitterly lamented. "That ended the frontier, ended the frontiersman; in came rapidly woman suffrage, prohibition, anti-gun laws, . . . and the frontier was gone—gone into history."

Only the famous Matchless mine was saved from the wreck of Tabor's fortune through the generosity of Stratton. But the Matchless was now practically exhausted. Within two months of Tabor's death his family was actually destitute, living in a small brick house, old and dingy, standing just a few feet off Larimer Street with its decaying buildings of earlier days. Having meantime quarreled with her brother Peter, Tabor's general manager, who had managed to survive the crash with a considerable fortune, Mrs. Tabor stubbornly refused to accept any aid from him. With the marriage of Elizabeth, the elder daughter, who departed to live in the Middle West, Silver Dollar was left alone with her mother to share for many years her hopeless struggle against adversity. Time did not improve their situation and ten years later the girl, now twenty, began to contribute verse to the local newspapers to earn an occasional few dollars. To her father she dedicated a song *On President Roosevelt's Colorado Bear Hunt.* She published other pieces on *Spirits, Love and Lilies, In a Dream I Loved You* and *The Outlaw Horse,* one stanza of which reads:

And the "Wild West" goes,
And the civilized grows
All in progression's course,
But there's still a flood
Of the dauntless blood:
That goes for the outlaw horse.

Silver Dollar next founded the *Silver Dollar Weekly,* of which only a few issues were published, and in a final literary effort the desperate girl sat down to write a lurid short novel entitled *The Star of Blood,* sentimentalizing the exploits of a notorious local criminal. Silver Dollar then took vows but did not enter convent life, soon drifting away to be gossiped about occasionally until in 1925 she was found dying under rather mysterious circumstances in a house in the back-of-the-yards district of Chicago. Terribly burned and scalded, Silver Dollar expired a few hours later, insisting to the last that she had accidentally tipped over upon herself a pan of boiling water. But in the shabby room was found a man's photograph bearing the notation that if anything happened, this man "would know all about it." The original of the photograph, one Jack Reid, a former saloon-keeper, was held by the police but soon discharged. As Silver Dollar's body lay unclaimed for a time, neighbors began taking up a collection to bury her. In the end Peter McCourt sent $300 for funeral expenses. It was reported at the time that Mrs. Tabor had succeeded in obtaining funds to attend the funeral, but she was not present when the last rites were performed. Mrs. Tabor has since declared that Silver Dollar is not dead but in the convent where she once took vows.

Many years before this tragedy Mrs. Tabor had quit Denver and gone to Leadville to settle down in an old cabin beside the shaft of the Matchless. To this day she lives and toils there. Many times the mine has been almost wrested from her, but always she has managed to retain it by extreme efforts of her own or the generosity of friends and even strangers touched by her heroic willful fight against absolutely hopeless odds. From year to year she strives desperately to make the Matchless once more pour forth treasure, for not even the unanimous opinion of experts can convince her that the mine is altogether barren. No doubt she will die there struggling against misfortune and poverty, for in her eyes the Matchless has obviously become a symbol of the days when she was young, gay, beautiful and rich.

From her cabin on Fryer Hill, Mrs. Tabor looks down upon a Leadville growing smaller and more quiet with every year. Late in the 'Nineties the camp enjoyed a brief boom when gold was found deep under the exhausted carbonate veins. But the boom did not approach that of earlier days and since the turn of the century Leadville has steadily declined. Today it holds perhaps three thousand people, not one tenth as many as in '79. Many long streets of frame houses and cabins are altogether deserted. Chestnut Street is in ruins. Tabor's old Leadville Bank is boarded up. The Tabor Opera House still stands on Harrison Avenue, but no drama has been presented upon its stage for many years. In 1905 the entire building passed into the hands of the Elks who use as club and lodge rooms the huge apartments where Tabor, assisted by Bush, once managed his millions and received friends and rivals in almost regal state. State Street, once so crowded and boisterous, is a waste. All of its large gay resorts have either been burned or torn down. There remain only a few cribs, Mike's Annex and the old Pioneer Saloon. During the earlier years of Prohibition many in Leadville prospered from copper stills hidden away in abandoned shafts and tunnels. Leadville "moon" remains popular and the best to be had for hundreds of miles around. But even prosperity from this source has been undermined, according to local complaints, by increasingly severe competition.

Other older camps have been even more ravaged by the years. Buckskin Joe has entirely disappeared. All that remains of Montgomery are a few rows of roofless cabins. Although their span of life was longer, the Clear Creek camps are now deserted and decayed. There is no stir of life along the steep narrow streets of Black Hawk and Central City. Bleak and bare, Gregory Gulch is almost a forgotten name.

> *Here's where they cut the conifers and ribbed*
> *The mines with conifers that sang no more,*
> *And here they dug the gold and went away,*
> *Here are the empty houses, hollow mountains,*
> *Even the rats, the beetles and the cattle*
> *That used these houses after they were gone*
> *Are gone; the gold is gone,*
> *There's nothing here,*
> *Only the deep mines crying to be filled.*